Where to Watch
in Britain and Europe

Where to Watch Birds in Britain and Europe

JOHN GOODERS

CHRISTOPHER HELM
London

© 1988 John Gooders
Line illustrations by John Davis
Maps by Robert Thorne
Christopher Helm (Publishers) Ltd, Imperial House,
21–25 North Street, Bromley, Kent BR1 1SD

British Library Cataloguing in Publication Data

Gooders, John
    Where to watch birds in Britain and Europe.
1. Bird populations — Europe   2. Bird watching — Europe
I. Title
598'.07'2344   GL690.Al

ISBN 0–7470–1212–1

Typeset by Opus, Oxford.
Printed and bound in Great Britain
by Billings and Sons, Worcester

CONTENTS

CONTENTS

CONTENTS

INTRODUCTION

This book has one straightforward aim: to put birders in touch with birds in the most simple and efficient manner possible. To this end, the book contains a selection of the best spots for watching birds throughout Europe. Here are famous 'hot spots' such as the Camargue, Porto Lago and Hornborgasjön, but here too are more obscure places like Boulmane and Monfragüe, super areas that are largely ignored or unknown.

To cater for the increasingly mobile birder, neighbouring areas have been grouped together to form larger units without losing the detail that is often required to put bird and birder into contact. This has the effect of cutting down on the number of entries and a consequent saving of space compared with the first *Where to Watch Birds in Britain and Europe*, published in 1970. As a result, it has been possible to extend the boundaries of Europe to include nearby countries most frequented by birding travellers. Thus, Morocco, Tunisia, Asiatic Turkey, Cyprus and Israel are all included for the first time. I may well be guilty of giving somewhat fuller coverage to these 'new' regions and rather less to the countries of mainstream Europe. I may also be biased towards those countries that are particularly fruitful for the travelling birder at the expense of those that are not. Thus, there are more sites for such countries as Spain, Finland and Greece than there are for some central European countries. For a variety of reasons there are no entries at all for Albania, Andorra, Liechtenstein, Luxembourg and so on.

When someone decides to travel half way across Europe in search of birds, he or she expects to see birds that are not found at home. Someone from northern Europe visiting the Coto Doñana for the first time will be delighted by the herons and egrets, the vultures and eagles, the exotic Rollers and Azure-winged Magpies. Thereafter, a journey to the eastern Mediterranean may be in order to seek out all of those species not found in Spain. Greece may produce pelicans, Glossy Ibis, Rüppell's Warbler and Black-headed Bunting. These birds are all widespread and are easy to find. Gradually, however, birding holidays take on a more controlled form with more specific objectives. From Great Bustard and Lammergeier to Trumpeter Finch and Caucasian Snowcock, the search for the unusual and rare narrows the choice of destination. Of course, many birders seek the 'complete wipe-out' by seeing all possible species within a country in a single trip. In Morocco, for example, the aim is to see not only all the desert-type wheatears and larks, but also Houbara Bustard, the Bush Shrike and the Bulbul, Fulvous Babbler, Bald Ibis, Dupont's Lark, Crested Coot, Marsh Owl, Chanting Goshawk and, with real ambition, Desert Sparrow. Such species require perseverance, luck and good 'stake-outs', or all three.

Over the years, travelling birders have changed our ideas on the status and distribution of a host of species. By seeking the unusual, they have discovered that the Black-winged Kite is not confined to a pair or two in Portugal, that Trumpeter Finch and Dupont's Lark can both be found in Spain, that Lesser Crested Tern breeds in the Mediterranean, and so on. Of course, once a spot for a particular species has been found it becomes *the* place to see the bird, and great areas of equally suitable habitat are ignored in the rush from one stake-out to the next. In this book you will find most of the great birding areas of Europe, together with many of the best-known stake-outs. It would be satisfying to hear that there is more than one place for Caucasian Blackcock, more than two spots for Demoiselle Crane, more than two areas for Andalusian Hemipode and so on. That would mean that birders are still looking, still locating, still adding to our knowledge and ultimately to our enjoyment.

It is remarkable just how freely such information is given today. Not so long ago all was darkness and secrecy, whereas today there is a sense of helpfulness and comraderie among birders. There are, of course, dangers. Egg-collectors and falconry adherents are still a major plague, but the best (worst!) of them are as well informed as any birder and, in realising this, we open the way for a freer exchange of information. Thus, exact details of the most famous pair of Black-winged Kites in Europe are widely known and passed from hand to hand, but I cannot repeat here the method for finding Caucasian Blackcock in Turkey for fear of reprisals!

Once upon a time sailors used to leave messages and letters for each other under cairns on deserted islands. Today, travelling birders leave notebooks in cafés, hotels and other favoured establishments that become public property and record 'What's about', visit by visit. My favourite is one in a café in the deserts of southern Morocco which is said to be 'gripping stuff'. Knowledge of the existence of such birding logs may be the key to successful exploration of certain areas.

The accounts of the individual areas follow a tried and tested formula. A general description of the area, its habitats and the more interesting birds is followed by a seasonal listing of birds likely to be seen. Such lists are far from exhaustive, but again pick out the most interesting and regular birds. Under the title of 'Access', details on finding exactly where to go are followed by permit details and any other relevant information. The heading 'Route' covers the major approaches to the area in general. Maps show detailed access to many of the major bird spots, but should not be regarded as substitutes for really detailed local maps. Several countries have an equivalent of the British Ordnance Survey and these maps are an invaluable tool for birders wherever they may go. Stanford (address: 12–14 Long Acre, London WC2) are probably the best map-suppliers in Britain.

The names of birds are those used by *British Birds* magazine, save for a few idiosyncracies of my own. In all such cases, these alternatives are the names most commonly used by birders. By and large I have avoided jargon, though reference to, for example, Stilt, Audouin's, Griffon, Caspian is simply shorthand for species that are immediately picked out and where the 'Black-winged', 'Gull', 'Vulture' and 'Tern' respectively are assumed.

Finally, a plea. If you find this book at all useful in your travels, why not send me a copy of your notes or report so that the next edition can be even more thorough and even more helpful. All help will, of course, be acknowledged.

John Gooders, Ashburnham, East Sussex

Acknowledgements

No book of this nature could be written without the help of a huge number of people. Mostly they must go unacknowledged for the simple reason that I do not know who they are. Information is passed from birder to birder and in a little while no one knows who originally found the particular bird or the particular site. These items of information have then been passed on to me by friends and contacts, who may have checked them themselves and added to the detail.

Over the years masses of individuals and car-full crews have produced reports on their travels varying in quality from a simple checklist of species seen to a multifaceted diary-cum-checklist with a mapped stake-out appendix. Such documents are both a labour of love and extremely valuable. I have been fortunate in being allowed to use many such reports as bases for my accounts of particular areas. Indeed, no-one who was asked for such help has refused. Many of these reports come direct from the authors, but others were obtained via Steve Whitehouse, who runs a report distribution service at: 5 Stanway Close, Blackpole, Worcester WR4 9XL. To Steve I am particularly grateful.

Correspondents and friends in other countries have put up with bombardments of paper, forms and telephone calls with great patience. The most significant are listed below, together with authors of reports and others who have, over the years, sought to keep this guide up to date by writing to me with news of European birding areas.

Please do not stop now!

Particular help was received from: Lars Norgaard Anderson, Mark Andrews, Stephan Bandelin, John Belsey, Patrick Bergier, E. Alexander Bergstrom, E. Bezzel, Jeff Blincow, N. Borrow, Alistair Brown, R. D. and L. Carthy, R. G. Clarke, Andy Cook, Hans Deetjen, Henrik Dissing, Tom Elkins, Philip Etherington, Roy Frost, Iztok Geister, Alan Gosland, Robin Gossage, Marco Gustin, Peter Hakansson, George Handrinos, Laszlo Haraszthy, Simon Harrap, John Hillmer, Erik Hirschfeld, A. Hitchings, Dave Holman, Jon Hornbuckle, Noel Howe, Andy Howes, H. Jones, M. S. Kington, Steve Lister, Kalevi Malmstrom, Salvador Maluquer, G. D. Mountain, Patrimonio Olivier, Johnni Paakkonen, D. Page, Hamish Paterson, G. D. Rees, Guy Robbrecht, Jan Alex de Roos, R. Safford, Michael Shaw, Bengt Skugge, D. Smallwood, Karel Stastny, Tadeusz Stawarczyk, Antonio Teixeira, Michel Thevenot, X. de Tirade, Stella Tuckey, Edward Valentine, Mark van Beirs, A. P. van der Graaf, J. Warne, Gordon Webb, Richard Webb, Barry White, J. C. S. White.

I should also like to thank all those correspondents who contributed to the first edition and thus laid the foundations on which this guide is based. Finally, my thanks to Caron Hobden for producing such an excellent typescript, to David Christie for such careful editing, particularly regarding spellings, where his knowledge of different tongues is wide, and to Robbie who has suffered with me during the birth pangs and shared in the thrills of discovery.

AUSTRIA

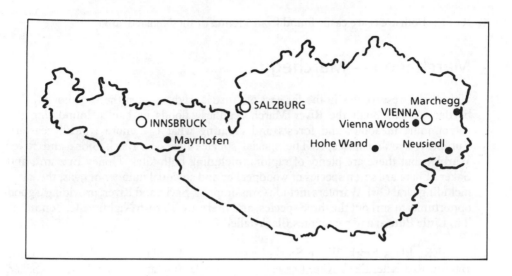

Hohe Wand, Rax and Schneeberg

These three mountain areas lie southwest of Vienna and offer the opportunity for really good, high-class birding at no great distance from either the city itself or the Neusiedl area.

The Hohe Wand (literally 'High Wall') is a vertical, rock outcrop about 12 km long by 3 km wide (7½ × 2 miles). It is well covered with forest and is a noted beauty spot that attracts many visitors in summer, particularly at weekends. The woods hold a good variety of birds, including Black Woodpecker, Capercaillie, Hazelhen, Nutcracker, Crested Tit, Ring Ouzel and Buzzard. As elusive as ever is the Wallcreeper, but it is definitely here.

Similar birds can also be seen in the Rax and Schneeberg Mountains that lie a little further southwest on either side of the village of Hirschwang. Rax is reached by cable-car, Schneeberg by rack-and-pinion railway from Puchberg. The high tops of both produce Golden Eagle, Alpine Chough, Raven and Ptarmigan, with Citril Finch on the way down. The secret is to walk down at least one stop/station, and the general opinion is that the railway up Schneeberg is the better bet.

SUMMER: Golden Eagle, Buzzard, Capercaillie, Hazelhen, Nutcracker, Three-toed Woodpecker, Black Woodpecker, Wallcreeper, Alpine Accentor, Ring Ouzel, Crested Tit, Water Pipit, Alpine Chough, Hoopoe, Red-backed Shrike, Snow Finch, Citril Finch.

ACCESS: Access is by road from Stolloff along the eastern side. Climb the zigzag road to the plateau. Turn left and keep right on the road that crosses to the western escarpment.

There is a car park near the 'Naturpark'. Tracks lead northwards through good woodpecker territory to a raised viewing platform. For Rax and Schneeberg see above.

ROUTE: Both areas are easily found from Vienna or the Neusiedl area.

Marchauen — Marchegg

This WWF reserve lies in the far east of Austria, right against the Czechoslovakian border. At this point the River March regularly floods its banks, inundating the surrounding meadows and forests and creating what is a more typically eastern European marsh landscape. The special species here are Black Stork and River Warbler, but there are plenty of raptors, including both kites, Honey Buzzard, and Saker. There are seven species of woodpecker and an equal number of owls, the latter including Ural Owl. Warblers include Grasshopper, Savi's and River, providing a good opportunity to sort out the three species, and there are Thrush Nightingale, Penduline Tit, Little Bittern and sometimes Black-tailed Godwit.

SUMMER: Black Stork, White Stork, Night Heron, Purple Heron, Spoonbill, Little Bittern, Red Kite, Black Kite, Lesser Spotted Eagle, Buzzard, Honey Buzzard, Saker,

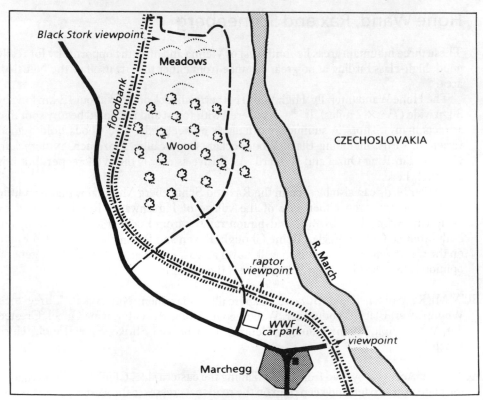

Hobby, Grey-headed Woodpecker, Green Woodpecker, Great Spotted Woodpecker, Middle Spotted Woodpecker, Ural Owl, Tengmalm's Owl, Pied Flycatcher, Collared Flycatcher, Thrush Nightingale, Grasshopper Warbler, Savi's Warbler, River Warbler, Short-toed Treecreeper, Golden Oriole, Penduline Tit, Hawfinch.

ACCESS: The village of Marchegg lies north of the Danube on Route 49. From the south continue through the village and, at the far end, take a track to the right to the reserve car park. A major floodbank runs northward from the car park. Walk along this for 3 km (2 miles) and then return via paths through meadows and, later, woods. The best views of Black Stork are in the north, over the meadow area. Walking south from the car park for a few hundred metres provides an excellent viewpoint for soaring birds of prey. Thereafter there is no access along the bank. Take mosquito repellent.

ROUTE: Little more than an hour's drive from Vienna or the Neusiedl area, but worthy of a thorough exploration.

Mayrhofen

This is a small resort town in the Austrian Tirol about 70 km (43 miles) southeast of Innsbruck. The surrounding hills are covered with conifers and, where these reach their highest point, there are grassy meadows. The valley floor is grassland, with smaller areas of cultivation. Two cable-cars give access up to about 2440 m (8000 feet) — the Penkenbahn and the Ahornbahn — with good zigzag paths down through the various habitats. The former is recommended as better birding.

Citril Finch, at the tree line, may be quite numerous, and the woods have Three-toed Woodpecker, Nutcracker, Bonelli's Warbler and Crossbill. The valley floor has Dipper and Grey Wagtail, while more widespread species include Goshawk and Alpine Swift.

For higher-altitude species the summer ski resort of Hintertux, with Snow Finch and Alpine Accentor, lies to the southwest.

SUMMER: Honey Buzzard, Goshawk, Buzzard, Alpine Swift, Great Spotted Woodpecker, Three-toed Woodpecker, Water Pipit, Grey Wagtail, Red-backed Shrike, Nutcracker, Alpine Accentor, Dipper, Bonelli's Warbler, Wood Warbler, Firecrest, Ring Ouzel, Fieldfare, Crested Tit, Citril Finch, Serin, Crossbill, Snow Finch.

ACCESS: The cable-cars are easily reached from the village, with relatively easy walks down. Hintertux lies to the southwest.

ROUTE: Leave Innsbruck, with its international airport, and take the motorway eastwards before turning south to Mayrhofen.

Neusiedl

Lake Neusiedl is Europe's fourth largest lake, extending over 30 km (19 miles) in length and 8 km (5 miles) in width, yet nowhere is it much deeper than 2 m (6½ feet).

Occasionally the whole lake dries up, but since it is fed by underground springs this is a fortunately rare event. This shallowness is responsible for its remarkable appeal. Huge reedbeds line almost every shore and, though they are initially annoying and frustrating to the birder seeking open water, they have had the effect of seriously reducing tourist development and thus maintaining the bird population.

Neusiedl is the only example of a steppe lake in western Europe, and offers a landscape more typical of the Hungarian plains than of our image of Austria as an alpine country. Indeed, to the east the plains of the Seewinkel and particularly those of the Hansag extend straight across the Hungarian border and still offer chances of birds such as Great Bustard, Goshawk and Lesser Spotted Eagle, more typical of that country.

For its many visitors, Neusiedl ranks alongside the Camargue, the Coto Doñana and Texel as the greatest bird spot in Europe. Its birds are plentiful, varied and, in some cases, most certainly rare. The Great White Egret has its major western stronghold here, while Spoonbills are as numerous as anywhere else in Europe. No fewer than seven species of woodpecker can be found, including Black and Syrian. There are Black-necked Grebes, Little Bitterns, and decidedly eastern birds such as River and Barred Warblers and Red-breasted and Collared Flycatchers. There are even Eagle, Pygmy and Tengmalm's Owls here, though they all need either extreme good fortune or local expertise to find them. Altogether, nearly 300 species have been recorded.

The Neusiedl area is not one that can be rushed through in a few days. Several tour operators find enough to occupy their groups for a fortnight, and many visitors return year after year.

SUMMER: Black-necked Grebe, Bittern, Little Bittern, Squacco Heron, Great White Egret, Little Egret, Purple Heron, White Stork, Black Stork, Spoonbill, Greylag Goose, Garganey, Ferruginous Duck, Honey Buzzard, Red Kite, Black Kite, Goshawk, Lesser Spotted Eagle, Short-toed Eagle, Hen Harrier, Montagu's Harrier, Marsh Harrier, Saker, Peregrine, Hobby, Red-footed Falcon, Great Bustard, Black-tailed Godwit, Black Tern, Roller, Hoopoe, Grey-headed Woodpecker, Black Wood-pecker, Syrian Woodpecker, Tawny Pipit, Woodchat Shrike, Lesser Grey Shrike, Great Grey Shrike, Savi's Warbler, River Warbler, Moustached Warbler, Marsh Warbler, Great Reed Warbler, Icterine Warbler, Barred Warbler, Bonelli's Warbler, Red-breasted Flycatcher, Collared Flycatcher, Bluethroat, Bearded Tit, Penduline Tit, Ortolan Bunting, Serin, Golden Oriole.

ACCESS: Save at the village of Podersdorf on the eastern shore, the whole lake is protected by a dense growth of reeds and access is, therefore, concentrated at several strategic points.

At the village of Neusiedl-am-See, where most birders tend to stay, a causeway leads to the See Bad where there is a marina and restaurant, but birding is probably best along the road itself. The local railway runs south of the village along the shore of the lake and is handy both for getting about and for offering one of the best bird-walks in the area. Eastward towards Weiden leads to areas of poplars where Penduline Tits nest, but there are plenty of warblers as well. Thereafter, head for the lake at the next level crossing by turning right, and then continue eastward on a cycle path.

Along the western shore there is access at Oggau, where a track leads past an army barracks towards the shore, and on the reserve of Gade-Lacke, where there are good heronries. There are some hides on stilts here that are for hunting purposes, but they can be useful for watching over the reed tops for Ferruginous Duck, Bittern and the ever-present Marsh Harrier.

Just to the north, near Schützen, is the Tiergarten, with Black and other woodpeckers, Golden Oriole and definitely no access: much can be seen from the road. Rust, to the south, is famous for its White Storks and for another walk through the reeds along a causeway to the See Bad. Here Little Bittern may oblige, as well as warblers.

To the east of Neusiedl lies the lakeland of Seewinkel. Each lake varies in its attractions and is, in any case, best found with the aid of a map. The most important are listed, with their specialities.

Zicksee has Black-necked Grebe and Bittern. It should not be confused with Zick Lacke near Illmitz. To the south is Hulden Lacke, not visible from the road, but worth the effort of finding, being good for passage waders and herons. The small woodland between Illmitz and Neusiedler See has Barred and Bonelli's Warblers, woodpeckers and Penduline Tit, and is excellent for passage flycatchers and chats. The Unterstinkersee (and Oberstinkersee) is the best water for passage waders, with all the usual west European species present in excellent numbers. There are also Black and White-winged Black Terns, occasional Caspian, and this is an excellent spot for Great White Egret. The walk between the two lakes is certainly worthwhile.

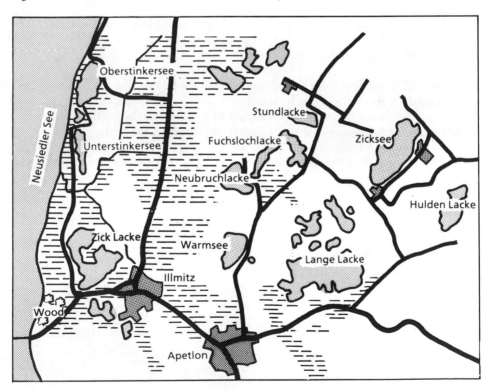

East of Apetlon is the Lange Lacke, a WWF reserve with Great White Egret, Spoonbill, Garganey, Avocet and more passage waders and terns. Further south near Pamhagen the border runs along the Einser Canal, with Barred and River Warblers, Black-tailed Godwit, Montagu's Harrier and drifting Spotted and Lesser Spotted Eagles, Goshawk, Honey Buzzard and Black Stork; many of the soaring birds are actually in Hungary, over the Kapuvarer Erlen Wald. The plains east of here and south of Tadten still hold small populations of Great Bustard, and there is a special reserve for these birds about two-thirds of the way from Tadten to the Hungarian border.

ROUTE: Vienna airport has worldwide flights and is even on the right side of the city.

Vienna Woods

The famed Vienna woods are adjacent to the city and are noted as the haunt of relatively scarce birds such as the woodpeckers and Red-breasted Flycatcher. Areas such as the Lainzer Tiergarten to the southwest of Vienna have attracted birders for many years. More convenient perhaps are the Schonnbrunn Palace Gardens, which are actually well within the city itself. Here Great Spotted and Middle Spotted and Green and Grey-headed Woodpeckers may all be seen in a remarkably confined area. Other species here include Short-toed Treecreeper, Golden Oriole and Serin.

SUMMER: Great Spotted Woodpecker, Middle Spotted Woodpecker, Green Woodpecker, Grey-headed Woodpecker, Red-breasted Flycatcher, Wood Warbler, Short-toed Treecreeper, Golden Oriole, Serin.

ACCESS: The Schonnbrunn Palace is most easily found by using the A23 motorway to Altmansdorf, from where the Palace is only 3–4 km (2–2½ miles) due north. Pass through the Palace archway, and walk across a flat area between high hedges to the pond. Then take the wooded track half-left and watch for the birds.

ROUTE: Vienna. Probably worth doing on a flying visit to Vienna or on the way to Neusiedl.

BELGIUM

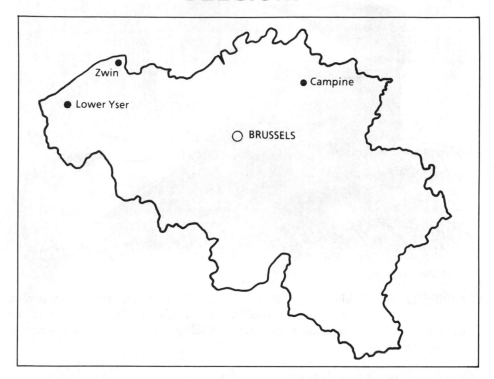

Campine

The Campine is the infertile stretch of Belgium lying north of Antwerp and extending from the estuary of the Schelde to the Dutch district of Maastricht. To all intents and purposes it lies north of the E9. Here are numerous heaths, plantations, forests, lakes, marshes and ponds, all of which sounds splendid. It is, however, such a vast area that concentration at particular points is essential.

In the west, the reserve at Kalmthout Heath has pine woods with Black Woodpecker, Black Grouse and Long-eared Owl. Much of the area is a reserve. To the east, the area around Herentals, Geel and Kasterlee has several small reserves, plus much excellent woodland with heath and marshes. Black Woodpecker, Teal, Curlew and Bluethroat all breed. Further east still is Genk, with a reserve at the nearby Stiemerbeck valley. The lakes and marshes here are favoured by Hobby, with Nightjar on the heaths, and Black Woodpecker, Goshawk, Honey Buzzard and Long-eared Owl in the woods.

Much of the land in this part of Belgium is a military zone and cannot be entered. Obey signs or pay the (ultimate?) penalty. There is, however, much to be seen at open areas and from roads.

SUMMER: Bittern, Hobby, Goshawk, Honey Buzzard, Water Rail, Curlew, Long-eared Owl, Nightjar, Black Woodpecker, Crested Tit, Bluethroat.

7

Black Woodpecker

ACCESS: Though the above areas are widely scattered reserves, they, as well as many other areas of the Campine, can be visited by roads and tracks. The forests in particular are superb, and the high population of raptors should present no difficulties to anybody wishing to find these species.

ROUTE: Off the E9 from Antwerp.

Lower Yser

The Yser is by no means a large river and its main ornitho-interest lies in its position on what is otherwise a rather inhospitable coastline for birds. The small estuary downstream from Nieuwpoort has many passage waders, as well as breeding Avocet and Kentish Plover. Part of the area, including the Yser channel, the Lombardzijde creek and some other creeks and dunes, has been declared a reserve. In autumn, Little Stint, Curlew Sandpiper, Wood and Green Sandpipers together with Spotted Redshank and Greenshank may build up to quite substantial numbers.

Further south, the right bank of the Yser near Woumen is a fine area of reed marsh, including the reserve of Blankaart. This is heavily overgrown with reeds and surrounded by water meadows. Despite its abundance in nearby Holland, the Black-tailed Godwit is a scarce bird in Belgium and finds here one of its few regular breeding areas. The reedbeds hold Bittern and Little Bittern and Marsh Harrier may also breed.

SUMMER: Bittern, Little Bittern, Marsh Harrier, Kentish Plover, Little Ringed Plover, Black-tailed Godwit, Avocet, Great Reed Warbler.

8

PASSAGE: Greenshank, Spotted Redshank, Wood Sandpiper, Green Sandpiper, Little Stint, Little Gull.

ACCESS: Both reserves can be visited by permit, obtained from Pol Houwen, Iepersesteenweg 77, 8150 Houthulst, but a great deal can be seen from roads and tracks at both areas.

ROUTE: Southwestward on the coastal road from Ostend to the Yser estuary, thence inland to Blankaart near Woumen.

Zwin

The Zwin reserve lies on the coast, tight against the Dutch border, and actually extends across the frontier. It is probably Belgium's most famous bird reserve and is, in fact, the former mouth of the River Zwin through which medieval ships sailed to the old port of Bruges. The marshes here do not, of course, compare with those of the Rhine delta to the north, but they do hold Avocet, Black-tailed Godwit and Kentish Plover. There are colonies of gulls, including regular Mediterranean, and terns, and Icterine Warbler is a regular breeder. During passage periods there is a good population of waders, and geese still frequent the inland fields during the winter.

This is a reserve 'for all the family' and the wildfowl collection and tea-room atmosphere may put off some birders as being far too dude. For those whose families insist on seeing Bruges, the Zwin offers an ideal escape.

SUMMER: Shelduck, Kentish Plover, Black-tailed Godwit, Avocet, Mediterranean Gull, Common Tern, Icterine Warbler.

PASSAGE: Waders.

ACCESS: Follow the minor road that skirts the old airfield and follow signs. Entrance fee.

ROUTE: Northward from Bruges on Route 67, then left to Knokke.

BRITAIN

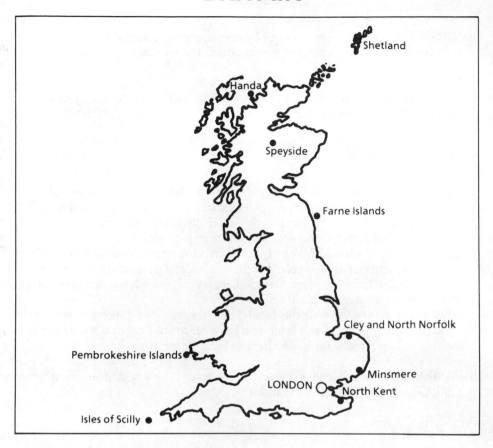

Cley and North Norfolk

A string of bird reserves now extends westwards from Cley along the North Norfolk coast, offering some of the best birding to be had anywhere in Britain. It is a cliché to call this 'the ornithologist's Mecca', but the area always has been, and remains, a major attraction to British birders. Not a day passes without birders scouring the marshes and fields, the woods and the saltings, and during the peak spring and autumn periods there often seem to be more watchers than birds.

Cley is a reedbed and lagoon reserve with plentiful hides, a good reserve centre and an excellent variety of species. Here one can see all the regular waders that pass through Britain, plus a few scarce species that breed at hardly any other location. Wildfowl are abundant in winter and the sea produces one of the best passages of birds to be found anywhere along the East Coast. 'Nancy's Cafe' by the windmill is the unofficial centre of the UK 'grapevine' and is the first port of call for most visitors.

Blakeney Point is a splendid ternery and an excellent place to see grounded migrants.

Being awkward to reach (long slog along the beach or by boat), it is less worked than it merits. Blakeney Harbour is a good estuary, with wildfowl and the more regular waders. The adjacent fields have begun to become the retreat of birds in need of peace and quiet away from birders.

Holkham is known primarily for its ability to produce rarities, especially warblers in autumn. These haunt the pines or rough scrub behind the beach, but the foreshore has geese and waders, as does Wells Harbour. Parrot Crossbills bred here in the early 1980s and are worth looking for.

Scolt Head is a low, sandy island reached only by boat. It is home to a substantial ternery and is best visited, after contacting the warden, in early summer. Next, to the west, is Titchwell, where the RSPB has created a superb lagoon and reedbed reserve of completely free and unhindered access. Bittern, Marsh Harrier and Bearded Tit breed, and the passage of waders vies in quality with that of Cley. Black Tern and Little Gull have become passage specialities. There are plentiful large hides and a good reserve centre and shop.

Just 'round the corner' and into The Wash is another RSPB reserve at Snettisham. Here the old gravel workings with islands lie just inland of one of Britain's top estuaries, and the number of waders that fly past, or in to roost, is simply staggering. Mostly these are the more common species, but all manner of things do occur here.

SUMMER: Marsh Harrier, Bittern, Water Rail, Ruff, Black-tailed Godwit, Common Tern, Sandwich Tern, Bearded Tit, Savi's Warbler.

PASSAGE: Manx Shearwater, Gannet, Brent Goose, Hen Harrier, Wood Sandpiper, Green Sandpiper, Curlew Sandpiper, Little Stint, Temminck's Stint, Whimbrel, Spotted Redshank, Greenshank, Arctic Skua, Little Gull, Short-eared Owl, Bluethroat, Barred Warbler, Snow Bunting, Lapland Bunting.

ACCESS: The whole of this coast is easily reached northwards from Norwich. Many visitors start at Cley and work their way westwards, choosing their sites according to season. Along the way one is bound to meet other birders and exchange information. Cley permits can be obtained from the reserve centre at the eastern end of the village, but many just walk the loop from the Coastguards along the beach to the East Bank and then back through the village.

Blakeney Point can be visited by boat from Morston — well advertised in this small village. The walk along the beach from Cley Coastguards is somewhat tedious. The Harbour is adjacent to Blakeney Quay. Take the wall directly north, alongside the quay car park.

Holkham lies directly north of Wells Harbour and has a large car park at the eastern end of the pines. These sites are of free access. The pines can also be approached via Holkham Gap, opposite the entrance to Holkham Hall. Scolt Head is really only for the terns; boats can be arranged in Overy Staithe or Brancaster Staithe. Access is free, but the terneries are protected by fences.

Titchwell reserve lies just west of the village to the north of the coast road. There is a car park, and access to hides is free at all times. Snettisham reserve is approached by driving to the beach car park and continuing southwards on foot to the reserve with useful hides overlooking the lagoon.

11

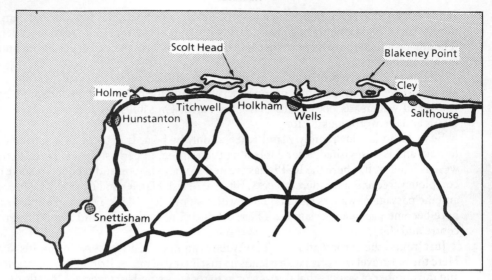

ROUTE: Norwich has good transport connections southward to London by road and railway.

Farne Islands and Lindisfarne

The Farnes consist of some 30 small islands lying off England's northeast coast between Tynemouth and the Scottish border. The majority of the islands belong to the National Trust and are of straightforward public access, though The Brownsman is closed during the breeding season. Seabirds are the main attraction and include auks, Kittiwake and Fulmar on the cliffs, Puffin and Eider inland, and four British terns on the low-lying areas. In particular this is a famous stronghold of Sandwich and the rarer Roseate Tern, though Eiders vie for popularity with the closeness of their sitting and immense numbers. There is a variety of waders and other species on passage.

Immediately west of the Farnes is Lindisfarne. Most of this area is intertidal and rich in birds, particularly during passage periods and in winter. To the birdwatcher the names of the various areas conjure up pictures of different exciting species. Fenham Flats, Skate Road, Ross Links, Holy Island Lough, Budle Bay — all are outstanding for birds. Wildfowl include a wintering flock of the light-bellied race of the Brent Goose, odd parties of Greylag Geese and a herd of up to 350 Whooper Swans. Skate Road is the favourite haunt of sea-duck, divers and three species of grebe. The number of waders in Lindisfarne runs into thousands. Even the summer visitor to the Farnes should not miss Lindisfarne.

SUMMER: Fulmar, Eider, Oystercatcher, Ringed Plover, Kittiwake, Common Tern, Arctic Tern, Sandwich Tern, Roseate Tern, Guillemot, Razorbill, Puffin.

AUTUMN AND WINTER: Divers, Slavonian Grebe, Red-necked Grebe, Brent

Goose, Pink-footed Goose, Greylag Goose, Whooper Swan, Bewick's Swan, Eider, Scoter, Whimbrel, Wood Sandpiper, Spotted Redshank, Sanderling.

ACCESS: The Farnes are reached by motor boat from Seahouses village and there is a landing charge. The best island is the Inner Farne.

The Lindisfarne reserve is of free public access, though the surrounding farmland is private. The most important access points are: Fenham near Mill Burn, north of Fenham le-Moor at Lowmoor Point; the road east of Beal and the causeway (beware: covered at high tide) across to Holy Island; north of Elwick to Whitelee Letch; east of Ross a footpath leads across Ross Links to Ross Back Sands and Skate Road; northeast of Budle; northwest of Budle at Heather Cottages; on Holy Island, the road leading north to the Links; east of Holy Island to Sheldrake Pool.

ROUTE: The A1, direct from London, passes within 2 km (1¼ miles) of the area, north of Newcastle.

Handa

Handa is a small island off the northwest coast of Scotland about 5 km (3 miles) north of Scourie. It is everyone's idea of what a seabird colony should be, with 100,000 breeding birds creating an incredible spectacle of non-stop movement and noise. Most of the species one could expect are here, and the Rock Doves are the genuine article.

SUMMER: Red-throated Diver, Fulmar, Shag, Kittiwake, Guillemot, Razorbill, Puffin, Black Guillemot, Arctic Skua, Great Skua, Rock Dove.

ACCESS: Day trips can be arranged easily from Scourie Harbour, but not on Sundays.

ROUTE: Leave the A894 at Tarbet. Nearest airport is at Inverness.

Minsmere

Minsmere is one of the best places to go birdwatching anywhere in Britain, and if the number of species seen is the test of a good day then Minsmere comes out tops. It is a reserve of the RSPB and lies on the Suffolk coast. The cross-section of habitats from the sea westwards comprises the dune beach (outside the reserve), with some interesting areas of *Suaeda* bushes; a sand-covered protective seawall; 'the Scrape', reedbeds and open pools; flat farmland; deciduous woodland; and open heather heath. The Scrape is the area of coastal pools that has been improved and extended to provide feeding grounds for waders on passage, and contains a series of islands, numbered to facilitate reference, for breeding birds. This direct interference with the process of nature has attracted Common Terns, and enabled the Avocet to breed successfully. Waders here are as good as in any other east coast area and a few rarities turn up every year. Further inland the reedbeds have Marsh Harrier, and these birds can be seen all

13

year round. Bearded Tits also breed, and Spotted Crakes have done so on occasions, though they are far from regular even as visitors. The farmland and woodland hold most of the birds one would expect to find in such areas of southern England, and the heath has Nightjar.

Minsmere is just one, albeit the best, of a series of coastal marshes in Suffolk that make an excellent birdwatching holiday.

SUMMER: Shoveler, Garganey, Spotted Crake, Marsh Harrier, Avocet, Sandwich Tern, Common Tern, Little Tern, Nightjar, Bearded Tit.

PASSAGE: Spoonbill, Spotted Redshank, Little Stint, Curlew Sandpiper, Black Tern.

ACCESS: Though Minsmere can be seen from two free public hides, entrance to the reserve is strictly by permit. These are available on various days of the week, varying from season to season. At present the reserve is closed only on Tuesdays. Parties should write in advance.

ROUTE: Leave the A12 eastwards just north of Yoxford, signposted Westleton. At Westleton take the Dunwich road and turn right after 3 km (nearly 5 miles), signposted Minsmere. Continue along a rough track, paying toll at summer weekends; park at the end and walk along the coast to the reserve entrance. One can go by train to Darsham, with connections to London, and hire a taxi from a nearby garage.

North Kent Marshes

The visitor to London, with only a day or two to spare for birding, need look no further than the marshes that line the Thames estuary in North Kent. Here, among the power stations and refineries, is some of the best birding in Britain. The Thames itself has exposed mudbanks at low tide that are the haunt of waders, ducks and geese. Behind the protective seawall are huge areas of rough grazing broken by dykes, fleets and flooding, providing roosting and additional feeding areas for these birds plus a home for many others. If time is really short, the visitor should concentrate on either Cliffe or Sheppey; if time allows, the area between the two is worthy of a full exploration.

Cliffe boasts a series of pits that have been excavated to provide material for the local cement industry. Mostly the water is deep, therefore providing a home for grebes and duck, with divers in winter. During passage periods, however, they also attract waders and terns and regularly boast a good rarity each season. From Cliffe Pools it is possible to walk the seawall eastwards, passing the marshes at Cooling to Egypt and St Mary's Bays, before cutting back inland to the RSPB reserve with its large heronry at Northward Hill. At Allhallows there is access to Yantlet Creek, a noted wader haunt, while further east lies the huge and rich Medway estuary.

Sheppey is a place on its own, separated from the mainland by the Swale channel, but connected by the Kingsferry Bridge. Here lies the RSPB reserve of Elmley. Often regarded as a winter birding area, Elmley is excellent at all seasons. It has good breeding birds, fine wader passage and a splendid collection of winter raptors.

SUMMER: Pintail, Wigeon, Greylag Goose, Marsh Harrier, Black-tailed Godwit, Red-shank, Avocet, Common Tern.

PASSAGE: Marsh Harrier, Montagu's Harrier, Curlew Sandpiper, Little Stint, Tem-minck's Stint, Spotted Redshank, Greenshank, Green Sandpiper, Wood Sandpiper, Black-tailed Godwit, Ruff, Grey Plover.

WINTER: Red-throated Diver, Bewick's Swan, White-fronted Goose, Brent Goose, Wigeon, Shoveler, Hen Harrier, Marsh Harrier, Rough-legged Buzzard, Merlin, Peregrine, Short-eared Owl, Knot, Grey Plover, Bar-tailed Godwit.

ACCESS: From Cliffe village turn left on a track out to the pools. Beyond the coastguard cottages the seawall leads eastward to the Cooling Marshes. Northward Hill can be reached at the far end of this walk, at the southeastern corner of St Mary's Bay. Alternatively, take minor roads from Cliffe to High Halstow, park at the village hall, and walk down Northwood Avenue to the reserve footpath. Continue to Decoy Farm and Swigshole to the Thames. Yantlet Creek is reached by walking eastwards along the seawall from Allhallows.

The huge Medway complex can be worked from its northern shores near Stoke Lagoon, just by the A228 where it crosses to the Isle of Grain. Alternatively, take the A249 toward Shellness and turn left just before the Kingsferry Bridge, signposted Lower Halstow. Turn westwards off this (with the aid of the OS map) and stop where a track leads to Chetney Cottages. Follow this and fork left to the seawall.

For Elmley, continue on the A249 over Kingsferry Bridge and turn right on the first farm track after 2 km (1¼ miles). Follow signs to the RSPB reserve.

ROUTE: Take the M2 from London, using the M25 ring road if starting in the west. Heathrow to Sheppey takes about two hours by road.

Pembrokeshire Islands

Pembrokeshire with its cliffs and islands is one of the most accessible and important of British seabird areas. Though Continental birdwatchers can go to the Channel Islands and the Sept Îles reserve on the Channel coast of France to see Gannets, in no way do those sites compare with the thousands of pairs that can be seen at Grassholm. What is more, the teeming colonies of auks, Kittiwakes and Fulmars of Skokholm, Skomer and the many mainland headlands are on a totally different scale from that of the Channel sites.

Though holding the gannetry, Grassholm is the smallest, least accessible and, Gannets apart, the least attractive of the islands. Skomer is only 2 km (1¼ miles) from the mainland and is the largest, the most easily accessible and the best island for birds. Its 200-foot (60-m) cliffs hold large numbers of common auks, Kittiwake, Fulmar and Chough, while inland there are vast puffinries and Manx Shearwater and Storm Petrel colonies. Short-eared Owl and Buzzard can be seen in summer.

Skokholm lies 5 km (3 miles) west of the mainland and the same distance south of

Skomer. Though breeding birds include Storm Petrel, Manx Shearwater, Guillemot and Razorbill, the emphasis on the island is on migration. Movements of chats, warblers and flycatchers are frequently very heavy, and in the latter part of the autumn movement of finches and thrushes is dramatic. Rarities of all shapes and sizes turn up with regularity.

SUMMER: Storm Petrel, Manx Shearwater, Gannet, Buzzard, Puffin, Guillemot, Razorbill, Chough, Short-eared Owl.

PASSAGE: Seabirds, chats, warblers, flycatchers, finches, thrushes.

ACCESS: For Grassholm, landing arrangements must be made with the West Wales Trust for Nature Conservation, 7 Market Street, Haverfordwest, SA61 1NF. Such landings are extremely infrequent. A nature trail is laid out for visitors to Skomer and the island is open daily in the summer, boats leaving under normal conditions at 10.30 hours from Martins Haven; there is a landing fee, though members of the West Wales Trust for Nature Conservation land free and may stay on the island in the hostel.

Access to Skokholm is via the West Wales Trust for Nature Conservation. For transport arrangements and enquiries, write to The Warden, Dale Fort Field Centre, Haverfordwest.

Isles of Scilly

These islands in the southwestern approaches have, over a period of 20 years, replaced Fair Isle (Shetland) as the prime producer of rare birds. Though the islands have a good collection of breeding seabirds, the main time for birding is October. Throughout that month there are upwards of 2,000 birders combing every nook and cranny of the five inhabited islands, as well as several that have no permanent residents. Their goal is the hyper-rare, the birds that make twitchers twitch, the 'new to Britain', 'new to Europe', 'new to the Palearctic'.

As the 'Scilly Season' has developed, so too has the infrastructure to cater for the hordes. At first the locals were disturbed by the damage to crops, but today the well-ordered birders are welcomed as a new tourist boom. A considerable array of functions, entertainments and meeting places is organised and a network of communications is designed entirely for birders. It may not be to everyone's taste, but the 'Scilly Season' is a quite remarkable gathering of skilful and enthusiastic people.

Birds vary from the commonplace to the rare. The interest is mostly in small lost passerines from North America, but Siberian birds are often present and there is generally a scattering of interesting waders. Frankly, anything can turn up here, and one has the feeling that very little is missed.

AUTUMN: Vagrants.

ACCESS: The main island is St Mary's and the majority of birders make their base there, near the Harbour for quick inter-island transportation. Accommodation may be in short supply and should be booked in advance.

ROUTE: Regular sailings and helicopter service from Penzance to St Mary's. Penzance has excellent rail connections with London.

Shetland Isles

The Shetlands lie 6° south of the Arctic Circle, and stretch 120 km (75 miles) from north to south and about half that distance from east to west. Only 19 of the hundred or so islands are inhabited. In such a vast and difficult landscape visiting ornithologists have inevitably to be choosy, as spending a full holiday on just a single island can be very rewarding. Nevertheless, the traveller, having come perhaps 1000 km (over 600 miles) to see northern birds, can be forgiven if he tries to cram everything in. This account, therefore, concentrates on those areas generally considered most worthwhile.

Shetland is a grim and rugged land with thick peat bogs underlain by hard igneous rock. The vegetation is mainly rough grass, supporting sheep and very little else, though Fetlar is called 'the green isle' because of its comparative fertility. This northern island group is one of the most convenient and accessible areas for seabirds in Europe, and has the advantage of several other northern species to see which usually involves visiting far higher latitudes. The seabirds are fantastic. Huge cliffs towering out of the sea are just splattered with birds. Vast numbers of auks, Kittiwakes and Fulmars line the ledges, and there are two colonies of Gannets both of which are easy to see. Manx Shearwater and Storm Petrel breed out of sight, though the former is often seen on the sea on early-season evenings. Of the northern species Great and Arctic Skuas are both numerous, and the Great Skua (called Bonxie locally) can be seen more conveniently here than anywhere else in the northern hemisphere. Red-throated Diver, Dunlin and

Razorbills, Guillemots, Kittiwake and Fulmar

17

two scarce birds — Whimbrel and Red-necked Phalarope — frequent the open land and inland lochs. Among wildfowl found in the same areas are Red-breasted Merganser, Wigeon and Scoter and the occasional pair of Whooper Swans. The visitor who carefully examines every gull in Lerwick Harbour may be rewarded by a summering but non-breeding Glaucous or Iceland Gull. A pair of Snowy Owls successfully bred in 1967–75, but only females have been seen since.

SUMMER: Red-throated Diver, Gannet, Fulmar, Manx Shearwater, Storm Petrel, Eider, Scoter, Red-breasted Merganser, Dunlin, Snipe, Common Sandpiper, Golden Plover, Whimbrel, Red-necked Phalarope, Arctic Tern, Common Tern, Arctic Skua, Great Skua, Kittiwake, Guillemot, Razorbill, Puffin, Black Guillemot, Wren, Twite, Hooded Crow.

ACCESS: Almost anywhere in Shetland is good for birds and a holiday could be had on any of the inhabited islands. Unst lies in the extreme north of the group and is 20 km by 8 km (12½ × 5 miles). The southern half is well cultivated and as green as nearby Fetlar. The cliff scenery is among the best in Britain, and Hermaness in the north of the island is the culmination of many a birdwatcher's dream. Cliff-nesting seabirds fill the air and offshore lie the stacks around Muckle Flugga with their large gannetry. The clifftops are honeycombed with the burrows of Puffins, while the moors inland are the stronghold of Great and Arctic Skuas. The Hermaness reserve was established in 1955, but there are no restrictions on access. The nearby Loch of Cliff is a favourite freshwater bathing place for many of the seabirds. Baltasound, the main village, is served by a regular boat from Lerwick, and the ferries between Mainland and Yell and between Yell and Unst provide an overland route.

Fetlar is the smallest of the main islands. Although its cliffs are not so impressive as many in Shetland, the usual auks, gulls and Fulmars manage to breed. Apart from waders, Fetlar also boasts both skuas and from 1967 to 1975 held breeding Snowy Owls.

Mainland is not to be overlooked by birdwatchers arriving hot-foot for the other famous Shetland islands. It has most of the specialities and with better services and facilities can provide a more varied holiday than any other island, and it is, of course, the best centre for seeing all the others by day trips. Gannets can be seen fishing in Lerwick Harbour and there are numerous cliffs with seabirds. Both species of scoter (only one breeding) regularly occur in Weisdale Voe, and Whiteness Voe is also worth a good look. Ronas Hill lies on the northwestern side of Mainland and extends along 20 km (12½ miles) of coast, including cliffs up to 750 feet (230 m) with seabirds and skuas. There is a wide choice of accommodation, including a wealth of guest houses.

Noss lies 5 km (3 miles) east of Lerwick and its cliffs, although they drop a mere 600 feet (180 m), seem as high as the famous 1400-foot (430-m) Conachair of St Kilda. Over 3,000 pairs of Gannets breed and the cliffs are covered with auks, Kittiwakes and Fulmars. On the top are Puffins and Great and Arctic Skuas. There are many tourist trips around Noss by boat from Lerwick which provide an ideal way of seeing the seabird cliffs.

Fair Isle lies mid-way between Orkney and Shetland and because of its isolation, geographical position and small size is world famous as a bird observatory. Though Fair

Isle is mainly a migration study station, it does have interesting breeding species such as Great and Arctic Skuas, auks including Black Guillemot, Storm Petrel, Fulmar and the Fair Isle subspecies of the Wren. Vagrants, however, are the Observatory's life blood and turn up weekly, if not daily, during the autumn. Loganair operate a twice-weekly service and an Observatory charter once a week. Accommodation is available on a full-board basis. Details from The Warden, Fair Isle Bird Observatory, Lerwick, Shetland, Scotland.

ROUTE: Regular daily air services between Sumburgh and Kirkwall (Orkney) and Aberdeen, and also from Wick on the Scottish mainland. There are connections with other parts of Britain. There are regular twice-weekly sailings from Aberdeen to Lerwick via Kirkwall, and Loganair operate a useful inter-island service.

Speyside

Continental birders visiting Britain expect two distinct types of birding: they expect the best seabird colonies in Europe, plus the chance to see several northern birds that are otherwise rather awkward. For the latter they are well advised to follow the path beaten by successive generations of British birders to the Spey valley. Here, around Aviemore, they find a land of moors and mountains, forests and lakes not much different from the landscape of Scandinavia. Here they can seek Golden Eagle, Peregrine, Hen Harrier, Ptarmigan, Dotterel and the otherwise localised northern grouse. Here too there are Scottish Crossbills, now recognised as a distinct species from their Continental (and English) counterparts. There are the more widespread Crested Tit and Osprey, and some very scarce waders, but above all there is some of the most beautiful countryside in the whole of Britain.

Once this landscape was the haunt of fishermen, stalkers and a few eccentric birdwatchers. Today, Speyside is a tourist resort in both winter and summer. The charm of Aviemore has disappeared, but the result has been to make the area more accessible to everyone, including birders.

SUMMER: Red-breasted Merganser, Capercaillie, Black Grouse, Red Grouse, Water Rail, Hen Harrier, Golden Eagle, Goshawk, Sparrowhawk, Merlin, Peregrine, Dotterel, Golden Plover, Wood Sandpiper, Crested Tit, Scottish Crossbill, Snow Bunting.

ACCESS: The remnants of the Caledonian forest at Rothiemurchus, Glenmore and Abernethy have been surrounded by modern plantations but still maintain their unique fauna. Everyone should visit Loch an Eilean and Loch Morlich and spend time walking the forest tracks. Loch Garten is the home of the Osprey and is well signposted from the A95 and elsewhere.

For higher-altitude birds, drive past Loch Morlich to the Cairngorm ski-lift terminal and take the easy way to the tops; weatherproof clothing, map and compass are essential, even in brilliant sunny summer weather. To the south, the RSPB reserve at Loch Insh is more than a winter home of wildfowl.

19

ROUTE: The A9 is a continuation of the motorway system of southern Scotland and runs right through the Spey valley. There are also regular trains from London stopping at Aviemore.

BULGARIA

Burgas

The town of Burgas has, over the years, become a well-known site for visiting birdwatchers. The main attraction is the three large lakes nearby that were formerly breeding haunts of a large and varied collection of waterbirds. Today, the blossoming commercialism of Burgas has all but destroyed these populations, though Lake Burgas itself does retain a fair amount of natural habitat. Lake Atanosov is now a series of saltpans, with good waders during passage periods together with breeding Avocet, Stilt and Kentish Plover. Lake Mandra is the most despoiled and should be searched if time permits after visits to the more northern lakes.

White Pelican is still regular and Glossy Ibis, Spoonbill and Great White Egret are invariably present on passage. It is, however, during these passage periods that the hordes of waders that are now the main attraction put in an appearance. Marsh, Terek and Broad-billed Sandpipers are always a possibility, and there are often outstanding numbers of Ruff and Little Stint together with Black and White-winged Black Terns. Though little studied, the movements of raptors along this coast could prove very interesting indeed.

SUMMER: White Stork, Little Egret, Kentish Plover, Avocet, Black-winged Stilt, Little Tern, Mediterranean Gull, Little Gull, Tawny Pipit, Short-toed Lark, Spanish Sparrow, Black-headed Bunting.

PASSAGE: White Pelican, Great White Egret, Spoonbill, Glossy Ibis, Ruddy Shelduck, Kentish Plover, Ruff, Little Stint, Black Tern, White-winged Black Tern, Gull-billed Tern, Little Gull.

ACCESS: Burgas is the ideal centre and offers a variety of accommodation. Route 11, to the north, gives good views over the saltpans of Lake Atanosov, and the road westward to Ezerovo provides access to Lake Burgas. Despite the boom in travelling, I get reports of birders being arrested more at this site than at any other. Anyone visiting this area should be prepared to see the inside of the local police headquarters for a few hours; take a copy (not a photocopy — in any case see copyright law) of this book, plus a field guide, and be prepared for interrogation. Though there is an apparently sensitive factory here, it seems to produce nothing more remarkable than pickles.

ROUTE: Most crews enter via Greece or Turkey.

Rila

The highest point of Bulgaria is Mount Stalin in the southwestern corner of the country, some 105 km (65 miles) south of Sofia. Here too is the famous Rila Monastery, with murals covering every inch of wall space inside and frescoes proliferating outside. This well-trodden tourist route makes a perfect base for birders intent on high-altitude and forest birds. Most of the real gems can be found here, but as always they are somewhat scarce and need searching for. Wallcreeper and Hazelhen fall into this category. They do not give themselves up lightly.

Woodpeckers, including Black and Grey-headed, can be found among the conifers on the slopes above the monastery, while higher still there are Golden Eagle, Alpine

J.D.

Sombre Tit

22

Chough, Rock Nuthatch and even Shore Lark and Alpine Accentor. The last two species do require some hiking through the forests to more open countryside above. Around the monastery itself the deciduous woods hold Sombre and Willow Tits, Treecreeper, Siskin and Hawfinch, while Nutcracker, Rock Partridge, Rock Bunting and raptors may be seen virtually anywhere.

A good spot for high-altitude species is above Borovets on the eastern side of the massif, where ski resorts and their paraphernalia make access considerably easier. Here Alpine Accentor, Shore Lark, Crag Martin, Rock Thrush and Water Pipit may oblige.

SUMMER: Golden Eagle, Short-toed Eagle, Booted Eagle, Capercaillie, Hazelhen, Goshawk, Buzzard, Honey Buzzard, Peregrine, Alpine Chough, Nutcracker, Scops Owl, Alpine Accentor, Alpine Swift, Crag Martin, Red-rumped Swallow, Wallcreeper, Rock Partridge, Shore Lark, Water Pipit, Black Woodpecker, Grey-headed Wood-pecker, Rock Thrush, Firecrest, Sombre Tit, Willow Tit, Crested Tit, Rock Bunting, Cirl Bunting, Siskin, Crossbill, Hawfinch.

ACCESS: Leave Sofia southwards on Route 2 and turn left (eastwards) on Route 164 at Kočerinovo. Rila has a tourist hotel and there are plentiful walks through the forests and above. For the Borovets area leave Sofia in the same direction on Route 2, but turn left at Stanke Dimitrov to Samokov, then right to Govedarci and the ski resorts beyond.

ROUTE: Sofia has an international airport.

Srebârna Lake

Lake Srebârna is the Bulgarian equivalent of the lower Danube marshes in Romania to the north, and visiting birdwatchers are just as likely to be turned away from this sensitive border zone. Nevertheless, this is a first-rate wetland and with the demise of the Burgas area to the south is the most important wetland in the country for breeding marsh birds.

The lake lies immediately west of Silistra in the northeastern part of the country and was declared a reserve in 1948. Open water is surrounded by reeds and thickets which hold Purple, Squacco and Night Herons, Little Egret and Little Bittern. There are also Marsh Harrier, Ferruginous Duck, Black and Whiskered Terns, Penduline Tit, Barred and Icterine Warblers and a good cross-section of the species that one could expect in southeastern Europe. Altogether, Srebârna and the surrounding land offer an excellent opportunity for first-rate birding in what is, in the west, a little-known area.

SUMMER: Red-necked Grebe, Great Crested Grebe, Dalmatian Pelican, Purple Heron, Little Egret, Squacco Heron, Night Heron, Little Bittern, Greylag Goose, Garganey, Red-crested Pochard, Ferruginous Duck, Marsh Harrier, Little Crake, Spotted Crake, Black Tern, White-winged Black Tern, Whiskered Tern, Penduline Tit, Roller, Golden Oriole, Hoopoe, Icterine Warbler, Savi's Warbler, Great Reed Warbler, Marsh Warbler, Barred Warbler.

ACCESS: Though the area is a reserve, much can be seen without disturbing the sanctuary. By contacting the authorities (warden) on the ground and seeking permission to visit, however, one may avoid any complications with the local police.

ROUTE: Drive westward on Route 23 from Silistra.

CYPRUS

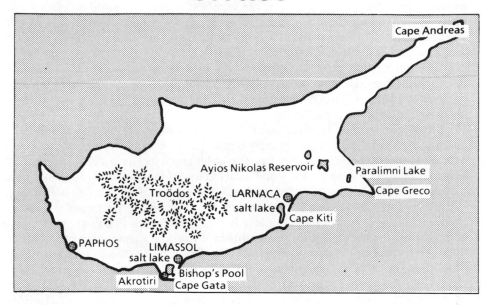

Cyprus has been well worked by a succession of distinguished and competent ornithologists over the years and there are several well-produced books to help the visitor get the best out of this beautiful island. Cyprus, at some 225 km (140 miles) from east to west and nearly 100 km (62 miles) north to south, is the third largest island in the Mediterranean. It is also the most easterly island and, lying south of Turkey, is on the major route between eastern Europe and the Middle East. Though it has several good-value breeding birds, among them the Cyprus Warbler and Cyprus Pied Wheatear (sometimes regarded as a subspecies of the Pied Wheatear) as well as Black Francolin and Dead Sea Sparrow, the main attraction is undoubtedly the migrants that pour through in spring and autumn. These include an interesting passage of birds of prey in the east, and hosts of warblers, chats and flycatchers that form the basic diet of very large colonies of Eleonora's Falcons.

Waders have a distinctly eastern bias and regularly include Greater Sand Plover along with Terek, Broad-billed and Marsh Sandpipers. There are often really substantial flocks of Little Stint in autumn. Gulls include Slender-billed and Audouin's, and White-winged Black is more abundant than Black Tern. Among the smaller birds, Cretzschmar's and Black-headed Buntings breed and Ortolans are regular. Masked Shrikes breed and three other species of shrike pass through, only Great Grey being absent. Collared Flycatchers are regular in spring and Semi-collared are probably overlooked among them. Most of the Mediterranean warblers breed and Olivaceous are widespread and common.

Cyprus has endured a somewhat tumultuous history, and even today there is conflict between the Turkish-speaking people of the north and the Greek-speaking population of the south. Indeed, the island is now effectively partitioned and visitors must choose which half to visit. Birders have little choice: the best bird spots are in the south and the

25

Greek part is, in any case, best served by flights, hotels etc. Unfortunately, several British military bases occupy some of the very best birding areas and access is either restricted or requires discretion. It is best not to carry a camera when birding around these areas, and wherever signs prohibiting photography are displayed it is wise not to use binoculars. The major birding areas, from east to west, are listed.

Cape Greco, where grounded migrants are often abundant, is itself out of bounds owing to the presence of a booster station for Radio Monaco. The surroundings, however, are still good and the invariably dry Lake Paralimni holds a good variety of open-country species.

The salt lake south of Larnaca holds Flamingo, as well as many waders and gulls, plentiful egrets and many open-country birds. To the west of the lake at the Tekke Mosque is an area of reeds and woodland that holds migrants. Spiro's Beach Restaurant is south of the main airport runway and adjacent to various pools that often hold good waders, as well as Flamingo. Further south still, Cape Kiti is often a good seawatch spot.

Probably the most famous birding area on the island is the peninsula of Akrotiri, south of Limassol. Here a large salt lake is a major haunt of Flamingo, waders and herons, while there are plentiful small birds in the varied surroundings of woodland, scrub, orchards, gravel pits, shoreline and cliffs. This is the best area for Greater Sand Plover and Broad-billed Sandpiper, as well as an outstanding one for small migrants. Cape Gata and the southern part of the peninsula lies within RAF Akrotiri and is generally out of bounds. It is, however, still possible to drive around the salt lake, picking up species such as Dead Sea Sparrow, Penduline Tit and Moustached Warbler. It is also possible to view Kensington Cliffs, where Eleonora's Falcon and Griffon Vulture breed. The mouth of the Paramali River to the west is excellent for small migrants and waders and is a noted haunt of Black Francolin, while further west still is Cape Aspro (no headaches here), where there are the largest colonies of Eleonora's Falcon.

Paphos is another excellent bird area, as well as an attractive place for a holiday. It is a small, historical, attractive area which has good birding sites nearby — an ideal set-up for family holidays. To the east, the Dhiarizos River has good reedbeds and a combination of scrub and pools that holds Black Francolin and many warblers. The western part of Cyprus is best for the endemic warbler. To the north, the Troödos Mountains hold Pallid Swift, Crag Martin and Griffon, while there is just a chance of Imperial Eagle.

Visitors to the Turkish sector of Cyprus have less choice of habitat and resort facilities, but Cape Andreas forms probably the best migration watchpoint of all. Again there is a military presence, but there is a great opportunity to update our information on bird migration here. Black Francolins breed in the scrub around the Apostolos Andreas Monastery.

SPRING: Little Bittern, Night Heron, Squacco Heron, Little Egret, Purple Heron, White Stork, Glossy Ibis, Flamingo, Honey Buzzard, Black Kite, Griffon Vulture, Pallid Harrier, Bonelli's Eagle, Imperial Eagle, Lesser Kestrel, Red-footed Falcon, Peregrine, Black Francolin, Spotted Crake, Little Crake, Crane, Demoiselle Crane, Black-winged Stilt, Collared Pratincole, Greater Sand Plover, Spur-winged Plover, Little Stint, Temminck's Stint, Broad-billed Sandpiper, Marsh Sandpiper, Slender-billed Gull, Audouin's Gull, White-winged Black Tern, Black-bellied Sandgrouse, Great Spotted Cuckoo, Scops Owl, Bee-eater, Roller, Calandra Lark, Short-toed

Cyprus Pied Wheatear (male, winter plumage)

Lark, Red-rumped Swallow, Tawny Pipit, Thrush Nightingale, Isabelline Wheatear, Cyprus Pied Wheatear, Moustached Warbler, Olivaceous Warbler, Cyprus Warbler, Rüppell's Warbler, Bonelli's Warbler, Collared Flycatcher, Semi-collared Flycatcher, Golden Oriole, Lesser Grey Shrike, Masked Shrike, Dead Sea Sparrow, Ortolan Bunting, Cretzschmar's Bunting, Black-headed Bunting.

AUTUMN: Osprey, Pallid Harrier, Red-footed Falcon, Eleonora's Falcon, Cyprus Pied Wheatear, Red-backed Shrike.

ACCESS: *Cape Greco*: Easily reached to the entrance of the Radio Monaco booster station. Finsch's Wheatear is a winter speciality along this road. Excellent seawatching and grounded migrants.

Lake Paralimni: Lies north of Greco. The surrounding fields are worth exploring, even when the lake is dry, for migrants.

Larnaca Salt Lake: Leave Larnaca southwards on the main road and work your way around the airport runway to the lake. Watch for Tekke Mosque on the right and later for the Meneou Kiti Beach road. Left off this leads to Spiro's Beach and pool and views of the main lake.

Akrotiri: Leave Limassol west and turn left signposted 'Ladies Mile Beach'. Continue to Zakaki Marshes and then take the track parallel to the beach, with side tracks leading to the eastern shore of the salt lake. Do not miss Kensington Cliffs. Tracks lead west around the southern shore; there is a gate that leads to Bishop's Pool, and eventually to the main Akrotiri base road. Turn right and explore the western shoreline. Before an area of woodland turn left to the reeds of Phasouri, or right to those at the salt lake. At this northwestern corner there are Dead Sea Sparrows.

Dhiarizos River: Stop on the road to Paphos at Kouklia and explore upstream and

27

downstream for Black Francolin. Other riverbeds nearby may be equally productive. To the north of Paphos, the area towards Lara can be rewarding.

ROUTE: The international airport is at Larnaca.

CZECHOSLOVAKIA

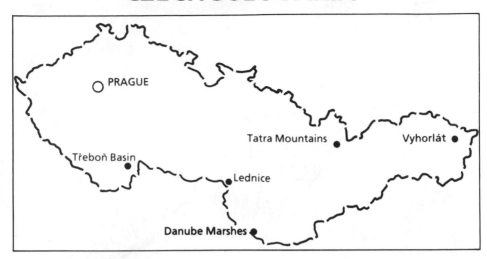

Danube Marshes

The Danube forms the common border with Hungary below Bratislava, in the south-central part of the country. As elsewhere in central Europe, it is prone to seasonal flooding and its banks are lined by marshes and flooded woodland. Many of these areas are quite excellent and have, over the years, been declared reserves. Purple Heron, Cormorant, Marsh and Montagu's Harriers, plus a fine collection of warblers, all breed and there are several sites worth exploring. The best marshes of all lie between Bratislava and Komárno. Between these two towns the Danube splits into two major channels, the Danube (Dunaj) proper and the Maly Dunaj, and the area is actually a huge island. This low-lying plain is also the major stronghold of the Great Bustard and there is a special reserve west of Komárno.

SUMMER: Cormorant, Little Bittern, Purple Heron, Marsh Harrier, Montagu's Harrier, Little Crake, Great Bustard, Stone-curlew, Black-tailed Godwit, Bearded Tit, Bluethroat, Moustached Warbler, Savi's Warbler.

ACCESS: Though the whole of this region is worth exploring, there are several major areas to visit. In the west the Dedinský ostrov, near Gabčíkovo, is a fine reedbed area, while just to the east is Istragov. Zilizský močiar is near Čilizská Radvaň, the Great Bustard reserve is Člatná na Ostrove, 13 km west of Komárno, while to the northeast of that town is Parížské močiare near Gbelce (see map on page 30).

ROUTE: Route 63 from Bratislava.

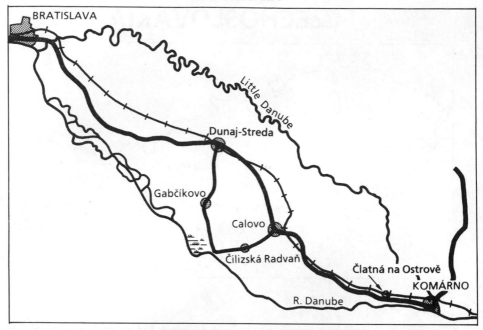

Lednice

At the border with Austria, immediately north of Vienna, two rivers join to form the March (see Marchegg in Austria). These rivers, the Morava and Dyje, meet near the town of Lednice among a maze of marshes, channels, islands and backwaters to form one of the most important wetland areas in the country. Indeed, at first sight it would seem that the Lednice area is another of these huge central European wetlands that are so rich in birds, but so difficult to work. Fortunately, there is a chain of lakes to the southwest of Lednice that hold most of the local specialities and can be viewed without difficulty. Here is a large colony of Black-necked Grebes, along with Greylag Geese, Red-crested Pochard, both storks, Bittern, Little Bittern, Night Heron, two harriers, Black Kite and a whole variety of other species. Here too there are River Warbler and Collared Flycatcher. The ponds at Pohořelice hold similar birds, while the nearby hills at Palava are noted for Rock Thrush.

SUMMER: Black-necked Grebe, Bittern, Little Bittern, Night Heron, White Stork, Black Stork, Greylag Goose, Red-crested Pochard, Honey Buzzard, Goshawk, Montagu's Harrier, Marsh Harrier, Black Kite, Black-tailed Godwit, Mediterranean Gull, Roller, Hoopoe, Black Woodpecker, Wryneck, Golden Oriole, Bearded Tit, Penduline Tit, Rock Thrush, Savi's Warbler, River Warbler, Marsh Warbler, Icterine Warbler, Barred Warbler, Woodchat Shrike, Lesser Grey Shrike, Collared Flycatcher, Ortolan Bunting.

ACCESS: The ponds near Lednice are crossed by minor roads and can easily be watched from these.

30

ROUTE: Brno is the nearest large town, but the crossing point from Austria, Drasenhofen — Mikulov, provides an opportunity for crews at Neusiedl to make a short trip here without difficulty. Please let me know the results.

Tatra Mountains

The various ranges of the Tatra (Tatry) Mountains occupy a huge area of eastern Czechoslovakia, culminating in the High Tatras at Mount Gerlach near the Polish border. This part of the wide Carpathian arch is certainly the highest and arguably the most beautiful part of this mountain chain. Here there are huge forests, mostly of spruce, but with smaller areas of deciduous and pine and a little meadowland. Some areas are well above the tree line and much of this is included in the Tatra National Park. Though noted for its mammals, which still include Bear, Lynx and Chamois, the whole area is excellent for birds, including Golden and Lesser Spotted Eagles, various owls, woodpeckers, Black Stork and high-altitude species such as Alpine Accentor, Rock

Ural Owl

Thrush and Wallcreeper. The forests hold Nutcracker, Capercaillie and Hazelhen. This is no place for a quick thrash for staked-out specials, but a good holiday of exploration should prove rewarding.

SUMMER: White Stork, Black Stork, Golden Eagle, Lesser Spotted Eagle, Goshawk, Black Kite, Hobby, Pygmy Owl, Long-eared Owl, Eagle Owl, Ural Owl, Tengmalm's Owl, Black Grouse, Capercaillie, Hazelhen, Golden Oriole, Nutcracker, Black Woodpecker, Middle Spotted Woodpecker, Three-toed Woodpecker, Grey-headed Wood-

31

pecker, Rock Thrush, Ring Ouzel, Wallcreeper, Dipper, Alpine Accentor, Firecrest, Crested Tit, Red-breasted Flycatcher, Icterine Warbler, Barred Warbler, Crossbill, Siskin.

ACCESS: The best centre is Starý Smokovec, where there are hotels, good transport and cable-cars up into the mountains. To the east, Tatranská Lomnica is the Park HQ, with a cable-car up Lomnický Štít. To the west, the Malá Fatra Mountains have more deciduous woods and can be explored from Žilina.

ROUTE: Check internal flights from Prague.

Třeboň Basin

The Třeboň Basin, Třebonská on the map, lies in the western part of Czechoslovakia, south of Prague and at no great distance from the Austrian border. This is a low-lying area with many ponds, some of which have been used since the eighteenth century for rearing carp. In particular the Velký (big) and Malý (little) Tisý (ponds) have been bird reserves for many years and their reedbeds hold a good population of Purple Herons and Marsh Harriers. There is also a Night Heronry, and even Great White Egrets breed occasionally. Other good breeding birds include Black-necked Grebe, Black Tern and a cross-section of warblers, plus Penduline Tit and Collared Flycatcher. Passage brings regular Osprey, Little Gull, terns and some waders, though the latter vary from pond to pond.

SUMMER: Black-necked Grebe, Bittern, Little Bittern, Night Heron, Purple Heron, White Stork, Greylag Goose, Little Crake, Spotted Crake, Honey Buzzard, Marsh Harrier, Hobby, Black Tern, Middle Spotted Woodpecker, Wryneck, Golden Oriole, Fieldfare, Icterine Warbler, Savi's Warbler, River Warbler, Penduline Tit, Great Grey Shrike, Collared Flycatcher, Serin.

PASSAGE: Osprey, Little Gull.

ACCESS: The largest area of ponds lies north of Třeboň, on either side of the Veselí n. Luž road, and can be seen from adjacent roads and tracks.

ROUTE: Southwards from Prague on the E14 to Veselí.

Vyhorlát

This range of hills in the easternmost part of the country is seldom visited by outsiders, despite its obvious attractions. Rising only to 1000 m (3280 feet), the hills are covered with mainly deciduous woods offering a home to a fine range of species, several of which are otherwise undoubtedly scarce in Czechoslovakia. Raptors are particularly important, and species include Golden, Lesser Spotted, Short-toed, Booted and probably even Imperial Eagles. Saker and Peregrine both breed, along with both kites. The woods also hold a good range of woodpeckers and even the decidedly difficult Ural Owl.

Though this area is almost the full length of the country away from Prague, it would seem well worth the efforts involved in making the journey and certainly worthwhile for anyone visiting the Tatras. The really intrepid might care to cross from Hungary by road via Slov Nová Město.

SUMMER: Golden Eagle, Lesser Spotted Eagle, Short-toed Eagle, Imperial Eagle, Booted Eagle, Black Kite, Red Kite, Saker, Peregrine, Goshawk, Ural Owl, Grey-headed Woodpecker, Black Woodpecker, Middle Spotted Woodpecker, White-backed Woodpecker, Syrian Woodpecker, Wryneck, Roller, Hoopoe, Dipper, Crested Tit, Rock Thrush, Red-breasted Flycatcher, Rock Bunting.

ACCESS: Base at Humenné or Michalovce and explore on minor roads and tracks.

ROUTE: Košice is the nearest large town, but see above.

DENMARK

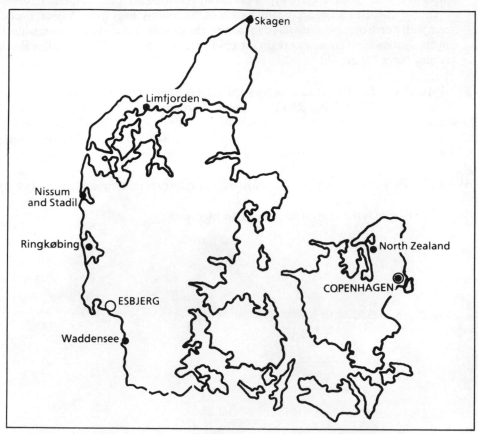

Copenhagen

The Copenhagen area is more than a convenient place for the busy traveller to get out and see a few birds in a short time. It is an outstanding area for birds in its own right, mainly as a result of its geographical position in the east of the country. There are a number of public parks, several of which have large lakes and which are known for the number of wildfowl, gulls and other waterbirds they attract. In particular, Utterslev Mose has a wealth of species in summer including three species of grebe, Greylag Goose, Pochard, Common Tern, Thrush Nightingale and sometimes Great Reed Warbler, all in a park completely surrounded by heavily built-up areas. Of the other parks, the most notable are Valbyparken (Red-throated Pipits regular in autumn) and Charlottenlund Skov, the latter being the best place for Icterine Warbler in summer.

The major bird areas, however, lie in the southern part of Copenhagen on the island of Amager. Sjaellandsbroen overlooks the largest area of open water in the harbour at the southern end, and holds large numbers of seabirds, including Smew, in winter. The little pond south of the bridge is always worth a look and in summer holds Little Grebe, a rather scarce bird in Denmark. Kongelunden is a mixed wood with thick undergrowth in the southern part of Amager and is an area of outstanding ornithological interest. Almost all of the passerines that one would expect to find in Denmark are present. Of interest to the visitor are Barred Warbler, Icterine Warbler and Thrush Nightingale. To the west of the forest is an area of saltmarshes that regularly hold numbers of waders on spring passage.

During autumn passage, the southward movement of birds of prey through Scandinavia can occasionally be seen over the streets of the city. September and October are the best months, and Honey Buzzard, Buzzard and Sparrowhawk are sometimes very numerous.

SUMMER: Great Crested Grebe, Black-necked Grebe, Red-necked Grebe, Little Grebe, Greylag Goose, Pochard, Common Tern, Thrush Nightingale, Great Reed Warbler, Icterine Warbler, Barred Warbler.

Barred Warbler

AUTUMN: Wildfowl, Buzzard, Honey Buzzard, Osprey, Sparrowhawk, Spotted Redshank, Temminck's Stint, Little Stint, Ruff.

WINTER: Duck, Smew, gulls, Dipper, Kingfisher.

ACCESS: All of the areas mentioned in this section can be visited conveniently by public transport. Utterslev Mose: a public park in the northeast of the city. Sjaellandsbroen: part of Copenhagen Harbour. Kongelunden: a wooded area in south Amager.

ROUTE: Copenhagen is an international centre and has a wealth of accommodation.

Faeroes

Geographically nearer to Iceland, Norway and Britain, the Faeroe Islands (Føroyar) nevertheless are politically and culturally part of Denmark, though in fact the people speak a language (Faeroese) of their own. There are 18 inhabited islands lying approximately half way between Shetland and Iceland. Visitors to the Faeroes must expect bad weather even during the best time for a visit, which is June. There can be drizzle for weeks on end, with continuous cloud down to sea level. The seabird colonies are among Europe's finest ornithological sights. There is a gannetry on Mykines, and vast colonies of Guillemot, Razorbill, Puffin, Kittiwake and Fulmar on almost all of the islands, but particularly on Streymoy, Mykines, Eysturoy, Kallsoy, Vidoy, Fugloy, Sandoy and Skúvoy. There are Great and Arctic Skuas on Streymoy, Svínoy, Sandoy and Skúvoy; also Leach's Petrel on Mykines and Manx Shearwater and Storm Petrel on Mykines and Skúvoy. Eider, Whimbrel, Golden Plover, Faeroe Snipe and Faeroe Wren breed all over the place, while one or two lakes hold Red-necked Phalarope, Red-throated Diver, Slavonian Grebe and several wildfowl species. In the northeastern group of the islands there is always a chance of Purple Sandpiper and Snow Bunting high up on the fjells.

SUMMER: Red-throated Diver, Slavonian Grebe, Gannet, Manx Shearwater, Fulmar, Leach's Petrel, Storm Petrel, Greylag Goose, Wigeon, Pintail, Scaup, Scoter, Red-breasted Merganser, Eider, Purple Sandpiper, Whimbrel, Golden Plover, Oyster-catcher, Snipe, Red-necked Phalarope, Great Skua, Arctic Skua, Kittiwake, Great Black-backed Gull, Arctic Tern, Guillemot, Black Guillemot, Razorbill, Puffin, Red-wing, Wren.

ACCESS: Visitors to the Faeroes must be prepared to charter taxis and boats, find accommodation where they can (outside Tórshavn) and generally be prepared to pay liberally. They should also remember that there is prohibition on the islands and that alcohol is not for sale — take your own!

Streymoy: The main island, with Tórshavn the Faeroe capital. The town's plantation holds breeding Redwing and the cliffs, mainly in the northwest, hold Wren, auks, and other seabirds. The valley near Saksum in the north of the island has an auk colony. There are hotels in Tórshavn, which is reached by boat and air from Copenhagen or Iceland. Accommodation in houses on this and other Faeroe islands can be arranged through The Faeroese Tourist Board, Føroya Ferdamannafelag, Tórshavn, Faeroe Islands.

Mykines: The most westerly island, with the Faeroes' only gannetry. There are colonies of cliff-breeding seabirds, Storm and Leach's Petrels, Manx Shearwaters and Arctic Skuas. There are boats from Vágar.

Eysturoy: Northeast of Streymoy. It has seabird cliffs at its northern tip and the lake of Toftavatn near the southern tip. The latter holds Red-throated Diver, Slavonian Grebe and Red-necked Phalarope. Possible accommodation can be arranged in homes.

Kallsoy, Vidoy and Fugloy: Part of the northeastern group of islands, with very large seabird colonies on their northern ends.

Svínoy: Has a Great Skua colony, and on both this and the previous islands there is a chance of Purple Sandpiper and Snow Bunting on the high tops. Access to the group is by boat from Tórshavn to Klaksvik, the second town of the islands.

Sandoy: South of Streymoy and one of the best islands for birds. The lakes, especially those around Sand (Sandsvatn and Grothusvatn), hold Red-throated Diver and most of the wildfowl and waders, including Red-necked Phalarope. Seabirds breed on the cliffs and Arctic and Great Skuas on the hills. There are regular boats from Tórshavn to Skopun and buses to Sand. Accommodation is possibly available in homes.

Skúvoy: A small island to the south of Sandoy with some magnificent seabird cliffs. Manx Shearwater and Storm Petrel breed on the grassy slopes and Great and Arctic Skuas in the hills, with waders including Purple Sandpiper. Boats go from Sandoy and Tórshavn and there is possible accommodation in houses.

Limfjorden

The Limfjord all but separates the 'cap' of Denmark from the rest of Jutland. It is a huge shallow inlet which, while being rich in birds, at first sight appears quite daunting to the visiting birder. Fortunately, the visitor can narrow down the search to the outstanding area along the northern shore between Thisted and the Aggersund Bridge. This excellent area is worthy of thorough exploration and a holiday here can be splendidly rewarding. Indeed, the visitor need look no further than the areas of Vestlige Vejler and Østlige Vejler, two splendid marshland reserves that hold all of the specialities for which any birding visitor to Denmark is looking.

Østlige Vejler is an area of wet grazing meadows with wet marshes and lagoons and the country's most extensive area of reedbed. It was created by the failure of a British engineer to construct a satisfactory seawall across one of the bays of the Limfjord in the nineteenth century — perhaps he was a birder? The resulting marsh has colonies of Little Gull and Gull-billed Tern, together with Red-necked and Black-necked Grebes, Bittern, Marsh Harrier, Godwit and Ruff. During passage and in winter it is a haunt of Bean and Pink-footed Geese, while passage also brings many waders.

Vestlige Vejler, to the west, has similar birds, though Red-necked Grebes are numerous in summer and there is a small colony of Avocets. The area includes Tømmerby Fjord, Vesløs Vejle, Østerild Fjord and Arup Holm.

The visitor to these areas should not ignore the migration possibilities of Hanstholm, a short distance to the northwest, where seabirds and wildfowl are the main attractions. During the breeding season there are Kittiwakes on the harbour walls, Wood Sandpipers on Vigsø Heath and a pair of Cranes on the Hanstholmreservatet. The latter is, however, of decidedly difficult access and Crane-watchers would be better advised to visit Sweden.

If holidaying hereabouts, the area of Agger Tange lies at the southwestern tip of the 'cap' beyond Thisted and affords good views of Avocet, Godwit and Ruff. It is also excellent for passage waders and wildfowl.

SUMMER: Red-necked Grebe, Black-necked Grebe, Bittern, Greylag Goose, Garganey, Shoveler, Marsh Harrier, Spotted Crake, Crane, Black-tailed Godwit, Wood

37

Sandpiper, Ruff, Dunlin, Curlew, Avocet, Little Gull, Black Tern, Gull-billed Tern, Crested Lark.

AUTUMN: Whooper Swan, Bewick's Swan, Bean Goose, Pink-footed Goose, Spotted Redshank, Little Stint, Curlew Sandpiper.

ACCESS: Østlige Vejler can be viewed from the dam at Bygholm east of Øsløs where there is parking. Vestlige Vejler can be seen from minor roads around Arup, which lies south of Østerild. Hanstholm is about 20 km (12 miles) northwest of Østerild, and though there is a track along the coast to the southwest this is closed during the breeding season; visible migration is best from the point east of the harbour.

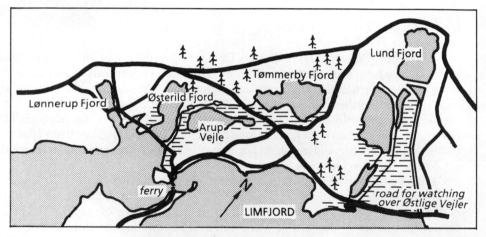

ROUTE: From the south, the area is reached by the A11 and the Oddesund Bridge in the west and Aggersund Bridge via Viborg in the east.

Nissum Fjord to Stadil Fjord

This stretch of the west Jutland coast abuts the Ringkøbing Fjord to the south and is in many ways very similar. It is treated separately to simplify what would otherwise be a very complex account.

Nissum Fjord is a shallow lake with a single outlet to the sea through the coastal dune system. There is an extensive area of pines between Bjerghuse and Husby to the south which hold Crested Tit. The beach, dunes and lakeshore are excellent during migration, especially for waders, which include most of the species one could expect to see in western Europe. In particular, Temminck's Stints are more numerous than further west. The marshes at Felsted Kog in the south of the fjord form a vast reedbed that is a particularly important breeding area for Garganey, Pintail, Shoveler and a variety of waders, including Black-tailed Godwit, Ruff and Avocet.

To the south of Nissum Fjord lies the pond of Husby Sø which, with its surrounding marshes, forms an excellent bird area, while further south still is the partly reclaimed but still excellent Stadil Fjord. This in fact leads into Ringkøbing Fjord. Black Tern, Black-tailed Godwit, Ruff, Dunlin, Avocet and Arctic Tern are all found in these two areas, which are noted for migrating wildfowl in autumn, especially Whooper and Bewick's Swans, Pink-feet and Greylag.

SUMMER: Bittern, Marsh Harrier, Montagu's Harrier, Pintail, Garganey, Shoveler, Black-tailed Godwit, Ruff, Dunlin, Avocet, Black Tern, Arctic Tern, Crested Tit, Crested Lark.

AUTUMN: Whooper Swan, Bewick's Swan, Pink-footed Goose, Greylag Goose, Brent Goose, Teal, Shoveler, Wigeon, Marsh Harrier, Spotted Redshank, Curlew Sandpiper, Temminck's Stint, Little Stint, Bar-tailed Godwit, Black Tern, Gull-billed Tern, Arctic Tern.

ACCESS: The coastal road along the dunes gives excellent views over the main area of Nissum Fjord and of the pines to the south. There is also access off minor roads in the northeast between Bøvlingbjerg, Nees and Vemb and the reserve of Felsted Kog can be visited after 1 October. Husby Sø can be seen from the Staby-Husby road, while Stadil to the south is an excellent start to an exploration of the Stadil Fjord and the marshes around Tiim.

ROUTE: The area is easily reached from Esbjerg.

Ringkøbing Fjord

Ringkøbing Fjord is the longest of the west Jutland fjords and also the most famous from a birding viewpoint. All of these lakes are shallow and cut off from the sea by only a narrow belt of dunes along which run various minor roads giving excellent views over the beach and the fjords. Where the dunes are not backed by lagoons, there are often large plantations of conifers which hold Crested Tit, with Crested Lark in the open sandy areas. Ringkøbing itself holds breeding grebes and Black Tern. The shores of the lake vary from the sandy beach to rich saltmarsh and water meadow.

The marshes on the island of Klaegbanke have been protected since 1894 and consist mainly of grass and reeds harbouring a rich breeding population of gulls including the occasional Little Gull, Sandwich Tern and Gull-billed Tern, Marsh Harrier and just possibly Spoonbill. To the south lies the peninsula of Tipperne, which consists of water meadows and saltmarshes surrounded by a vast area of shallow water with a few islands. Breeding birds include a large colony of Avocets, Black-tailed Godwit, Ruff, Sandwich Tern, Gull-billed Tern and a host of duck and gulls. Both of these reserves are exceptionally good during autumn passage, when almost all the waders and wildfowl that one can see in western Europe occur, often in large numbers. A single day once produced 50,000 wildfowl at Tipperne alone. Among these species, Pink-feet and Whooper and Bewick's Swans are most important. The similar Vaernengene area is well worth a visit.

Though the southern end is so rich, the whole of the Ringkøbing Fjord is worth exploring and will produce birds. The dune reserve of Nymindestrømmen and Holmslands Klit lies immediately south of Nymindegab and approximates to a southward extension of Ringkøbing.

SUMMER: Marsh Harrier, Montagu's Harrier, Kentish Plover, Black-tailed Godwit, Ruff, Curlew, Avocet, Black Tern, Sandwich Tern, Gull-billed Tern, Black Grouse, Crested Tit, Crested Lark.

AUTUMN: Whooper Swan, Bewick's Swan, Pink-footed Goose, White-fronted Goose, Greylag Goose, Brent Goose, Teal, Shoveler, Wigeon, Bar-tailed Godwit, Spotted Redshank, Temminck's Stint, Little Stint, Curlew Sandpiper, Wood Sandpiper, Ruff, Avocet, Black Tern.

ACCESS: The road running north and south along the beach and the roads between Skjern, Ringkøbing and Søndervig provide excellent views over the greater part of the fjord. The beach road north of Nymindegab overlooking the Tipperne peninsula is especially good, and there is free access to the dune reserve south of Tipperne village.

Klaegbanke is strictly out of bounds for all but the most scientific purposes. Tipperne, too, is strictly protected but can be visited on Fridays, Sundays and Wednesdays (in the afternoons) during June and July. The southern part of these marshes is excellent and is not part of the reserve.

ROUTE: The area is easily reached from Esbjerg. There are hotels at Ringkøbing that make an excellent base for this and the Nissum area.

Skagen

Skagen lies at the northern tip of Jutland and is primarily a migration watchpoint. Its huge sandy beaches, rolling dunes and stunted vegetation are reminiscent of such promontories in many parts of Europe. Spring, from April through to May, is by far the best season and movements are most dramatic during periods of easterly winds. At such times huge flocks of finches, thrushes and pipits can be seen passing along the coast before setting off across the sea towards Norway and Sweden. Birds of prey, mainly Buzzard and Honey Buzzard, are also to be seen and there are invariably numbers of grounded passerines. As at other such places, there are favoured spots for different times of the day and different types of birds. Visible migration is best on the north coast just east of the lighthouse. Birds of prey are best from the hill of Flagbakken, and small migrants are looked for among the bushes at the tip of the peninsula and among the trees to the north of the road before it enters the town.

Rarities do, of course, turn up and, while many such as Red-footed Falcon and Red-breasted Flycatcher are highly irregular, some are of annual occurrence. The latter category includes White-tailed Eagle, Golden Eagle and Golden Oriole. Both Glaucous and Iceland Gulls can be found in the harbour almost throughout the year.

SPRING: Red-throated Diver, Black-throated Diver, Buzzard, Rough-legged Buzzard,

Honey Buzzard, Hen Harrier, Red Kite, Sparrowhawk, Osprey, Hobby, Crested Lark, Tawny Pipit, Snow Bunting.

ACCESS: Flagbakken Hill for raptors lies west of the town of Skagen on the road south of the railway. It is best watched in the latter part of the morning and in the afternoon. The other spots are best found with the aid of a map.

ROUTE: Take the main A10 from Alborg.

Waddensee

The Waddensee, the single most important intertidal zone in Europe, extends from the coast of Holland and along the German coast to southwest Jutland. Here it terminates north of Esbjerg at the sandy promontory of Blåvandshuk. This area has a lighthouse and bird observatory (private) and is one of the best areas in Denmark for watching migration. Waders and wildfowl pass in huge numbers and, after westerly winds, there are often good movements of divers, grebes and even Gannet. The promontory is excellent for visible movements of finches, thrushes and pipits and there are frequently rarities of international status among grounded migrants, as well as semi-rarities such as Bluethroat, Lapland Bunting, Tawny Pipit and Barred Warbler.

Blåvandshuk also has other appeals, including breeding Black Grouse in the adjacent pine forest with Ruff in the meadows and even a pair of Red-necked Grebes. The latter are at the small lake of Graerup Langsø to the north, while Black Grouse lek on the edges of Kallesmaersk Heath. Inland, but extending to the south, lies the tidal inlet of Ho Bugt, a haunt of a good variety of waders including several hundred Avocets in autumn. These birds breed on the islands of Fanø and on Rømø to the south, as well as on the peninsula of Skallingen that separates Ho Bugt from the sea. Here too there are a few pairs of Kentish Plover.

Though breeding birds may be attractive, it is autumn that sees the area at its best. Wigeon are then present in their thousands and there are Greenshank, Spotted Redshank and Whimbrel in good numbers. Perhaps the outstanding feature of this season is the gathering of Avocets at the eastern end of the causeway that connects Rømø to the mainland — about 5,000 in August. Being so near to Esbjerg, this is an excellent area for a brief Danish excursion or the start of a fuller exploration.

SUMMER: Red-necked Grebe, Garganey, Spotted Crake, Kentish Plover, Curlew, Ruff, Black-tailed Godwit, Dunlin, Avocet, Black Grouse.

AUTUMN: Red-throated Diver, Black-throated Diver, Red-necked Grebe, Gannet, Brent Goose, Pink-footed Goose, Pintail, Wigeon, Shoveler, Velvet Scoter, Scoter, Eider, Merlin, Grey Plover, Whimbrel, Greenshank, Spotted Redshank, Bar-tailed Godwit, Curlew Sandpiper, Avocet, Kittiwake, Black Tern, Little Gull, Crested Lark, Shore Lark, Tawny Pipit, Bluethroat, Lapland Bunting.

ACCESS: Blåvandshuk lies west of Varde off the A12 north of Esbjerg. A road leads to the lighthouse and the best spot for visible migration is the extreme western tip.

Heathland: The various heaths with their small lakes are reached via Oksby on minor roads to Graerup and beyond. They lie just inland of Blåvandshuk. Graerup Langsø can be seen from the road to the east. Filsø can be viewed from the north at the car park at Klovbakken. Black Grouse can be seen from the road, but an early start is usually all but essential

Ho Bugt and Skallingen: Is best viewed from the Skallingen peninsula, which is reached by taking a small road south of the Ho near Blåvandshuk. The breeding meadows of Godwit and Ruff are quite near the village. The bay can also be seen by leaving Oksbøl eastward and taking a right to cross the river Varde; immediately take another right to the river mouth.

Fanø: Can be reached via a ferry, but has much the same birds as Rømø, to the south, which is easily accessible via a causeway.

Rømø: Take the A11 south from Esbjerg to Skaerbaek and turn left to Rømø. The causeway across the Waddensee is an outstanding birding spot and has convenient parking places. The Avocet concentration is usually to the south immediately on starting the crossing. The island itself has dunes, with ponds and some meadowland in the north that hold Godwit, Ruff and Avocet during the summer.

ROUTE: Esbjerg enjoys regular ferry contact with Britain and has excellent road links with the north, south and east.

North Zealand

North Zealand has a number of natural beech woods, with a scattering of oak and lime, and plantations of conifers and some marshes. The best known are Gribskov to the north of Hillerød, which is the largest forest in Denmark, and Dyrehavn, a Royal deer park with areas of rough pasture not too far north of Copenhagen. Icterine Warblers are the most characteristic birds, though they depart in early August. Thrush Nightingale is easily located when singing, and there are Red-backed Shrikes in more open areas. The Black Woodpecker is, however, the star species. It breeds in both these woods and also in Tisvilde Hegn and Jaegerspris, both to the northwest.

A few Green Sandpipers breed, as do both Buzzard and Honey Buzzard, but raptors are best seen on passage in spring. At this time Gilbjerg Hoved is the best place, particularly in April and May and when there is a southeasterly wind. The northernmost point of Zealand is popular with local birders, who gather at a clifftop watchpoint some 2 km (1¼ miles) west of Gilleleje. Finch and thrush movements can be dramatic and raptors vary from none to a hundred per day. Sparrowhawk is the dominant species, but all three buzzards may be seen in season.

SUMMER: Buzzard, Honey Buzzard, Green Sandpiper, Black Woodpecker, Nightjar, Red-backed Shrike, Icterine Warbler, Thrush Nightingale, Hawfinch, Crossbill.

SPRING: Sparrowhawk, Buzzard, Rough-legged Buzzard, Honey Buzzard, thrushes, finches, larks, pipits.

ACCESS: *Gilbjerg Hoved*: Take the A6 from Helsingør and turn northwards through Tikob to Gilleleje. Continue 2 km (1¼ miles) past the town heading westwards, and park on the right just before some pines. Walk northwards to a mound with a large stone at a point overlooking the sea.

Gribskov: Leave Hillerød northwards toward Gilleleje. Free access.

Dyrehavn: Leave Hillerød southwards toward Copenhagen and the woods are just outside of town.

Tisvilde Hegn: Pines along the coast north of Liseleje, which is reached via Frederiksvaerk.

Jaegerspris: These woods are reached via Frederikssund. Leave westwards over the bridge across Roskilde Fjord and turn north (right) to Jaegerspris. The woods lie to the east (right) of the road and hold Green Sandpiper and Honey Buzzard, as well as Black Woodpecker.

ROUTE: This area is easily worked from Copenhagen, though those intent on migration-watching may be able to get a chalet near Gilbjerg Hoved.

FINLAND

Karigasniemi
Inari
Pallas-Ounastunturi
ROVANIEMI
Oulanka National Park
Oulu
TAMPERE
Parikkala
Lahti
HELSINKI

Helsinki

Despite being both the capital and the largest city in the country, Helsinki is one of the best areas for birds in Finland. There are many scarce eastern species to be found, a wide variety of habitats and an efficient 'grapevine' that is only too pleased to help visitors find the specialities of the area. It thus offers considerably more than a chance for the hard-pressed businessman to fit in an hour or two between appointments. Right in the middle of the city is Vanhankaupunginselka Bay (it is a lot easier to say if you break it up into syllables). At Sannalahti is an extensive reedbed with Marsh and Great Reed Warblers, possible Bittern and Little Gull. Grönträsk is a reed-fringed lake of more manageable proportions in the northwestern suburbs where Red-necked and Slavonian Grebes breed and where Caspian Terns are regular. Laajalahti is a large bay in the western suburbs with the area of Otaniemi on its western shore. This is another Caspian Tern spot, but there may also be a few interesting landbirds hereabouts.

SUMMER: Red-necked Grebe, Slavonian Grebe, Water Rail, Caspian Tern, Arctic Tern, Marsh Warbler, Sedge Warbler, Great Reed Warbler.

ACCESS: A good map of Helsinki shows all of these sites.

ROUTE: Helsinki.

Lake Inari

Lake Inari lies 260 km (162 miles) north of the Arctic Circle and measures more or less 70 km by 30 km (nearly 45 × 20 miles). It is huge, remote, but well worth the effort both in getting there and in exploring its surrounding marshes and forests. The numerous bays, inlets and islands hold important populations of breeding duck, including Smew and Goldeneye. The woods, which in places come right down to the lakeshores, hold many typically Arctic species, including Siberian Jay, Siberian Tit, Pine Grosbeak and the elusive Arctic Warbler. More open areas have a tundra-type fauna, including Lapland and Snow Buntings as well as Long-tailed Skua.

Throughout this part of Lapland there are strategically sited mountain huts offering basic accommodation to walkers. Those near the roads may be used as a handy base for investigation, though the more adventurous visitors may walk from hut to hut in their exploration. Accommodation and information maps on the hut system can be obtained via the Inari Tourist Hotel which overlooks the rapids of the River Juutuanjoki. This may well be the worst area for mosquitoes in Finland: 'Jungle Formula' (now available in the UK) is the only answer.

SUMMER: Whooper Swan, Velvet Scoter, Goldeneye, Red-breasted Merganser, Smew, Goosander, Hen Harrier, Rough-legged Buzzard, Merlin, Willow Grouse, Capercaillie, Crane, Broad-billed Sandpiper, Spotted Redshank, Greenshank, Long-tailed Skua, Hawk Owl, Great Grey Shrike, Siberian Jay, Siberian Tit, Pine Grosbeak, Rustic Bunting, Lapland Bunting, Little Bunting, Snow Bunting.

ACCESS: Most birders stay around Inari or at the wooden huts to the northwest. Exploration by road gives access to a number of interesting areas, but some have found the open rocky areas around the huts as good as anywhere. The route eastward toward Akujärvi has a small road to Veskoniemi on the left after 4 km (2½ miles); this leads to the lake. Continue to Akujärvi and keep left to Virtaniemi. Explore here and around Nellimö.

ROUTE: Ivalo has an airstrip with connections to Helsinki, but many will arrive via the larger town of Rovaniemi to the south.

Karigasniemi

To the north of Inari the road divides, offering two routes into Norway. Most birders take the eastern route to the Varanger Fjord, but some use the westerly one toward the Porsanger Fjord. Both provide excellent birding along the way, with a marsh some 10 km (6 miles) north of Utsjoki regularly attracting stops on the way to Varanger. On the westerly route Karigasniemi serves the same purpose. Actually there is nothing much here but a few huts, a couple of hotels, a youth hostel and a camp site, but it is an excellent base for the surrounding countryside.

This is mainly open tundra, with dwarf birches in the valleys and many marshes. Some 11–13 km (7–8 miles) from Karigasniemi and a little to the east is a marsh with a splendid reputation for breeding waders. Broad-billed Sandpiper, Spotted Redshank, Temminck's Stint and possibly Bar-tailed Godwit usually breed, and there are invariably Golden Plover, Whimbrel and Rough-legged Buzzard to be seen. The river valleys hold Waxwing and Arctic Warbler (try the Tenojoki River towards Utsjoki), while the peak of Ailigas to the north has real tundra species such as Shore Lark, Lapland Bunting and possibly Gyrfalcon.

This is splendid country, with fine birding in every direction. Do, however, treat it with the respect that any remote wilderness deserves: compass, map, emergency rations and lots of warm and waterproof clothing even in midsummer.

SUMMER: Whooper Swan, Long-tailed Duck, Gyrfalcon, Rough-legged Buzzard, Wood Sandpiper, Spotted Redshank, Ruff, Whimbrel, Broad-billed Sandpiper, Temminck's Stint, Dotterel, Red-necked Phalarope, Long-tailed Skua, Ptarmigan, Shore Lark, Great Grey Shrike, Waxwing, Siberian Tit, Red-throated Pipit, Bluethroat, Arctic Warbler, Pine Grosbeak, Lapland Bunting, Snow Bunting.

ACCESS: Use Karigasniemi as a base or extended stop-over and explore up and down the road on foot. A smaller road leads northward along the Tenojoki River.

ROUTE: Buses do run along the road, but most birders arrive by car from the south or from Norway.

Lahti

Lahti is a considerable town no great distance north of Helsinki and is an easy-to-get-to place for a taste of Finnish birding. To the north of the town the twin lakes of Kutajärvi and Vesijärvi are among the top ranked of the country's wetlands. They hold good numbers of breeding and migrating ducks and waders, as well as typical forest birds in the surrounding woodland. A little further north is the Vesijako Natural Park with its old forest and several interesting lakes. Here all the usual Scandinavian woodland birds can be seen, along with reasonably regular Osprey, Pygmy and Ural Owls and Red-breasted Flycatcher. The last three are, however, always elusive species.

SUMMER: Osprey, Pygmy Owl, Ural Owl, Pied Flycatcher, Red-breasted Flycatcher, Goldcrest, Siskin.

ACCESS: Leave Lahti northwards on Route 58 and turn left after 60 km (37 miles) at

Arrakoski; bear left and the park is on the left after 3 km (nearly 2 miles). The twin lakes extend northwards from the city; try Route 58 on the way towards the Park or Vaasky.

ROUTE: Directly north from Helsinki past the airport.

Oulanka National Park

Oulanka lies just south of the Arctic Circle, near the Soviet border, and is an outstandingly beautiful wilderness area with mountains, forests, lakes and streams. There are excellent meadows, deep ravines, spectacular rapids and waterfalls, and some really good birds in a reasonably accessible area. The whole is served by a network of paths and tracks — quite different from the wilderness further north. Widespread species include Brambling, Siberian Tit, Wood Sandpiper, Tengmalm's Owl and Golden Eagle.

Red-flanked Bluetail

For those with a little time on their hands, the gorge of Ristikallio formed by the Oulankajoki River is beautiful and the haunt of Red-flanked Bluetail. Try in the wee small hours of the morning. To the south lies the peak of Rukatunturi, with a prominent ridge reaching towards the road. This may prove interesting, though some have been disappointed. Nobody, however, has failed to be entranced by the woods of this delightful area. Guide books are available.

SUMMER: Black-throated Diver, Crane, Golden Eagle, Wood Sandpiper, Eagle Owl, Tengmalm's Owl, Hawk Owl, Siberian Tit, Crested Tit, Red-flanked Bluetail, Siberian Jay, Crossbill, Parrot Crossbill.

ACCESS: From Kuusamo (do not ignore the lakes to the east, as they have Broad-billed

47

Sandpiper and Little Bunting), head northwards, pausing at the ridge of Rukatunturi, to a right-hand turning to Käylä. Here fork right to Kiutaköngas, the park centre. There is a path from here along the Oulankajoki. For Ristikallio, return to Käylä and continue northwards on the road toward Salla. Watch for the crossing of the Oulankajoki River.

ROUTE: There are hotels in Kuusamo and most visitors drive here after working Oulu.

Oulu

Once a fur and fish trading station, Oulu is now the most important town in northern Finland. It is heavily industrial, has a very busy oil port and is an essential stop-over on any birding trip to Finland. The main attractions are two decidedly scarce breeding birds that are otherwise really difficult to find outside the Soviet Union: Terek Sandpiper and Yellow-breasted Bunting. Even here these birds are no doddle, and there is inevitably the atmosphere of a twitch as one waits around for them to put in an appearance. There are, however, many other species to be found in the area, among them Crane, scarce owls, Scarlet Rosefinch and Arctic waders including Red-necked Phalarope and Jack Snipe.

To the south, the marshes at Liminka are still largely ignored by the 'head-down' brigade, though there is a fine collection of species to be seen, including Red-necked Phalarope, Ruff and Marsh Harrier.

SUMMER: Crane, Garganey, Red-breasted Merganser, Marsh Harrier, Hen Harrier, Rough-legged Buzzard, Spotted Crake, Temminck's Stint, Ruff, Spotted Redshank, Greenshank, Terek Sandpiper, Turnstone, Red-necked Phalarope, Caspian Tern, Hawk Owl, Scarlet Rosefinch, Siskin, Yellow-breasted Bunting.

ACCESS: Oulunsalo and Limingoviken lie across the bay from Oulu near the airport and are the best areas for Yellow-breasted Bunting. Follow signs for the airport (Lentoasemat), turning right off the main road southwards after 6 km (3¾ miles); after 500 m (550 yards), stop and explore a damp bushy area on the right of the road down to the shore. Other species include waders and duck. Continue through Oulunsalo to Varjakka for mature pine forests on dry ground.

For Terek Sandpiper head northward, but take the Hietasaarentie road before leaving town. Continue to the oil port. The oil-port lagoon should be inspected, as well as the shoreline immediately to the north. Terek tends to turn up just after the tide turns and starts to come in, or in the afternoon. Do not forget that you can bird all night in the summer.

Liminka lies just off the main road 23 km (14¼ miles) south of Oulu where meadows and marshes can easily be explored. The nearby Limianlahti Bay is the primary Finnish wetland for breeding and migrating birds.

ROUTE: Fly Helsinki — Oulu.

Pallas-Ounastunturi

This huge National Park is situated in northwestern Finland, only a short distance from the Swedish and Norwegian borders, and is centred on a mountain ridge of the same name. It lies just south of the coniferous-forest limit, but a little altitude takes one into basically tundra country, with all of the species that one would expect further north. It is, in fact, the combination of landforms that makes the whole area so fine for birds. The park is best penetrated from the south, but the delightful Lapp village of Enontekiö, to the north, is situated by a lake well away from the 'main road'. This area is typical taiga, with lakes, bogs, marshes and open land holding Crane, Whooper Swan, Smew and many waders. The forests have Siberian Jay, as well as the elusive Great Grey Owl.

The park itself can be explored via Mafkmaja, where the Pallastunturi Tourist Hotel is a fine base. The route northwards is well marked, with well-spaced huts offering accommodation along the 60-km (37-mile) walk to Enontekiö. This walk may produce Snowy Owl, Long-tailed Skua, Lapland and Snow Buntings and possible Bar-tailed Godwit. The Gyrfalcon breeds among the gorges around the Könkämä River west of Enontekiö and may be seen flying above the valley.

SUMMER: Scaup, Long-tailed Duck, Velvet Scoter, Whooper Swan, Gyrfalcon, Crane, Ptarmigan, Rough-legged Buzzard, Greenshank, Spotted Redshank, Red-necked Phalarope, Dotterel, Long-tailed Skua, Snowy Owl, Great Grey Owl, Hawk Owl, Siberian Jay, Shore Lark, Ring Ouzel, Bluethroat, Twite, Lapland Bunting, Snow Bunting.

ACCESS: Leave the road to Norway at Sarkijärvi, south of Muonio, for the park. The hotel can offer help with maps and advise on a mountain trek. Alternatively, take the road to Enontekiö from Palojoensuu further north and explore from there. There is a tourist hotel at the village, but do not rely on unbooked accommodation in northern Finland. A road follows the Könkämä River for Gyrfalcon, to Lake Kilpisjärvi. High above this the hill lakes hold many tundra specials.

ROUTE: Most visitors to this part of the world use a car to cover Inari, Varanger Fjord, North Cape and then the present area.

Parikkala

Parikkala has long been famous as *the* available haunt of Blyth's Reed Warbler in western Europe. The westward extension of this species' range in recent years has done nothing to harm the reputation of this splendid wetland, which is now a WWF reserve. Parikkala is situated on the shores of a large lake with extensive stands of reeds and a shoreline of willow scrub. The best area is called Siikalahti Marsh and all birders head for this like a magnet. The surrounding countryside is predominantly agricultural, though there are large areas of conifers. The region is, however, often called 'Finland's Lake District', for there is certainly as much water as there is land in this part of the country.

49

Blyth's can be found among the willows at the edge of the marsh, rather than in the stands of pure reed. Most visitors manage to get this bird, but it is not numerous and considerable patience may be required, especially for good views.

Otherwise, there is a good variety of summer birds hereabouts, including Red-necked and Slavonian Grebes, Bittern, various duck, Marsh Harrier, Osprey, Hobby and a variety of smaller birds that includes Thrush Nightingale and Scarlet Rosefinch.

SUMMER: Great Crested Grebe, Red-necked Grebe, Slavonian Grebe, Bittern, Pintail, Garganey, Shoveler, Marsh Harrier, Osprey, Hobby, Spotted Crake, Sedge Warbler, Blyth's Reed Warbler, Thrush Nightingale, Scarlet Rosefinch.

ACCESS: There are no restrictions on access to the Parikkala area or to Siikalahti Marsh. Do, however, be careful not to approach the Soviet border too closely or someone may take an interest in your optics.

ROUTE: Leave Helsinki eastwards through Kouvola, Lappeenranta, Joutseno (another Blyth's place), Imatra to Parikkala.

FRANCE

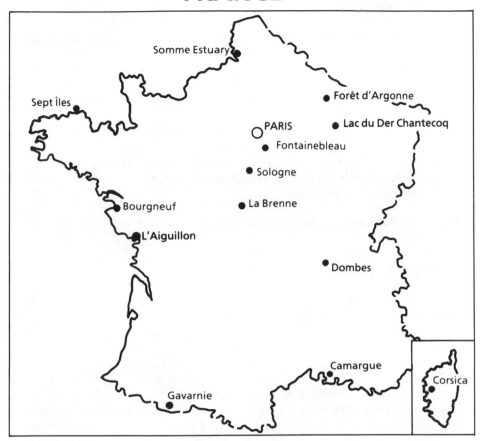

Somme Estuary
Sept Îles
Forêt d'Argonne
PARIS
Lac du Der Chantecoq
Fontainebleau
Sologne
Bourgneuf
La Brenne
L'Aiguillon
Dombes
Camargue
Corsica
Gavarnie

Baie d'Aiguillon

The Biscay coast of France is broken by some of the most splendid and important wetlands in western Europe. Arguably the best and certainly among the most significant is the Baie d'Aiguillon, north of La Rochelle. This huge intertidal inlet is so shallow that it almost empties out completely at low tide, offering vast feeding grounds for waders. As a result there is little or no development along the shoreline, but a continuing threat of a barrage scheme instead. The marshes that back the estuary are intersected by a network of dykes, with some wet and reedy areas that hold a good collection of birds. Here Stilt, Black-tailed Godwit and Black Tern breed and harriers hunt throughout the year. It is, however, during passage and, especially, winter that Aiguillon is at its best. Autumn brings almost a quarter of a million waders, half of which stay through the winter. Knot, Dunlin, Grey Plover, Avocet and especially Black-tailed Godwit are present in their thousands. This is also an important wintering ground for Spotted Redshank, as well as several duck species. In spring, the flocks of Black-tailed Godwit are among the most important in Europe.

51

SUMMER: Montagu's Harrier, Marsh Harrier, Garganey, Black-tailed Godwit, Black-winged Stilt, Black Tern.

PASSAGE: Whimbrel, Ruff, Black-tailed Godwit, Bar-tailed Godwit, Little Stint, Golden Plover.

WINTER: Brent Goose, Shelduck, Pintail, Wigeon, Golden Plover, Grey Plover, Black-tailed Godwit, Bar-tailed Godwit, Spotted Redshank, Dunlin, Knot, Avocet.

ACCESS: Several roads run through the surrounding marshes to the Baie. The best area, however, is the north where the D60 runs south from St Michel-en-l'Herm. This is connected to the D46A via La Dive and thus southwards along the Digue de l'Aiguillon. Best of all is the reserve at Point d'Arcay, south of la Faute — l'Aiguillon. This is the major high-tide roost for the whole area.

ROUTE: La Rochelle is the nearest large town.

Forêt d'Argonne

The Argonne, as it is usually called, is a ridge of densely forested hills east of Reims. Immediately to the south lies a less well defined area of forests, lakes and ponds, while to the west are huge rolling cereal plains. The Argonne comes as an extraordinary contrast to the boring cereal plains and its birds are both more numerous and diverse. The Argonne is, above all, known for its birds of prey, and Osprey, Honey Buzzard, Black and Red Kites, Goshawk and Hobby all summer. There are also some other species that can be seen closer to home here than anywhere else in Europe. Black Stork, Little Bittern, Great Reed Warbler and Bluethroat all fall into this category. Good woodpeckers, the occasional Little Bustard and Collared Flycatcher (perhaps as rare as any) can all be found.

SUMMER: Great Crested Grebe, Teal, Gadwall, Osprey, Buzzard, Honey Buzzard, Marsh Harrier, Hen Harrier, Montagu's Harrier, Black Kite, Red Kite, Goshawk, Hobby, Little Bittern, Bittern, Black Stork, Stone-curlew, Little Bustard, Crested Lark, Barn Owl, Grey-headed Woodpecker, Great Spotted Woodpecker, Middle Spotted Woodpecker, Wryneck, Red-backed Shrike, Golden Oriole, Dipper, Kingfisher, Short-toed Treecreeper, Crested Tit, Firecrest, Blue-headed Wagtail, Bluethroat, Marsh Warbler, Savi's Warbler, Great Reed Warbler, Bonelli's Warbler, Collared Flycatcher, Cirl Bunting, Hawfinch, Crossbill.

ACCESS: The small town of Sainte Menehould east of Châlons-sur-Marne is the access point for the Argonne, with the most interesting area lying to the south and east. Basically, the ridge that lies to the east of the Vouziers to Sainte Menehould road is the Argonne proper, and the minor roads that criss-cross the area offer most of the woodland species including raptors. The many lakes to the south are all worth visiting and many have Marsh Harrier. Étang de Belval is one of the best, but the others should not be ignored. Minor roads leading north from Sommeilles into the Forêt de l'Îsle are good for Honey Buzzard, Goshawk and Golden Oriole. Near Châlons on the D1 is Marson, from where a road leads high into the chalk hills for Little Bustard and Crested Lark. Eastwards some 6 km (3¾ miles) beyond le Fresne, the D1 passes through woodland with Bonelli's Warbler. The whereabouts of the small colony of Collared Flycatchers must, unfortunately, remain unpublished for security reasons.

The Argonne is an area with an established reputation, but one which will still repay careful exploration. It is worth a week of anyone's time, particularly if you like seeing raptors every day.

ROUTE: The A4 passes north of Châlons and then just south of Sainte Menehould. From there head southwards to Givry-en-Argonne, which makes an excellent base.

Bourgneuf

This huge bay lies on the west coast of France immediately south of the mouth of the River Loire. It is partially enclosed by the Île de Noirmoutier, which is joined to the mainland by a causeway and which has developed into a booming seaside resort over the past 20 years. Huge intertidal flats make this one of the primary wetlands of France, but they are backed by the saltpans around Bouin and the fresh marshes of Machecoul. Further inland, towards the Loire, lie the great impenetrable marshes of the Lac de Grand Lieu.

The area is a noted haunt of waders and recent reclamation, notably between Port des Champes and Port du Bec, west of Bouin, has done nothing to reduce their numbers. The variety of species is particularly impressive during passage periods, but several species including Stilt and Avocet breed. Wildfowl are good in winter — there are good numbers of Brent — while in autumn the seawatching from the far point of Noirmoutier can be excellent with a southwesterly wind. To the south of the causeway, the huge dune beach towards St-Jean-de-Monts has extensive pine forest with Bonelli's Warbler, Woodlark, Hoopoe and Tawny Pipit.

SUMMER: Little Egret, Shoveler, Montagu's Harrier, Marsh Harrier, Black Kite, Quail, Black-winged Stilt, Avocet, Kentish Plover, Black-tailed Godwit, Curlew, Short-toed Lark, Woodlark, Tawny Pipit, Hoopoe, Pied Flycatcher, Bluethroat, Bonelli's Warbler.

PASSAGE: Kentish Plover, Spotted Redshank, Greenshank, Avocet.

WINTER: Brent Goose, Wigeon, Grey Plover, Curlew.

ACCESS: The town of Bouin is probably the best base and saltpans can be found in all directions. The polders lie to the west and are approached via Port des Champes (D21) and Port du Bec (D51). The Lac de Grand Lieu has many species but is impossible to work. The village of Passay is as near open water as one can get, but several birders have explored the surrounds on local roads and seen a few bits and bobs. Black Kite is regular, but a boat would seem to be the answer.

The woods and dunes to the south can be explored from La Barre-de-Monts or Notre-Dame-de-Monts via the D38.

ROUTE: From Nantes take the D751 westward, turning left to Bourgneuf on the D758 and continuing on this road to Bouin.

La Brenne

A glance at a map is sufficient to show that the area of La Brenne in central France is a highly attractive one for birding. A huge area of ponds and lakes (about 500 in all) is broken by large forests, smaller woods and areas of agriculture. Compared with the Sologne district to the north, 'Chasse Gardé' notices are nowhere near as numerous. Though the major waters are grouped together between Rosnay and Mézières, there are so many outlying lakes that a thorough exploration would occupy a good week's birding holiday.

The ponds are shallow, with a good growth of emergent vegetation offering breeding security to many species. This vegetation is mostly reeds and in some areas quite extensive reedbeds have developed. As a result, all three harriers breed along with Bittern, Little Bittern and a good variety of duck. Crakes include Baillon's, and both Black and Whiskered Terns breed. The surrounding dry land holds a good cross-section of species that one would expect in central lowland France, together with Little Bustard and Stone-curlew.

Winter brings large numbers of other species to La Brenne, with wildfowl being particularly impressive from November onwards. Terns and waders appear on passage, and raptors pass through in numbers every autumn.

An up-to-date map is essential and the 1:25,000 of the Institut Géographique National is excellent and available locally. This is particularly so as fresh ponds are still being created, and these newly flooded waters are rich in food, attracting many wildfowl and waders. Near the Étang du Sault, for example, a series of three small ponds was created in the late 1970s and immediately attracted a fine range of species.

SUMMER: Great Crested Grebe, Black-necked Grebe, Purple Heron, Little Bittern, Bittern, Shoveler, Garganey, Marsh Harrier, Montagu's Harrier, Hen Harrier, Red Kite, Black Kite, Baillon's Crake, Water Rail, Snipe, Curlew, Little Bustard, Stone-curlew, Black Tern, Whiskered Tern, Savi's Warbler, Great Reed Warbler.

PASSAGE: Osprey, Honey Buzzard, Black Kite, Common Sandpiper, Greenshank, Common Tern, Black Tern.

ACCESS: Most of the ponds and lakes are worth a look, and can be watched from the network of surrounding roads with the aid of a good map. The following are easily seen and number among the more productive waters: Notz; Moury — with large areas of reeds; Couvent — a reedbed; Miclos — with reeds and terns; Beauregard — reeds;

Gabrière — one of the larger waters, with duck; Gabrieu — water lilies, with breeding grebes and terns; Hardouine — reed-fringed; La Mer Rouge — huge water, with terns and duck; Montiacre — reedbeds and open water; Blizon — with reeds and islands; Le Sault — with reed-fringed banks and the nearby string of three small lakes. The Étang du Condreau has a Black-headed Gullery with Whiskered Terns, and the Auberge de la Gabrière, adjacent to the lake of the same name, makes an ideal centre.

ROUTE: From Paris, take the A10 to Tours and turn southeastward on the N143 towards Châteauroux. At Châtillon turn right on to minor roads to La Brenne.

Camargue

The Camargue remains as popular with European birders as it has ever been, despite the radical changes that have affected this wilderness on the French Mediterranean coast. The reasons are easily found: it has a wealth of species second only to Spain's Coto Doñana and yet is decidedly closer to northern Europe. The Camargue proper lies between the two arms of the River Rhône, south of Arles, yet it is unthinkable not to include in any account of the area the Petite Camargue to the west, the stony wastes of La Crau to the east, the Roman town of Les Baux to the northeast and the Pont du Gard to the north. Such a huge area must, of necessity, take time to explore thoroughly, and most birders will take at least a week to seek out all the species that are regularly found here.

The Camargue is changing. There are more tourists than ever and, while most of them confine their attentions to the coastline, the former *cabanes* of the 'cowboys' are now mostly holiday cottages or bijou second homes. Rice is still grown in the north, salt extracted in the south, and even the stony Crau area has been partly converted to agriculture. The roads are better, there are many hotels and, of course, more bird-watchers. The heart of the Camargue, however, remains the Réserve Naturelle on the Étang de Vaccarès and this is still protected as the major French wetland for birds.

The beach has breeding Kentish Plover and the dunes both Tawny Pipit and Short-toed Lark. The southernmost lagoons are saline and the salt-extraction industry has a vested interest in keeping them so. Here is the Flamingo breeding area, and Black-winged Stilt and Avocet both benefit. Passage waders may be both numerous and exciting here in season. Still saline, but not commercially exploited lagoons lie to the north and here are the best colonies of gulls and terns, including Gull-billed Tern and a few Slender-billed Gulls. The surrounding vegetation and larger islands hold Specta-cled Warbler, Crested Lark, Great Grey Shrike and Bee-eater. Further north still, drainage ditches and overgrown reedbeds hold Penduline Tit and Fan-tailed Warbler (much depleted after a series of hard winters), as well as offering opportunities for breeding Black Kites — now common throughout the Camargue — harriers and Scops Owl. It is, however, the great lagoons and marshes that are the first areas that most visitors will see, and these are full of warblers, herons, egrets, waders, terns and Marsh Harriers. Woodland should not be ignored, for there are Melodious Warbler and Golden Oriole here. Among the rice-growing areas are Whiskered Terns galore, joined over the lagoons by the other marsh terns on passage.

To the east, La Crau is actually the delta of the youthful River Durance. Though much reclaimed for agriculture, there are still areas with Little Bustard, Stone-curlew, Black-eared Wheatear, Calandra Lark and sometimes Pin-tailed Sandgrouse. The rubbish tip at Entressen may produce Egyptian Vulture, though this species is now decidedly scarce.

To the north, Les Baux in the Alpilles is excellent for Alpine Swift, Blue Rock Thrush, Subalpine Warbler and sometimes Egyptian Vulture. Frankly, it is worth the entrance fee to the Roman ruins to sit atop the cliffs and watch the birds go by. Continuing along the Val d'Enfer gets one away from the tourists and offers the chance of Peregrine, Wallcreeper, Alpine Accentor and even Eagle Owl.

West of Avignon is the Pont du Gard, a magnificent Roman aqueduct that crosses a deep gorge across the Gardon valley which is full of birds. Alpine Swift, Rock Sparrow and Bonelli's Warbler are all regulars here. The Camargue has a wealth of breeding birds, but is splendid at all seasons.

SUMMER: Purple Heron, Little Egret, Squacco Heron, Night Heron, Little Bittern, Bittern, White Stork, Flamingo, Garganey, Red-crested Pochard, Egyptian Vulture, Golden Eagle, Bonelli's Eagle, Red Kite, Black Kite, Honey Buzzard, Marsh Harrier, Montagu's Harrier, Short-toed Eagle, Peregrine, Hobby, Lesser Kestrel, Spotted Crake, Little Bustard, Kentish Plover, Redshank, Avocet, Black-winged Stilt, Stone-curlew, Collared Pratincole, Slender-billed Gull, Whiskered Tern, Gull-billed Tern, Little Tern, Pin-tailed Sandgrouse, Great Spotted Cuckoo, Scops Owl, Eagle Owl, Pallid Swift, Alpine Swift, Bee-eater, Roller, Hoopoe, Wryneck, Calandra Lark, Short-toed Lark, Crag Martin, Golden Oriole, Penduline Tit, Bearded Tit, Wall-creeper, Rock Thrush, Blue Rock Thrush, Black-eared Wheatear, Cetti's Warbler, Savi's Warbler, Moustached Warbler, Great Reed Warbler, Melodious Warbler, Spectacled Warbler, Dartford Warbler, Sardinian Warbler, Subalpine Warbler, Fan-tailed Warbler, Tawny Pipit, Great Grey Shrike, Lesser Grey Shrike, Serin, Rock Sparrow.

SPRING AND AUTUMN: Osprey, Red-footed Falcon, Whimbrel, Black-tailed God-wit, Green Sandpiper, Wood Sandpiper, Greenshank, Marsh Sandpiper, Little Stint, Temminck's Stint, Curlew Sandpiper, Ruff, Little Gull, Black Tern, White-winged Black Tern, Caspian Tern, Orphean Warbler, Woodchat Shrike, Red-backed Shrike.

ACCESS: The heart of the Camargue, the Étang de Vaccarès, can be viewed from a variety of minor roads and tracks extending along the west, north and eastern shores. The Cartes Touristiques 1:100,000 published by IGN are excellent, but the Michelin series is almost as good and more generally available. The area is reached from Arles via the N570 and its subsidiary the D36. The latter leads to Salin de Giraud, the saltworks town, and gives variable views of the riverine forest along the Grand Rhône, which has several large heronries. Beyond Salin de Giraud lies a network of tracks that lead to the shore, as well as among the lagoons.

The D36B is the most famous of the Camargue roads, giving excellent views of Vaccarès as well as access off to the west to Étang du Fangassier, Étang de Galabert and Étang du Fournelet, all of which should be explored. The Salin du Midi here has

Flamingo, passage waders, terns and many typical birds. In the north, the lagoons and marshes around Mas d'Agon hold Great Reed and Moustached Warblers, Penduline Tit, Whiskered Tern and Collared Pratincole.

La Crau is reached by taking the N113 and turning right on to the N568. Watch for good habitat and explore on foot. Further east, at the intersection of the N113 and the D5, turn left and take the track on the right through the fields of the Croix de Crau area for Little Bustard and Pin-tailed Sandgrouse — especially in winter. Returning to the D5, head southwards, cross the N113 and after 1 km (just over ½ mile) turn left (east) on a track leading along the northern edge of a disused airfield. This is another area for these two special species. Continuing southwards leads to the Entressen area.

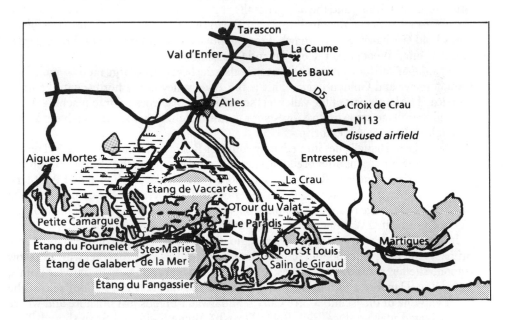

To see Les Baux, take the N570 northwards from Arles and then turn right on the D17 and follow the signs. The road along the Val d'Enfer to the west is strongly recommended; and this area, together with the route from the Castle to the Cathedral in the cliff face, both regularly produce Wallcreeper (particularly in winter). Taking the D27A to the D5, turn left (north) and watch for the road to the radio station at La Caume. Here are Wallcreeper, Alpine Accentor, Alpine Swift and Eagle Owl, the latter often in the gully northeast of the radio station.

For the Pont du Gard, take the N570 northwards to Tarascon, cross the river to Beaucaire and continue on the N86L, past the A9, to its junction with the N86 at Remoulins. Pont du Gard is 3 km (nearly 2 miles) to the north.

ROUTE: The nearest airport is Marseilles, though those serving the Côte d'Azur are not too distant. The French motorway system enables the Camargue to be reached from the Channel ports in a day and a bit of hard driving, but it is autoroute all the way. The advantage of tourist development is that there are now more hotels available than ever.

Corsica

Corsica is a splendid island with some quite magnificent scenery and some excellent birds that have been sadly ignored by the non-French visitor. There are still several pairs of Lammergeier, as well as Golden and Short-toed Eagles, Red Kite, Goshawk, Osprey, Peregrine, and a good spread of other species. This is not a place to be rushed and is certainly worthy of a week in early summer. One species, however, continues to attract a string of birders: the endemic Corsican Nuthatch. The Vizzavona Forest, one of three acknowledged sites for the species, lies in the centre of the island, northeast of Ajaccio. Here there are also Red Kite, Citril Finch, Dipper, Crossbill and Cirl Bunting. Another nuthatch site, and the one generally regarded as the best by French birders, is the Forest of Aitone to the northwest near Porto (not Porto Vecchio). Here the mixed pines hold Goshawk, Sparrowhawk, Dipper, plus a local subspecies of Treecreeper, Great Spotted Woodpecker, Coal Tit and Crossbill.

Yet another site for Corsican Nuthatch is also the best for the large raptors, including Lammergeier and Golden Eagle. This is the Asco valley in the north-central part of Corsica. The lower part of the valley has some excellent gorges prior to reaching Anso; beyond the village are extensive forests for the nuthatch. Other species include Alpine Chough and Alpine Accentor.

The Lake of Biguglia lies immediately south of Bastia and is the best wetland on the island. Its reedy margins offer breeding sites to typical species such as Purple Heron and Marsh Harrier, along with Reed and Great Reed and Cetti's and Fan-tailed Warblers. Hobby, Montagu's Harrier, Red-crested Pochard and Water Rail also breed. On passage a wide range of species includes reasonably regular Red-footed Falcon, Little Egret, Moustached Warbler and Penduline Tit.

In spring, the Cap Corse area at Barcaggio, in the extreme north of the island, is the primary migration watchpoint. Here the dunes and maquis area, together with a shallow lagoon, shelter a variety of species, including scrub warblers such as Marmora's, Subalpine, Dartford and Sardinian. Other good coastal areas are at Bonifacio at the other extreme of the island, where Cory's Shearwater breeds just offshore and where the mainland may produce Blue Rock Thrush, Alpine Swift and Spanish and Rock Sparrows. Eleonora's Falcon is often a migrant here. Near Calvi, in the northwest, is the reserve of Scandola, where both Osprey and Peregrine breed; it is best approached via boat.

SUMMER: Cory's Shearwater, Manx Shearwater, Shag, Red-crested Pochard, Golden Eagle, Lammergeier, Short-toed Eagle, Red Kite, Goshawk, Sparrowhawk, Marsh Harrier, Montagu's Harrier, Osprey, Peregrine, Hobby, Water Rail, Dipper, Corsican Nuthatch, Alpine Swift, Pallid Swift, Spotless Starling, Alpine Accentor, Blue Rock Thrush, Marmora's Warbler, Subalpine Warbler, Dartford Warbler, Sardinian Warbler, Reed Warbler, Great Reed Warbler, Cetti's Warbler, Fan-tailed Warbler, Citril Finch, Crossbill, Cirl Bunting.

ACCESS: Vizzavona lies on the main road, the N193, across the island between Ajaccio and Bastia. Along this road is a sign to 'La Gare de Vizzavona'. A little way along, on the Ajaccio side of this side road to the station, is the Office National des Forêts. Opposite this (on the western side), beside a hut, is a footpath leading over a bridge, around a picnic site, past a 'fire' sign, over another bridge and then zigzagging up into the pines. Follow this path, watching and listening for the nuthatch. Citril Finch has been seen below the pines. It is easy to make a loop back towards the railway station.

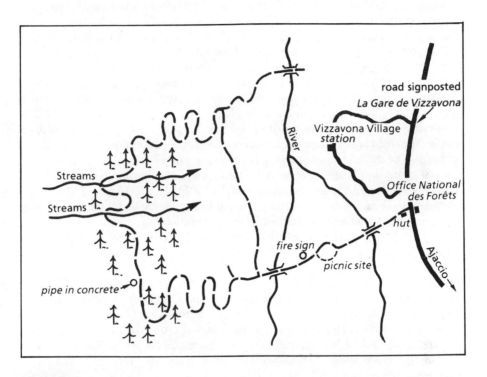

The Aitone Forest lies near the village of Evisa, some 25 km (15½ miles) from Porto due west of Corte. There are numerous tracks through the forest for exploration, but no definite stake-outs. The Asco valley is reached by leaving Bastia towards Corte, but turning right towards Calvi at Ponte Leccia on the N197. After 25 km (15½ miles) turn left on the D47 toward Asco. The gorges are before the village, the woods beyond.

Lake Biguglia lies east of the N198, south of Bastia near the airport. The southern end is generally the most productive. To the north of Bastia, the Barcaggio area of Cap Corse is reached by following the road to Ersa and then taking the D253 to Barcaggio. Here take the track to the east of the village crossing the river towards the Tour d'Agnellu.

At Bonifacio, which is very picturesque, descend the cliffs to a point opposite the island of Grain de Sable. At night you can hear Cory's Shearwaters coming in to their burrows. For the reserve of Scandola, go to Calvi and take a boat trip to the south. Boats are not allowed to stay more than 24 hours at Scandola.

ROUTE: Regular daily ferries from Nice and Marseilles to Bastia and Ajaccio and flights to both towns.

Dombes

The ponds of the Dombes north of Lyons are considerably more than a convenient stop-over on the way to or from the Camargue. Indeed, were they not so close to that famous area they would probably become a major ornitho-tourist site. A glance at a map is sufficient to indicate the possibilities. There are literally a hundred or more areas of water centred on the town of Villars and all neatly enclosed in the valley of the River Rhône between the Alps and the Massif Central. Most of the waters are shallow, with emergent vegetation forming considerable reedbeds in some areas. Though there is still some commercial fishery exploitation, the main change in recent years has been the development of water sports in several areas. The nature reserve south of Villars has been partially developed into an ornithological park — a sort of glorified zoo with Chilean Flamingoes, captive wildfowl, a snack-bar and various dioramas with stuffed birds. The free car park here does, however, facilitate exploration of the two large lakes either side of the A83 where parking is otherwise unavailable.

The most significant birds of the Dombes are the herons, which include good colonies of Purple, Night, Squacco and Little Egret. Red-crested Pochard, Stilt, Whiskered Tern, harriers and Black Kite all breed. Being so far south in France, the Mediterranean influence is evident in the populations of several birds found in the general area. The surroundings are mostly agricultural, but there are woods to the east beyond Chalamont.

SUMMER: Black-necked Grebe, Grey Heron, Purple Heron, Night Heron, Little Egret, Squacco Heron, Bittern, Little Bittern, Garganey, Gadwall, Red-crested Pochard, Marsh Harrier, Montagu's Harrier, Black Kite, Goshawk, Spotted Crake, Black-winged Stilt, Black-tailed Godwit, Black Tern, Whiskered Tern, Woodchat Shrike, Red-backed Shrike, Hoopoe, Bee-eater, Great Reed Warbler, Fan-tailed Warbler, Savi's Warbler, Melodious Warbler.

ACCESS: The N83 cuts through the heart of the Dombes, with Villars at the centre making an ideal base. The huge number of lakes should be explored with the aid of a map, for most can be seen from the network of minor roads. The best lakes are the Étang de Glareins and the Grand Étang de Birieux situated on either side of the N83 south of the town. This is where the free parking at the 'bird centre' comes in handy.

ROUTE: Leave the Autoroute du Soleil at Villefranche.

Fontainebleau

The Forest of Fontainebleau lies some 60 km (37 miles) southeast of Paris immediately east of the Autoroute du Soleil (A6), and has been used by generations of birders as a convenient stop-over on the way down to the exotics of the Mediterranean. The extensive woods, both coniferous and deciduous, are home to a good range of species, including those Continental woodpeckers that have such an appeal to the British. Grey-headed, Middle Spotted and Black Woodpeckers can all be found here, along with Short-toed Treecreeper, Crested Tit, Goshawk and other typical woodland birds of north-central France.

SUMMER: Buzzard, Honey Buzzard, Goshawk, Green Woodpecker, Grey-headed Woodpecker, Middle Spotted Woodpecker, Great Spotted Woodpecker, Black Wood-pecker, Wryneck, Short-toed Treecreeper, Bonelli's Warbler, Crested Tit, Hawfinch.

ACCESS: The specialities do, of course, occur throughout the area. The spots detailed here are thus, more than most, those where others have managed to find particular birds over the years. This docs, of course, create self-perpetuating 'hot spots'. All of these areas are less than 4–5 km (3 miles) from the centre of Fontainebleau, within the minor 'Route Ronde' around the southern part of the town marked in white on the best map, the Michelin 61.

On the D409, stop near the Gorges de Franchard and turn south on the ring road. Stop after a short distance and explore the mixed woods on the left-hand side of the road for preference.

Leaving the town on the N152, stop where it passes under the Aqueduc de la Vanne at

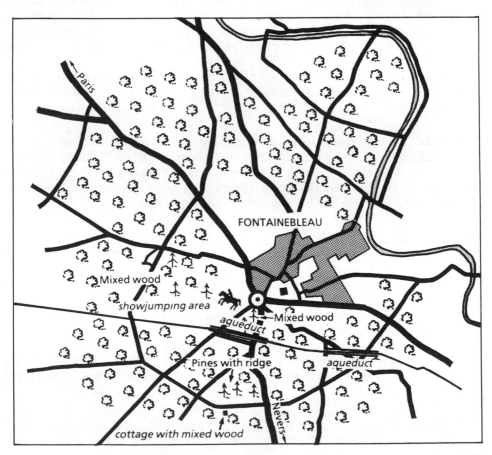

an open horse-jumping area. Take the track south of this. Similarly, the area just north of where the Aqueduc crosses the N7 is also worth exploring. Just a little south of the Aqueduc on the N7 a small turning forks right (west) — the D63E. After 1 km (just over ½ mile) there is an area of pines near a small ridge; explore on both sides of the road.

About half way between the D63E and the N7, along the ring road, there is a cottage on the south side of the road. Stop here and walk southwards behind the cottage to an open area.

ROUTE: The Paris motorway ring gives access to the A6; exit at Ury on to the N152 to Fontainebleau.

Gavarnie

Gavarnie is the primary birding site in the French Pyrenees. The Spanish side has more species and is warmer, but this French spot has most of the specialities and is considerably easier to get to. Though Gavarnie itself is a high mountain village, the lowland approach from Lourdes should not be ignored: Booted Eagle is seldom found at any height and Egyptian Vulture is usually a low-level species. The valley is lined with pine forests as you approach, but these gradually give way to more open areas and become progressively more rocky. The scenery is spectacular.

Outstanding here are Lammergeier (they do breed on the French side), Bonelli's Eagle, both choughs, Alpine Accentor and Wallcreeper, but there are many more birds besides.

SUMMER: Lammergeier, Griffon Vulture, Egyptian Vulture, Booted Eagle, Bonelli's Eagle, Goshawk, Chough, Alpine Chough, Wallcreeper, Black Woodpecker, White-backed Woodpecker, Alpine Swift, Alpine Accentor, Crag Martin, Water Pipit, Blue Rock Thrush, Black-eared Wheatear, Dipper, Red-backed Shrike, Bonelli's Warbler, Firecrest, Citril Finch, Rock Bunting, Crossbill, Snow Finch.

ACCESS: The approach road should be explored. On arrival at Gavarnie, there are several areas (all easily found) that should be explored. Just before the village is an intersection. Take the road leading to Port de Gavarnie — the pass to Spain (open only in August and September). This leads to the ski centre, where the road is blocked. Stop and explore along the line of the ski lift for Accentor and Snow Finch.

The Cirque de Gavarnie is reached by track above the village. This leads through woodland to a disused hotel, behind which there is Citril Finch, with Bonelli's Warbler in the lower woods and Accentor high up in the Cirque.

The route to the Vallée d'Ossoue lies off the road to the Port de Gavarnie — continue straight on where that road veers off to the left. The sheer rock face here is excellent for raptors and Wallcreeper.

ROUTE: Easily reached via Lourdes. For those wishing to continue to Spain, the route is a huge circle westwards via Escot and Urdos to Jaca (except in August and September).

Lac du Der Chantecoq

South of Paris, between Troyes and Saint-Dizier, lies a remote backwater of France drained by the great rivers of the Seine, the Marne and their tributaries. Much of the area is forested, the agriculture poor and the land devoted mainly to grazing: a sharp contrast to the great rolling arable plains to the north and west. Here two huge reservoirs have been constructed, virtually along the traditional migration route of the European Crane population. Not surprisingly, then, birds quickly took advantage of the new opportunities and began to use the northernmost reservoir, Lac du Der, as a safe roost and staging-post on their journey between the southern Baltic and winter quarters in Spain. The area proved so much to their liking that variable numbers have, in recent years, stayed on to winter.

The southern lake, Lac de la Forêt d'Orient, has not become a Crane roost, though the birds often occur there. Instead this has become one of the most regular spots in France for wintering White-tailed Eagle. Together, and along with the surrounding forests, these two lakes have become one of the classic winter birding spots in Europe. White-tailed Eagles often also occur at Lac du Der, and the 'Digues' along the southwestern corner often boast birders from three or four countries during a February weekend. This is an excellent spot for the eagles, as well as for the late-afternoon roosting flights of Crane.

There are, of course, other attractions too. Hen Harrier is regular, Buzzard abundant, Bean Geese common and Great Grey Shrike, Middle Spotted Woodpecker and Short-toed Treecreeper regular. Duck include Smew and Goosander, and there is generally a Peregrine present. Some have tried the lakes in spring and summer, though they have not lived up to their winter reputation.

WINTER: Red-necked Grebe, Bean Goose, Greylag Goose, Shoveler, Gadwall, Wigeon, Goosander, Red-breasted Merganser, Smew, Hen Harrier, Buzzard, Red Kite, Peregrine, White-tailed Eagle, Crane, Ruff, Great Spotted Woodpecker, Middle Spotted Woodpecker, Great Grey Shrike, Crested Tit, Hawfinch, Crossbill.

ACCESS: Both lakes can be explored quite freely from the surrounding roads, some running along the banks in the south and west of Lac du Der. The classic spot is the northern end of the Digue de Nord. The boating port east of Giffaumont Champaubert is a good viewpoint, as is the area reached on the D55 across the bay. Cranes feed to the southwest and are best left undisturbed. The Lac de la Forêt d'Orient is best in the north (a bird hide here) and the east, but it too can be explored at various points. Most of the surrounding forests can be explored by tracks and on foot.

ROUTE: The area is easily reached from Paris or the Channel ports via Reims and Châlons. The best routes are toll motorways.

Sept Îles

These islands lie off the northern coast of Brittany, approximately half way between

Rennes and Brest, near the resort of Perros-Guirec. They form the best seabird colonies in France and, in particular, hold two species, Puffin and Gannet, that reach their southernmost breeding stations here. The Gannet first started to breed on the island of Rouzic during the Second World War and has since become well established, reaching 3,800 pairs by 1975. They can now be seen in the area throughout the summer, and many pass through the maze of islands off western Brittany on their way to and from Biscay. A good selection of other seabirds can be seen, though the Peregrine is unfortunately no longer here.

SUMMER: Storm Petrel, Fulmar, Gannet, Shag, Kittiwake, Sandwich Tern, Razorbill, Guillemot, Puffin.

ACCESS: The Sept Îles are a nature reserve and landing is not allowed on Rouzic, Malban and Cerf — they are, of course, the most interesting of the islands. Local boatmen from Perros-Guirec, however, regularly run 'round-the-islands' tours giving excellent views of all the species. Please note: these do not start until early June.

ROUTE: Leave Rennes westward on the N12 to Guingamp, take the D767 to Lannion and follow signs to Perros-Guirec. Many birds can be seen from Ploumanach to the north.

Sologne

The Sologne is an area of heaths and woodland broken by innumerable pools, ponds and lakes. Much of the vegetation is mature deciduous woodland and in many areas this effectively hides the various waters from the public highways. This region has long been famous as one of the primary hunting regions of France and is, as a result, heavily 'keepered. Prohibiting notices and barbed-wire fences are a decided detraction from what is otherwise a superb birding area.

Most of the ponds are shallow with a fringe of reeds, the latter often forming quite extensive reedbeds. There are drainage schemes in process of completion and much valuable habitat has already been lost. Nevertheless, there are still plenty of good birds to be seen, including three harriers, Purple and Night Herons, Black Tern, Black-tailed Godwit, Black Kite, Goshawk, Honey Buzzard and several woodpeckers.

In the north there is more heath than woodland, though here there is considerable reclamation for agriculture and invasion by birch scrub. There are also large areas of conifer plantations, some of which are old enough to have attracted their own particular bird fauna.

SUMMER: Great Crested Grebe, Black-necked Grebe, Purple Heron, Night Heron, Little Bittern, Bittern, Shoveler, Marsh Harrier, Hen Harrier, Montagu's Harrier, Black Kite, Goshawk, Honey Buzzard, Curlew, Black-tailed Godwit, Black Tern, Whiskered Tern, Great Spotted Woodpecker, Lesser Spotted Woodpecker, Black Woodpecker, Savi's Warbler, Great Reed Warbler.

AUTUMN: Crane, Black Kite, Black Tern.

Night Herons

ACCESS: The huge number of lakes precludes any but a highly selective list of recommendations. In the central area the following can be seen from the road: Marguilliers (marsh and reeds), Favells, Pontbertas, Menne, Malzone and Panama. The Étang de Beaumont requires permission, but is generally productive, while the Étang de Bièvre can be poorly viewed from the northeast corner and permission should be sought to walk the 25 m down a track to get better views.

In the northwest of Sologne the Forêt de Chambord is worthy of exploration. It is a hunting reserve, but the many roads and tracks make exploration relatively straightforward. There are, however, several other large areas of woodland nearer the central area, including the Forêt de Bruadan.

ROUTE: From Paris take the A10 (L'Aquitaine) to Orléans and then the N20 to Nouan-le-Fuzelier (the A10 may be completed to Nouan by the time of publication). From Nouan, head westward on the D923 and start exploring. There is a hotel at Chaumont, but I have received no recommendations for this area.

Somme Estuary

The Somme is regularly ignored by birding visitors to France, which is a pity, for this is a major haunt of waders and wildfowl with a good reserve on the northern shore. In fact the reserve is bordered by a uniquely French experiment called 'Parc Ornithologique du Marquenterre', which caters for casual visitors and birders in much the same way as does the Wildfowl Trust in Britain. With the Somme as a background, there are wader pools, open marshes and saltings all to be explored, as well as a bird collection, picnic spot, information centre and so on. It's a bit dude, but definitely worth a stop.

At low tide the Somme reveals extensive flats of mud and sand, and during the summer masses of holidaymakers descend on the cockle and whelk beds. During passage periods and in winter, the birds have these foods to themselves and there is an excellent collection of waders. Wildfowl still mostly pass through. High-tide roosting flights can be seen from the reserve.

PASSAGE: Red-throated Diver, Brent Goose, Shelduck, Spoonbill, Black-tailed Godwit, Bar-tailed Godwit, Whimbrel, Little Stint, Curlew Sandpiper.

WINTER: Pintail, Wigeon, Greylag Goose, Dunlin, Bar-tailed Godwit.

SUMMER: Garganey, Shoveler, Pintail, Greylag Goose, Kentish Plover, Fan-tailed Warbler.

ACCESS: The northern shore is accessible at several places, including the Parc Ornithologique du Marquenterre between April and November, north of Le Crotoy. There is an admission charge to the Parc. The dunes north of Le Crotoy are free.

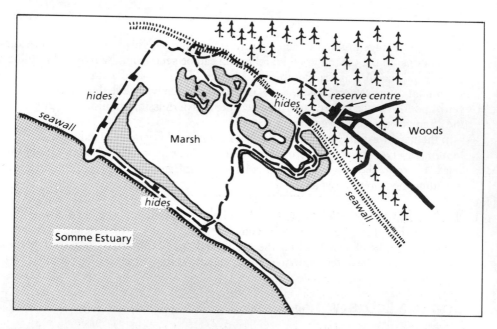

ROUTE: Easily reached from the Channel ports.

GERMANY (FEDERAL REPUBLIC)

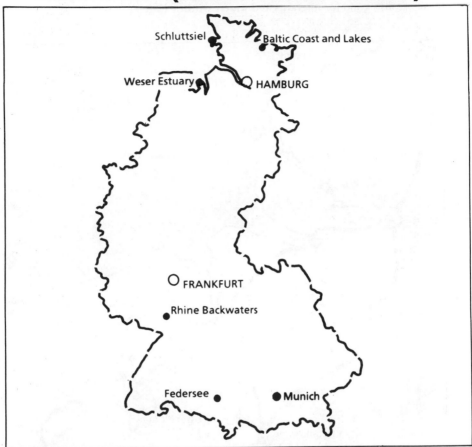

Baltic Coast and Lakes

The northeastern corner of West Germany has so many splendid birdwatching areas that it is worth a holiday at almost any time of the year. For the sake of simplicity this account is divided into two halves — the coastal area and the inland lakes — though in use birders will doubtless flick from one to the other in planning their next move.

The lakes of Schleswig-Holstein are the equivalent of the Muritz Lakes in East Germany and the Masurian Lakes of Poland. As in those areas the lakes are many and varied, and many more than those detailed here are worthy of attention. To the east the White-tailed Eagle breeds, and may well still do so in Schleswig-Holstein. Certainly it was breeding at the Warder See northwest of Lübeck when the first *Where to Watch Birds in Britain and Europe* was published in 1970.

One of the best lakes in the area is Lebrade, to the north of Plön, where both Black-necked and Red-necked Grebes breed, along with Bittern, Little Bittern, Marsh Harrier and Great Reed Warbler. Lake Plön itself has Black-necked Grebe, Bittern,

Goosander, Goldeneye, Ruff and Thrush Nightingale. Like other lakes in this area, these are also good for migrants and winter wildfowl.

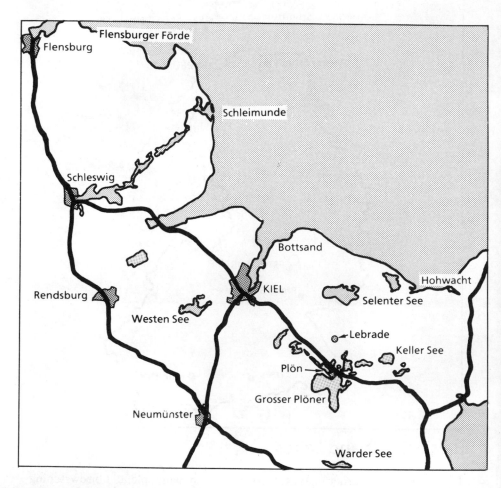

SUMMER: Black-necked Grebe, Red-necked Grebe, Greylag Goose, Mute Swan, Gadwall, Pochard, Goldeneye, Bittern, Little Bittern, White-tailed Eagle, Marsh Harrier, Ruff, Common Gull, Common Tern, Thrush Nightingale, Great Reed Warbler.

The coastline of Kiel Bay is one of the very best areas to watch birds in Germany. There are several estuaries, many marshes and some outstanding seabird colonies. There is much worth exploring and, once again, selection has had to be rather rigorous. The area at the mouth of the Flensburger Förde north of Gelting is a noted winter haunt of waders and wildfowl, including good numbers of Barnacle Geese. To the south, the sandbars at the mouth of the River Schlei (Schleimunde) are intersected by creeks, marshes and meadows, which offer a home for over a thousand pairs of terns, Avocets and Red-breasted Mergansers. This same area also holds many waders, duck and Brent Geese during passage and winter periods. The peninsula to the south is approached via Olpenitz and is wardened during the breeding season.

Bottsand is a low half-island of sand with adjacent saltmarsh that holds breeding Shelduck, Red-breasted Merganser, Kentish Plover, Avocet and Little Tern. It is also a major wader area during passage. Bottsand is on the eastern shore at the mouth of the Kieler Förde and is reached by taking the Probsteier road in the direction of Barsbeker and continuing past Barsbeker Lake to the coast. Further to the east is Hohwacht, a good area for migrants, with the nearby Kleiner Binnensee separated from the Baltic by only a dune beach. Breeding birds include Goosander and Avocet.

Having worked the whole of the Kiel Bay coastline, it would be a pity to miss the marshes of the island of Fehmarn. In the west there are several waters with Greylag Goose, Red-crested Pochard, Red-necked Grebe, Bittern, Marsh Harrier and Red-breasted Merganser. The island is now connected to the mainland via a bridge.

SUMMER: Red-necked Grebe, Greylag Goose, Red-crested Pochard, Red-breasted Merganser, Bittern, Marsh Harrier, Kentish Plover, Black-tailed Godwit, Avocet, Common Tern, Sandwich Tern, Little Tern.

PASSAGE: Greylag Goose, Barnacle Goose, Brent Goose, Bewick's Swan, Whooper Swan, Wigeon, Pintail, Scaup, Eider, Long-tailed Duck, Scoter, White-tailed Eagle, Osprey, Honey Buzzard, Spotted Redshank, Greenshank, Knot, Little Stint, Curlew Sandpiper, Broad-billed Sandpiper, Snow Bunting.

ACCESS: Routes and access details are indicated above within the main text.

ROUTE: From Hamburg north to the sites area.

Federsee

Anyone visiting or passing through southern Germany should certainly make a detour to include the Federsee on their itinerary. It is only a small reed marsh and lake, lying just west of Biberach near Buchau, but over 100 species have been recorded breeding here. Among these, Black-necked Grebe, both bitterns, Marsh Harrier, Black Kite, Common Tern and even Black Grouse can be found. Today, Federsee is something of a summer tourist resort, with boardwalks, display signs and visitor amenities, but it is still worth more than the hour or so that most non-birding visitors spend here. The staff are usually pleased to meet anyone seriously interested in birds, and can be very helpful in guiding one in the best direction.

SUMMER: Black-necked Grebe, Great Crested Grebe, Garganey, Gadwall, Bittern, Little Bittern, Marsh Harrier, Black Kite, Red Kite, Hobby, Spotted Crake, Little Crake, Water Rail, Curlew, Common Tern, Long-eared Owl, Black Grouse, Willow Tit, Savi's Warbler, Reed Warbler, Grasshopper Warbler.

ACCESS: From Bad Buchau follow signs to Federsee Museum, where there is a free car park. There is a small entrance fee, and boardwalks lead to open water where boats may be hired.

ROUTE: Leave the E11 Autobahn at Ulm and take Route 311 to Riedlingen. Turn left outside the town to Buchau.

Munich

One of the best areas for birds in southern Germany lies between Munich and the Austrian border, towards Salzburg and Passau. There are many lakes of various sizes here, but not all are worth exploring and attention should be concentrated on the following: Ismaninger Teichgebiet, Chiemsee, Eching and Moosburg and, especially, the Innstauseen. If in any doubt at all head for the latter, which are often referred to as the Inn Lakes.

The River Inn forms the border between Germany and Austria for the lower part of its course, before joining the youthful Danube at Passau. Construction of a series of five dams here has turned an area of meadows into a major wetland, though only part of Lake Ering-Frauenstein in Austria has been declared a nature reserve. Soon after their creation, the River Warbler spread westward to colonise the area, and other breeding birds include Purple Heron and Night Heron, Little Bittern (100 pairs), Red-crested Pochard and many other duck, Penduline Tit and the occasional Black-winged Stilt. Waders are often abundant on passage, with several thousand Ruff in spring and autumn, and winter sees thousands of wildfowl including Mallard, Teal, Tufted and Pochard.

Chiemsee lies just north of the Munich–Salzburg Autobahn and is a huge and deep lake. It does, however, have some extensive reedbeds that offer breeding sites for Bittern and Red-crested Pochard. Though much used for recreation, there are still passage waders and winter wildfowl.

The Eching and Moosburg Reservoir lies near the town of the latter name in the valley of the River Isar, northeast of Munich. It is mainly a passage and winter haunt of duck, with quite large numbers of Goosander.

Ismaninger Teichgebiet is a substantial reservoir with an adjacent area of fishponds to the northeast of Munich. These rich habitats make the area one of the best in Germany for waterbirds, and there is a substantial colony of Black-necked Grebes associated with a large Black-headed Gullery. There are good numbers of breeding duck including Red-crested Pochard, as well as Little Bittern, Water Rail and Penduline Tit. During passage periods many waders pass through, and in autumn there are thousands of duck, many of which winter here.

SUMMER: Black-necked Grebe, Purple Heron, Night Heron, Bittern, Little Bittern, Pintail, Garganey, Shoveler, Gadwall, Tufted Duck, Pochard, Red-crested Pochard, Water Rail, Black-headed Gull, Common Gull, Common Tern, Penduline Tit, River Warbler, Savi's Warbler.

WINTER: Teal, Shoveler, Wigeon, Pintail, Tufted Duck, Pochard, Ferruginous Duck, Red-crested Pochard, Goldeneye, Goosander.

ACCESS: The Inn Lakes are easily found by following the road along the river south of Passau as far as Simbach. Chiemsee is also easy to locate north of the Munich–Salzburg Autobahn. The reservoir at Moosburg lies just off Route 11 to the northeast of Munich, while Ismaninger Teichgebiet lies in the same direction on the road to Ismaning. The last area is the private property of an electricity company and accessible only to *bona fide* ornithologists. Membership of one of our national societies should suffice. Write to Deutscher Bund für Vogelschutz, Achalmstrasse 33a, D7014, Kornwestheim, for details of their current Munich branch.

ROUTE: Munich has excellent communications by road and air.

Rhine Backwaters

Between Karlsruhe and Mainz the Rhine formerly meandered over a wide floodplain, creating a multitude of backwaters and oxbows. Today, many of these remain as lakes and marshes, in some cases isolating islands from their surroundings. The largest and most famous of these wetlands is the Kühkopf, but there are many others, including the Roxheimer Altrhein on the west bank above Worms and Lampertsheimer Altrhein on the eastern bank. Kühkopf itself lies downstream to the west of Darmstadt. It is a former island of the Rhine, with areas of open water, reedbeds, damp meadows and belts of woodland. This range of habitats provides opportunities for over a hundred species to breed, with another hundred recorded as visitors. Breeders include duck, crakes, Little Bittern, kites, Goshawk, Black Woodpecker, Golden Oriole and Bluethroat. In fact, now that the island is connected to the mainland by bridge, this is a really attractive and easily accessible summer birding spot.

The two other wetlands to the south do not support anything like the same variety of species, though Roxheimer has a good population of Little Bittern, Great Crested Grebe and Little Ringed Plover. Both this area and Lampertsheimer are, however, important for wildfowl and waders on passage and in winter.

SUMMER: Grey Heron, Little Bittern, Garganey, Shoveler, Goshawk, Red Kite, Black Kite, Buzzard, Honey Buzzard, Hobby, Spotted Crake, Little Crake, Corncrake, Quail, Curlew, Little Ringed Plover, Long-eared Owl, Short-eared Owl, Grey-headed Woodpecker, Middle Spotted Woodpecker, Black Woodpecker, Great Grey Shrike, Woodchat Shrike, Red-backed Shrike, Hoopoe, Golden Oriole, Bluethroat, Icterine Warbler, Firecrest, Serin.

PASSAGE: Garganey, Pintail, Pochard, Tufted Duck, Snipe, Green Sandpiper.

ACCESS: Kühkopf is reached by bridge from Stockstadt, which is on Route 44 north of Mannheim. Roads facilitate exploration, though the heronry is fenced off. Lampertsheimer is off the same road to the east, only a short distance from Mannheim, while Roxheimer is reached via Route 9 along the western bank of the Rhine.

ROUTE: Mannheim is well connected to the rest of Germany via the Autobahn network.

Schluttsiel

This wetland and coastal area lies on the Waddensee coast of Jutland, some 25 km (15 miles) south of the Danish border, at the northern end of what is a fine birding area. In fact, good bird habitat extends right along this coast from the border to Hamburger Hallig and beyond. At Schluttsiel, a road runs behind the seawall and is separated from a lake by an area of damp meadows. There are good reedbeds that attract Bittern and Marsh Harrier, and among the colony of Black-headed Gulls there are regular Mediterranean. Little Gulls also breed and flocks build up in summer to quite reasonable numbers. The meadows hold Black-tailed Godwit, plus a good variety of passage species. There is a good movement of birds over the beach at high tide.

To the south, the sandbanks offshore hold good populations of Common, Arctic and Sandwich Terns and quite incredible numbers of passage waders. The figure of a million birds has been mentioned. To these can be added a quarter of a million ducks and a few thousand Barnacle Geese, among which Red-breasted Goose is comparatively regular. Though these populations are centred on the offshore islands, much can be seen from the mainland.

SUMMER: Bittern, Marsh Harrier, Black-tailed Godwit, Avocet, Mediterranean Gull, Little Gull, Arctic Tern, Common Tern, Sandwich Tern.

PASSAGE: Dunlin, Knot, Redshank, Oystercatcher.

WINTER: Bewick's Swan, Barnacle Goose.

ACCESS: The whole of this area can be explored by road and, though there are several nature reserves here, there are few restrictions on access.

ROUTE: Husum is the nearest big town.

Weser Estuary

The north coast of Germany is lined by the Waddensee and broken by several major estuaries, including those of the Ems, Elbe and Weser. Each is excellent for birds at all seasons, and it is somewhat invidious to pick out one as being better than the others. In fact, there are splendid birding opportunities along the entire length of this coast and almost anywhere makes a good base for a holiday.

The Weser, downstream from Bremerhaven, is typical of this coastline, with huge areas of intertidal mud and sand backed by seawalls and lush grazing meadows. Immediately to the west is Jadebusen, a shallow sea bay with sandbanks, mudflats and an intricate network of creeks. Together, these two areas form a superb feeding ground for waders and wildfowl and are noted as a haunt of wintering geese and Avocet. Offshore, at the mouth of the complex, the island of Mellum is a strictly controlled nature reserve with breeding Shelduck and a huge gullery. It is also a major high-tide roost for many of the winter waders.

In the summer the surrounding marshes hold good numbers of Avocet, Black-tailed Godwit and Ruff, while during passage periods waders pass through in both number and variety.

SUMMER: Avocet, Black-tailed Godwit, Ruff, Sandwich Tern.

WINTER: Greylag Goose, White-fronted Goose, Brent Goose, Wigeon, Pintail, Shelduck, Bar-tailed Godwit, Black-tailed Godwit, Knot, Curlew.

PASSAGE: Whimbrel, Black-tailed Godwit, Little Stint, Little Gull.

ACCESS: The Jadebusen can be worked at several points, though the area around Dangast is as good as any. Even within a short distance of Wilhelmshaven there are excellent marshes, and the ferry to Eckwarderhörne may prove splendid in winter. The area around this peninsula between the two great tidal zones is known as Butjadinger Land and the coastline here is fine for marsh and shoreline birds. The island of Mellum may be visited only under guidance of the warden.

ROUTE: Both Wilhelmshaven and Bremerhaven make good starting points.

East Germany

Several correspondents have written about their birdwatching experiences in the German Democratic Republic (GDR) and were quite clear that birdwatchers can go where they please and watch what they like. German citizens can obtain a day visa; non-Germans can get a visa for lengthier periods, but must stay at Interhotels. This 'hotel-for-foreigners' chain has establishments in most large towns. It may thus be possible to explore the Baltic coast and the nearby Muritz lake system. Certainly there are some good reserves here, some Crane stop-overs and even a population of Great Bustards.

GREECE

Aspróvalta

The area between Aspróvalta and the mouth of the River Strimón has long been a convenient stopping-off point between Thessaloníki and Kaválla. Here the main road runs behind the beach, making for easy access to both the shoreline on the one side and the rather lush orchard and grassland on the other. The sea here regularly produces both Slender-billed and Audouin's Gulls, and Cory's and *yelkouan* Shearwaters are often noted. The smaller birds, however, regularly include Masked Shrike, Rufous Bush Chat, Black-eared Wheatear and Black-headed Bunting.

To the east, after the River Strimón is crossed, there is a large lagoon with plentiful waders, terns, gulls and regular Great White Egret. Further east still lies the formerly splendid Néstos delta. Here there are rubbish tips, fish factories and some splendidly level, rich agricultural land all of which was once prime bird habitat. There are still birds here, and the village of Keramoti is an attractive base for visits to the delta and to the island of Thásos offshore. It is, however, but a shadow of its former self and, if time presses, is mostly passed by.

SUMMER: Cory's Shearwater, *yelkouan* Shearwater, Little Egret, Great White Egret, Short-toed Eagle, Levant Sparrowhawk, Hobby, Red-footed Falcon, Eleonora's Falcon, Stone-curlew, Black-winged Stilt, Kentish Plover, Mediterranean Gull, Slender-billed Gull, Audouin's Gull, Little Gull, Scops Owl, Pallid Swift, Roller, Crested Lark, Golden Oriole, Red-rumped Swallow, Masked Shrike, Woodchat Shrike, Lesser Grey Shrike, Rufous Bush Chat, Olivaceous Warbler, Orphean Warbler, Black-headed Bunting.

ACCESS: Take the E5 eastward from Aspróvalta (100 m and onwards) and stop to explore north and south throughout the area. The Europa Camp site has Eleonora's at dusk.

ROUTE: Thessaloníki has an international airport.

Corfu

Corfu has become one of the most popular holiday destinations in the eastern Mediterranean yet retains that delightful timelessness that is such a feature of Greek island life. Over the centuries it has endured many invasions and occupations; there is a cemetery, in Corfu town (Kérkira) itself, where the gravestones document the British period of control — it also boasts a wide variety of carefully protected wild orchids. Corfu is the 'green' island of Greece, and its trees and meadows present a sharp contrast to the mainland only a few kilometres to the east. Basically, it consists of a high rocky area in the wide north and a low-lying narrow region to the south. Though most of the best bird areas lie in the north, at no great distance from Corfu airport, there is one major attraction at the Alikes saltpans that must draw the visitor to the extreme south of the island. The other main birding areas are Lake Antinioti in the north, alongside the coastal road; the northern mountains, rising to over 3000 ft (900 m) at Pandokrátor; the plain of Ropa in the 'mid-west'; Lake Korisson in the southwest; and the saltpans at Alikes, right in the south. There are, of course, several other excellent spots, but visitors with time at a premium should certainly include these areas in their itinerary.

Corfu is best regarded as a splendid migration spot, rather than the home of a wealth of exciting birds. Of most interest to visitors are Cretzschmar's Bunting, which breeds, and spring migrants such as Collared and Semi-collared Flycatchers, Red-throated Pipit, White-winged Black Tern and Red-footed Falcon, with the chance of Great Snipe, Olive-tree Warbler or Saker Falcon. From April through to mid-May there are always birds coming and going, and a daily watch at a favoured area can be very rewarding. Do not expect Black-headed Bunting before May.

SUMMER: Little Grebe, Pygmy Cormorant, Dalmatian Pelican, Little Bittern, Little Egret, Squacco Heron, Purple Heron, Glossy Ibis, Garganey, Golden Eagle, Short-toed Eagle, Buzzard, Marsh Harrier, Montagu's Harrier, Hobby, Red-footed Falcon, Quail, Stone-curlew, Little Ringed Plover, Kentish Plover, Great Snipe, Temminck's

Stint, Ruff, Black-tailed Godwit, Curlew Sandpiper, Black-winged Stilt, Collared Pratincole, Mediterranean Gull, Black Tern, White-winged Black Tern, Gull-billed Tern, Scops Owl, Alpine Swift, Pallid Swift, Roller, Hoopoe, Wryneck, Red-rumped Swallow, Golden Oriole, Red-throated Pipit, Tawny Pipit, Red-backed Shrike, Woodchat Shrike, Short-toed Treecreeper, Blue Rock Thrush, Black-eared Wheatear, Cetti's Warbler, Moustached Warbler, Great Reed Warbler, Icterine Warbler, Orphean Warbler, Subalpine Warbler, Sardinian Warbler, Pied Flycatcher, Collared Flycatcher, Semi-collared Flycatcher, Cirl Bunting, Cretzschmar's Bunting, Black-headed Bunting, Spanish Sparrow.

ACCESS: Lake Antinioti lies on the north coast to the west of Kassiópi and can be viewed from the roadside. Its open waters and reeds are a haunt of Little Bittern among others.

Pandokrátor is the highest point of Corfu and can be reached by road. It is worth walking the last few kilometres as this is Cretzschmar's habitat. Golden Eagle has been seen near Episkepsia and at times a Lammergeier has flown across from Albania. The occasional White-tailed Eagle follows the same route to Lake Antinioti.

Plain of Ropa lies south of Corfu golf course and is best approached along the road down the eastern side. The plain is crossed by a track that leads toward Yiannádhes and to a bridge over the river. Stop, and walk up and down the river for Great Reed and Moustached Warblers, Red-footed Falcon, harriers, etc.

Lake Korisson is reached by taking the main road south and stopping at the café-garage at Linia before you get to Aghios Georgios Beach. Walk the track to the lake through good small fields with shrikes and wheatears. Continue to the beach and watch for migrants among the junipers.

Alikes saltpans are right in the south of Corfu and reached by turning left at a difficult-to-spot road in the town of Lefkímmi. Access is free enough, but avoid weekends and holidays. The pans can be explored on foot and may be disappointing, or staggeringly full with waders, terns, gulls, Osprey, depending on the circumstances.

ROUTE: Corfu airport has regular flights from most major European cities. As you land, watch for Little Egrets in the lagoons next to the runway. Plentiful accommodation, but book in advance for the lovely old houses on the northeast coast.

Crete

The island of Crete is some 300 km (180 miles) in length, but only 25 km (15½ miles) wide at its narrowest point. It rises steeply to over 8000 ft (2440 m) and is essentially a huge mountain chain emerging directly from the sea. Its west-to-east axis creates a formidable obstacle to birds moving directly north and south and, in poor weather with low cloud, day-flying migrants can be seen to alter course to find their way around, rather than over, the barrier. In some of the high passes, grounded migrants are often abundant during similar conditions.

Most ornithological exploration has been concentrated in the past 20 years or so and only comparatively recently has the island developed into a major tourist centre. This has had the advantage of providing a wide and plentiful variety of hotel and villa accommodation, as well as a new major west-to-east road. It has, however, accelerated the process of filling all the rivers and marshes with rubbish and debris. The rivers of Crete mostly run from south to north (the north is more gently sloping and holds most of the human population), but they are inevitably short with only seasonal flows and narrow mouths. The infilling and dumping has only highlighted Crete's lack of substantial wetlands.

Being almost as close to Libya as it is to Athens, Crete enjoys substantial southern influences. The Sirocco often blows warm air over the island and there are even wild palm groves in the extreme east at Vai. As this site is so far south, huge areas of polythene have sprung up for vegetable-growing and these too have reduced the area of lowland available to birds. Unfortunately, these southern influences have had no effect on the bird population — there are no exotic babblers or bulbuls to be found. Also, being so isolated, Crete is not a regular port of call for either migrant raptors or storks. Such soaring birds as do occur are resident.

After what is a rather depressing picture of disappearing habitat, rapid development and, in any case, a somewhat impoverished fauna, it is good to be able to report that Crete is a fine place for birds. It has a good population of Lammergeier, is of crucial importance for Eleonora's Falcon, is doing well by its Griffon Vultures and has a splendid passage of migrants in both spring and autumn.

To explore the island fully it is necessary to use two bases; Aghios Nicholas (east) and Chania (west) are perfect. While Ag. Nick. (as it is generally known) is fast developing as Crete's most popular resort, Chania remains a fine Venetian city with one of the world's finest waterfronts. Because of the lack of any major wetlands, birding can start almost anywhere. The grounds of a good hotel, an olive grove, a scrub area, a rubbish tip — all can, and do, produce birds. Rüppell's Warbler, always an important bird for every visitor, is widespread, though everywhere outnumbered by Sardinian Warbler. Migrants too can turn up anywhere, and not just on the south coast in spring and the north coast in autumn. Collared and Semi-collared Flycatchers outnumber Pied, Red-throated Pipit may occur in small flocks, there are Whitethroat and Lesser Whitethroat, Black-eared Wheatear and Great Reed Warbler and hosts more.

Rüppell's Warbler apart, Crete has other specialities. The Lammergeier inhabits all the main mountain massifs and is relatively easy to see around the Lasithi Plateau (east) and at the top of the Samaria Gorge (west). Griffons are particularly numerous on the climb up to Lasithi from Ag. Nick. and may easily be seen at the Selinari Gorge on the main road west of Ag. Nick. Eleonora's Falcon arrives in May and can then be seen in flocks several hundred strong in the areas of Sitía and Heráklion. The world's largest colony of these birds, estimated at some 180–230 pairs, lies on the island of Diá north of Heráklion, while the Dionisides Islands off the northeast coast hold some 290 pairs in total. Between them these two colony-groups account for an important percentage of the world total of this falcon. Good views can be obtained on the mainland between Sitía and Piskokefalon, or in the valley of Skopi where the falcons feed every day.

If these three are the major specialities there are others: Black-headed Bunting, Bonelli's Eagle, Marsh and Montagu's Harriers, together with the occasional Pallid, Red-footed Falcon, Audouin's Gull, Glossy Ibis and Peregrine, are all regular, but frankly there is nothing quite like the spring passage period.

SUMMER: Black-necked Grebe, Cory's Shearwater, Squacco Heron, Great White Egret, Little Egret, Sparrowhawk, Buzzard, Booted Eagle, Bonelli's Eagle, Short-toed Eagle, Lammergeier, Griffon Vulture, Marsh Harrier, Peregrine, Hobby, Lesser Kestrel, Eleonora's Falcon, Red-footed Falcon, Chukar, Scops Owl, Pallid Swift, Alpine Swift, Hoopoe, Short-toed Lark, Woodlark, Crag Martin, Tawny Pipit, Blue-headed Wagtail, Ashy-headed Wagtail, Black-headed Wagtail, Red-backed Shrike, Woodchat Shrike, Masked Shrike, Cetti's Warbler, Savi's Warbler, Moustached Warbler, Great Reed Warbler, Icterine Warbler, Olivaceous Warbler, Olive-tree Warbler, Sardinian Warbler, Rüppell's Warbler, Wood Warbler, Bonelli's Warbler, Black-eared Wheatear, Blue Rock Thrush, Spanish Sparrow, Italian Sparrow, Golden Oriole, Chough, Alpine Chough, Citril Finch, Black-headed Bunting, Rock Bunting.

SPRING: Great White Egret, Glossy Ibis, Little Bittern, Purple Heron, Black Kite, Mediterranean Gull, Little Gull, Audouin's Gull, Little Ringed Plover, Little Stint, Curlew Sandpiper, Ruff, Spotted Redshank, Greenshank, Green Sandpiper, Wood Sandpiper, Black-winged Stilt, Tree Pipit, Red-throated Pipit, Whinchat, Redstart, Thrush Nightingale, Collared Flycatcher, Semi-collared Flycatcher.

ACCESS: The Lasithi Plateau is easily reached from Ag. Nick. The steep, twisting climb may produce vultures and the occasional eagle, but it is the hills on the south side that are best for Lammergeier. The valley floor holds Cirl Bunting among others.

Lammergeier

The village of Kritsa (Byzantine church) lies at the mouth of a gorge with breeding vultures, Chough, Buzzard etc, and is only a short drive or bus ride from Ag. Nick. Just outside the town (to the east) lies the tiny marsh of Almyros, with Penduline Tit.

In the far east, the Sitía area is good for Eleonora's (see above) and the harbour for Mediterranean and Little Gulls. Beyond, the road leads to Kato Zákros via a deep gorge for vultures, raptors, Crag Martin, Alpine Swift and possible Bonelli's Eagle. The shoreline cover often holds migrants and the adjacent agricultural area should be explored for wagtails and pipits.

West from Ag. Nick., the main road passes through the Selinari Gorge for breeding Griffon Vultures and, in winter, possible Peregrine, Buzzard and even Lammergeier. Beyond, and off to the right, lies the Minoan site of Mallia, and it is worth exploring the fields and wet scrub to the west for Penduline Tit, Wryneck, Red-throated Pipit, Marsh Harrier and Buzzard in season.

The Heráklion area is quite productive, with the harbour being good for gulls, terns and sometimes shearwaters following the fishing boats. Agia Reservoir and Lake Kournas are no great distance away and between them offer the best opportunities for wetland birds: Black-necked Grebe, Great White Egret plus duck, waders and 'wet' warblers. Further south lies the site of Phaestos, where in spring a variety of falcons, including Eleonora's, Hobby and Peregrine, can regularly be seen. At one time the adjacent Geros River was the best spot on Crete, but rubbish-dumping and pollution has changed it beyond recognition. Unfortunately, it is impossible to drive far through the remaining marsh owing to the presence of a military base, but a walk along the northern riverbank should still produce Penduline Tit, Marsh Harrier, Buzzard, Woodchat and warblers. I would be delighted to hear from anyone who persists along this route as far as the sea: Great Snipe may be the reward.

An exploration of Mount Ida on minor roads may be rewarding, before heading westwards to Chania. Along the north coast the rivers have cut deep gorges that offer chances of several birds, but especially Bonelli's Eagle. That of the Petres River is excellent, with a small marsh at the coast as well, while the Sfakoriako River, just west of Réthimnon at Prassies, is also good for the same birds. Beyond the village, watch for a farm with lots of chickens and goats and then walk directly east to the gorge for Bonelli's Eagle etc.

From Chania, excursions southward to the Omalos Plateau for larks and pipits and to the Samaria Gorge are excellent. Many tourists walk the gorge; the birder can stay at the café at the top for Lammergeier, Peregrine, etc, and walk only a few hundred metres down for Bonelli's Warbler, Crossbill, Citril Finch, etc. Chóra Sfakíon on the south coast is first-class for spring migrants, and Frankokastelo to the east has a few damp pools, plus excellent bush cover.

ROUTE: Heráklion has an international airport with scheduled flights from Athens and summer charters from northern Europe. Accommodation is plentiful and seldom fully booked outside the main holiday period.

Delphi

Twenty years ago Delphi was on everyone's list of places that it was unthinkable to miss. Today it is inundated with tourists, crowded by coaches and seemingly one of the most unlikely birding spots in this book. Yet, by staying nearby and entering at opening time the delightful open-air theatre, the Temple of Apollo, the stadium and the other wonders of Ancient Greece can be enjoyed along with Sombre Tit, Rock Nuthatch, Cretzschmar's Bunting and even Rüppell's Warbler. There are other warblers, including Orphean, and other buntings, including Ortolan, Rock and Cirl. Crag Martins are abundant and Alpine Swifts should be seen. This is a quite delightful place provided that an early-morning visit is arranged. Once the coaches have arrived — forget it.

Above Delphi lies Parnassós, which can be explored by road. Stops can be made to watch for the birds of prey that still inhabit this splendid area. The vultures formerly found here have declined rapidly in recent years, but there may still be the odd Lammergeier, and Short-toed and Golden Eagles are still seen.

SUMMER: Griffon Vulture, Golden Eagle, Short-toed Eagle, Rock Partridge, Alpine Swift, Lesser Grey Shrike, Woodchat Shrike, Crag Martin, Red-rumped Swallow, Rock Nuthatch, Blue Rock Thrush, Black Redstart, Sardinian Warbler, Rüppell's Warbler, Orphean Warbler, Olive-tree Warbler, Olivaceous Warbler, Sombre Tit, Cretzschmar's Bunting, Rock Bunting, Ortolan Bunting, Cirl Bunting, Rock Sparrow.

ACCESS: Lies west of Athens along the northern shore of the Gulf of Corinth. The ruins are worthy of a thorough exploration and above the Arena, after a bit of a scramble, is the boundary fence. This is broken in several places (presumably by impecunious tourists) and gives access to a track leading northeastwards. By climbing up to where the ruins are just about to disappear you enter Rüppell's Warbler territory. It is possible to reach this track north and then east of Delphi town.

Below the entrance to the ruins, a track leads downhill to the southwest and joins a major track south of the town. This is worth a walk for Red-rumped Swallow, Rock Partridge and Cretzschmar's Bunting.

To the southwest of Delphi, around Itéa, is an area of olive groves offering a variety of species, including Olivaceous and particularly Olive-tree Warbler. Watch for a BP garage less than 1 km (1000 yards) east of Itéa. Continue eastwards past a track, past a small church and stop just beyond a small spur of rocky terrain. A track leads north among excellent groves.

For Parnassós and the higher-altitude species, take the road northwards from Arákhova and explore as you climb. A large plateau is worth a stop, and a right turn soon after leads to the mountain for Shore Lark, etc.

ROUTE: Via Athens.

Évros Delta and Ávas Gorge

Were it not for the fact that the River Évros forms the frontier between Greece and Turkey, the Évros Delta would be one of the most popular bird resorts in Europe. As it is, the Évros is an outstanding wetland, despite the inroads that continuous drainage programmes have made. Much is now arable or grazing, but there are still lagoons with areas of reed and it is among these that the best birds can be found. Spur-winged Plover, White Stork, Black Kite, Rufous Bush Chat, Spanish Sparrow and Isabelline Wheatear can all be seen and there are often many migrating waders, including the essentially eastern and much sought-after Marsh, Broad-billed and Terek Sandpipers, Slender-billed Curlew, Greater Sand and Sociable Plovers. There are Bee-eater, Lesser Grey Shrike, Sombre Tit, Olive-tree Warbler, Masked Shrike and often impressive forma-tions of migrating raptors. Spotted and Lesser Spotted Eagles, Honey and Long-legged Buzzards, Levant Sparrowhawk, Goshawk and Red-footed Falcon all put in an appear-ance. There is a chance of White-tailed and Steppe Eagles, Great Black-headed Gull, Palm Dove and even Rufous Turtle Dove and Black Lark.

In winter the 100,000 wildfowl include smallish numbers of Lesser Whitefronts and Red-breasted Geese, as well as the occasional Bewick's Swan and Saker.

To the north lies the Ávas Gorge, an impressive ravine beloved of Griffon and Black Vultures, Booted, Golden, Imperial and Short-toed Eagles and three species of buzzard. There is a pair of Eagle Owls here, as well as species such as Blue Rock Thrush, Crag Martin and Dipper. Among the olive groves below the gorge there are Isabelline Wheatear along a railway embankment and Masked Shrike — this is the number one European spot for this bird. Some 12 km (7½ miles) beyond Ávas village the road ends at Essimi. Beyond is military territory.

SUMMER: White Pelican, Dalmatian Pelican, White Stork, Black Stork, Little Egret, Squacco Heron, Purple Heron, Ruddy Shelduck, Garganey, Ferruginous Duck, Egyptian Vulture, Griffon Vulture, White-tailed Eagle, Booted Eagle, Bonelli's Eagle, Short-toed Eagle, Spotted Eagle, Lesser Spotted Eagle, Golden Eagle, Imperial Eagle, Marsh Harrier, Honey Buzzard, Buzzard, Long-legged Buzzard, Goshawk, Levant Sparrowhawk, Lanner, Peregrine, Hobby, Red-footed Falcon, Stone-curlew, Spur-winged Plover, Black-winged Stilt, Avocet, Collared Pratincole, Caspian Tern, Gull-billed Tern, Eagle Owl, Hoopoe, Bee-eater, Roller, Grey-headed Woodpecker, Syrian Woodpecker, Masked Shrike, Red-backed Shrike, Lesser Grey Shrike, Golden Oriole, Blue Rock Thrush, Isabelline Wheatear, Black-eared Wheatear, Rufous Bush Chat, Subalpine Warbler, Barred Warbler, Orphean Warbler, Olive-tree Warbler, Collared Flycatcher, Sombre Tit.

SPRING AND AUTUMN: Little Stint, Curlew Sandpiper, Broad-billed Sandpiper, Wood Sandpiper, Spotted Redshank, Marsh Sandpiper, Terek Sandpiper.

ACCESS: There are three distinct routes into the delta. The two southern ones (to the best areas, naturally) require permits. These may be obtained from either the police or the military headquarters in the boulevard near the lighthouse in Alexandroúpolis. Armed with a piece of paper, one can then enter the delta from the Town Hall in Ferrai where an earth road leads to a military post and then along the main dyke to the Hunting Lodge (soon a biological station) and the Palukia Lagoon. The second route involves leaving the E5 just beyond Monastiraki where a track leads right just after a small hill. After crossing the railway, there is a good chance of Isabelline Wheatear, Rufous Bush Chat and more or less certain Spanish Sparrow. The track continues on the north side of a river to the pumping station, turning right past Drana Lagoon back to the E5. This route can, of course, be reversed by leaving the E5 on the east side of the Loutros Bridge on a track to the south. Those with permits on the Monastiraki route can cross the river and turn right to the pumping station, then south to Palukia Lagoon and the Hunting Lodge.

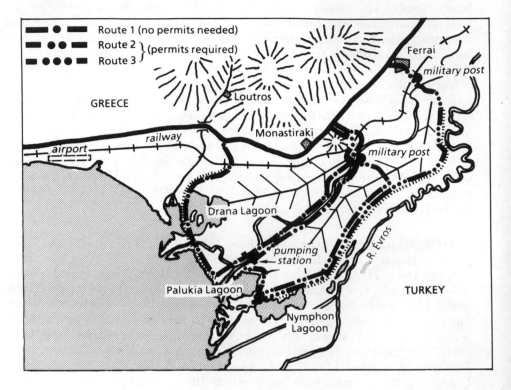

The Ávas Gorge is reached on a minor road that crosses the railway north of Alexandroúpolis and leads toward Aisymi. Only a few kilometres north of Alexandroúpolis and 2–3 km (1–2 miles) south of Ávas village, take a left turning just past some ruins. Park where a track leads right and walk northwards along the track for Masked Shrike, Olive-tree Warbler and Syrian Woodpecker. Continue through Ávas to the gorge to and beyond the bridge for Eagle Owl. Higher still, watch for Imperial Eagle two hours after dawn.

ROUTE: Nearest airport is at distant Thessaloníki, but there are excellent birding spots along the way.

Ioánnina

The area of northwestern Greece around the town of Ioánnina is in almost every way a backwater and remains little explored by international birders. Those intent on the wonders of Porto Lágo and Évros may make a detour to Préspa and those exploring the whole of Greece find their high-altitude birds at Mount Olympus, so Ioánnina remains underworked. This is a pity, for the town has an excellent lake noted for passage of waders and terns, as well as reedbed species, and the nearby mountains have an excellent raptor population.

The town itself has a strong colony of Lesser Kestrels, good numbers of White Stork, and a rubbish tip that attracts vultures and other scavengers. The lake has Little Bittern, Squacco and Purple Herons and regular Glossy Ibis. There are often Gull-billed Terns and sometimes Caspian, along with Great Reed, Moustached and other small marsh birds.

To the north, Mount Astraka, with Snow Finch, Alpine Accentor and Alpine Chough, rises over 5000 ft (1500 m), while the whole of the area can produce most of the more widespread Greek birds. There is even Wallcreeper for those with patience.

SUMMER: White Stork, Griffon Vulture, Golden Eagle, Short-toed Eagle, Booted Eagle, Long-legged Buzzard, Lesser Kestrel, Water Rail, Rock Partridge, Roller, Hoopoe, Alpine Accentor, Rock Nuthatch, Wallcreeper, Dipper, Alpine Chough, Sombre Tit, Bearded Tit, Snow Finch, Spanish Sparrow.

AUTUMN: Purple Heron, Squacco Heron, Little Bittern, Glossy Ibis, Long-legged Buzzard, Black-winged Stilt, Gull-billed Tern, Black Tern.

ACCESS: Ioánnina is reached by the major road, the E19, that runs northwards through western Greece north of Árta. Alternatively, it may be reached from Athens via Tríkkala and the E87. The lake lies east of the town, and the excellent southern shore is reached by heading southwards on the E19 and then turning eastwards on a rough lakeside track. After 1 km (just over ½ mile) park and walk to the lakeside reedbeds, which may, at times, make open-water viewing impossible.

For Astraka, take the road northwards out of Ioánnina and turn right after about 45 km (28 miles) to Aristi. Continue to Papingon and then walk the mule track to the cliff face of Astraka.

ROUTE: Via Athens.

Kastoría Lakes

About 150 km (94 miles) north of Metéora and at no great distance from the famed Lake Préspa, in northwestern Greece, lies a series of four large lakes, at the western end of which is the town of Kastoría. By some strange quirk of fate these lakes have been largely ignored by visiting birders and are, therefore, little known. Yet what we do know is enough to show their potential. Lake Kastorías lies immediately east of the town of the same name and is strangely the most awkward of access. To the east is Lake Cheimaditis, with a smaller subsidiary lake 1 km (just over ½ mile) to the north. Next eastwards is Lake Petrou, which is too deep for waders, but has pelicans, grebes and other 'swimming' birds. Here, near to the Yugoslavian border, there are notices prohibiting photography, so telescopes and binoculars should be used with discretion. Furthest east is Lake Vegorrítis, the largest of the four.

Birds in spring have proved quite outstanding, with good numbers of many species. White Pelican, Little Egret, Squacco and Purple Herons, Little Bittern, Spoonbill, Ferruginous Duck, Black-winged Stilt, Little Stint, Water Rail, Bearded Tit, together with Black, White-winged Black and Caspian Terns, are regularly present. The surrounding land has Rock Nuthatch, Hoopoe, Black-eared Wheatear, Lesser Grey and other shrikes, together with raptors and the usual warblers and buntings etc.

SPRING: Black-necked Grebe, Dalmatian Pelican, White Pelican, Little Egret, Squacco Heron, Purple Heron, Little Bittern, Spoonbill, Gadwall, Ferruginous Duck, Marsh Harrier, Long-legged Buzzard, Water Rail, Kentish Plover, Black-winged Stilt, Sanderling, Ruff, Little Stint, Collared Pratincole, Black Tern, White-winged Black Tern, Caspian Tern, Hoopoe, Roller, Wryneck, Red-backed Shrike, Woodchat Shrike, Lesser Grey Shrike, Black-eared Wheatear, Cetti's Warbler, Great Reed Warbler, Fan-tailed Warbler, Rock Nuthatch, Tree Sparrow.

ACCESS: Lake Kastorías lies east of Kastoría and is best reached by leaving the town to the southeast and turning left signposted 'Yugoslavia'. Some 100 m before reaching the turning to Marrokórion there is a small bridge with an adjacent track to the left. This leads to the lake. Lake Cheimaditis lies south of the 'Yugoslavia' road mentioned above, and is reached by turning right before reaching E90. Do not ignore the smaller, shallow lake to the north. Lake Vegorrítis lies south of the road to Petrou and is best at the shallow southern end. The E90 toward Ptolemaís often has huge flocks of Rollers, shrikes and Kestrels during passage periods.

ROUTE: The international airport at Thessaloníki is ideally suited for visiting this area on the way to Préspa.

Kerkini Lake

The damming in the late 1950s of the River Strimón near the Bulgarian border created one of the most important wetlands in Greece. For reasons unknown, it still does not feature on the schedules of crews working the coast of Macedonia. Perhaps this account will correct this absurdity.

Kerkini has shallow northern margins with extensive growths of reeds and other emergent vegetation. These have attracted a wide range of species, including Glossy Ibis, Spoonbill, several herons, Penduline and Bearded Tits and Whiskered Tern. Nearby breeders, and regular visitors, include White-tailed, Lesser Spotted and Imperial Eagles plus a variety of other raptors and a host of smaller birds typical of this part of Greece.

During passage periods, White Pelican, Marsh Sandpiper, Caspian and Black Terns, shrikes and many more pass through. In winter there are 30,000–40,000 duck, plus up to 300 Dalmatian Pelicans, 4,000 Pygmy Cormorants, 1,000 Great White Egrets and also Spotted Eagle and Black-necked Grebe. At all seasons Kerkini is full of birds and is an absolute must for all visitors to this part of the country.

SUMMER: Night Heron, Squacco Heron, Purple Heron, Little Egret, White Stork, Black Stork, Spoonbill, Glossy Ibis, Greylag Goose, White-tailed Eagle, Lesser Spotted Eagle, Imperial Eagle, Short-toed Eagle, Booted Eagle, Long-legged Buzzard, Black-winged Stilt, Collared Pratincole, Gull-billed Tern, Whiskered Tern, Bee-eater, Roller, Syrian Woodpecker, Red-rumped Swallow, Penduline Tit, Bearded Tit.

PASSAGE: White Pelican, Marsh Sandpiper, Wood Sandpiper, Caspian Tern, Black Tern, Golden Oriole, Lesser Grey Shrike, Woodchat Shrike.

WINTER: Black-necked Grebe, Dalmatian Pelican, Cormorant, Pygmy Cormorant, Great White Egret, Spotted Eagle, Sandwich Tern.

ACCESS: The nearest large town is Sérrai. From here head northwards to Sidhirókastron and continue, taking a left to Vironeia on the Kilkis road. From Vironeia railway station, a track leads to the Strimón River. Immediately after crossing the bridge, turn left on the main dyke. There are good tracks right around the lake except on the northern shoreline. Also, try the old bed of the Strimón for waders.

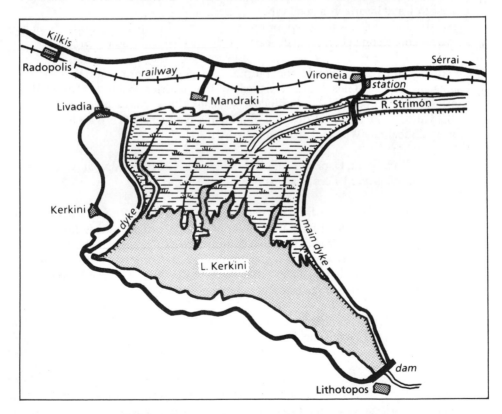

ROUTE: From Thessaloníki on the E20 to Sérrai.

85

Lake Korónia

Lake Korónia, or Lake Vassilios as it is sometimes called, lies only a short distance from Thessaloníki in northeastern Greece and is a shallow, reed-fringed lagoon. Along with Porto Lágo, Korónia is generally regarded as one of the prime migration sites in this part of Europe and regularly produces excellent passage of both waders and terns. Though over 10 km (6 miles) long and 5 km (3 miles) wide, most of the action is concentrated at the margins. As the lake is so shallow, a slight difference in water level can have a serious effect on the position of the margin. At low levels the margin may be well beyond the fringing reeds, while at higher levels water may extend to the grassy surroundings. In either case waders will be found. Problems start when the margin is actually among the reeds and waders may then be concentrated out of sight tight against the vegetation. The surrounding land is mainly agricultural, with occasional clumps of bushy cover that can hold good numbers of migrating warblers.

Though a good variety of birds, including Little Egret, breeds here, the main attractions are migrants. These include Dalmatian and White Pelicans, Booted Eagle, Marsh Harrier and Night and Purple Herons. There are often Glossy Ibis, occasionally Black Stork and invariably a good variety of waders.

Nearby, Lake Vólvi is too deep for many birds, but the Apollonia woods have both storks and the Rentina Gorge, to the east, has Eagle Owl and Booted Eagle.

SUMMER: Little Egret, Night Heron, Purple Heron, Pygmy Cormorant, White Pelican, Dalmatian Pelican, Glossy Ibis, Buzzard, Marsh Harrier, Kentish Plover, Black-winged Stilt, Avocet, Collared Pratincole, Calandra Lark, Short-toed Lark, Crested Lark, Tawny Pipit, Hoopoe, Bearded Tit, Cetti's Warbler, Savi's Warbler, Orphean Warbler, Subalpine Warbler, Spanish Sparrow.

PASSAGE: Black Stork, Osprey, Little Ringed Plover, Green Sandpiper, Greenshank, Black Tern, Whiskered Tern, Caspian Tern.

ACCESS: The lake is obvious from the main road running eastward from Thessaloníki, and can be explored along its southern shore. At the eastern end is the village of Langadikia, reached via a rough road that continues to a stream (fordable) and then out to the lake. This area has some of the largest reedbeds at Korónia. In the northwestern corner there is an excellent sandspit that holds waders, and this can be reached by walking around the edge of the lake from the main road.

ROUTE: Thessaloníki has an international airport with car-hire facilities and a variety of accommodation to suit most pockets.

Lesbos

Lesbos, formerly Mytilene, lies just off the western coast of Turkey. Though the fourth largest of the Greek islands, it remains largely untouched by mass tourism. Nevertheless, some package-tour operators do include the island in their offerings and this is an ideal way of getting its special birds. Lesbos is a rugged island, with scrub-covered hillsides broken by valleys with olive groves and small-scale agriculture. Mitilíni is the capital and the only town of any size. The airport is nearby.

As Lesbos lies so near Turkey, there are considerable eastern influences on its avifauna. Most visitors want Krüper's Nuthatch and Cinereous Bunting, but there is more and certainly sufficient for a good week. Both storks, Levant Sparrowhawk, Eleonora's Falcon and Lanner, plus Cretzschmar's Bunting, Rock Nuthatch, Masked Shrike, Middle Spotted Woodpecker and Olivaceous and Olive-tree Warblers are all regularly seen.

Unfortunately, the best birding sites are scattered throughout the island and a hired car or motorbike is essential. There is thus no ideal centre. A bus service goes almost everywhere each day.

SUMMER: White Stork, Black Stork, Ruddy Shelduck, Long-legged Buzzard, Levant Sparrowhawk, Hobby, Lanner, Eleonora's Falcon, Chukar, Black-winged Stilt, Avocet, Bee-eater, Scops Owl, Middle Spotted Woodpecker, Krüper's Nuthatch, Rock Nuthatch, Masked Shrike, Woodchat Shrike, Blue Rock Thrush, Subalpine Warbler, Olivaceous Warbler, Olive-tree Warbler, Cretzschmar's Bunting, Cinereous Bunting, Rock Sparrow.

ACCESS: Saltpans lie at the head of the huge sea inlet in the southwest of the island and can be seen from the road south of Kallloní. There is a garage opposite the turning to Agios Paraskevi and a track leads to the beach some 200 m (220 yards) further west. Take this and walk around the pans to buildings, from where access can be achieved.

Míthimna is a good base for exploration eastward along the north coast (follow signs to Eftalou). After 3 km (nearly 2 miles) the olive grove on the right (opposite Hotel Alcreos) has Masked Shrike. Continue as far as possible — a path was being converted into a road in 1986 — for Eleonora's at the cape.

Eressós lies in the west of the island, about 50 km (30 miles) from Kallloní. Above the town is a farm lying beside (but below) a ridge. To the northwest of this is a twin-peaked hill. From the northern peak to the ridge above the farm is the best area for Cinereous Bunting. There are also Cretzschmar's Bunting and Rock Nuthatch here.

Agiássos lies due west of Mitilíni, in the hills. Before reaching the village from the north there is a major fork, with Agiássos signposted 4 km (2½ miles) in each direction. Take the left and turn left again immediately on entering the village (the road straight on becomes cobbled); continue out of the village and on to an unmade surface with pines on the left. After 2 km (1¼ miles) there are pines on both sides. Stop and explore for Krüper's Nuthatch.

ROUTE: Fly on a package tour or from Athens. Alternatively by boat from Piraeus.

Mesolóngion

Since this area first appeared in an earlier edition of WWBBE, reports have arrived in a steady stream more or less equally balanced between 'pros' and 'cons'. Some rated

Mesolóngion as high as anywhere in Greece; others found it virtually birdless. Clearly it is an area that should be visited at the correct time — mid-April into May.

These lagoons and marshes lie on the northern shore at the mouth of the Gulf of Corinth on the Greek west coast. South of the town a raised causeway extends seawards, giving excellent views over lagoons to the west and saltpans to the east. The latter are excellent, with Avocet, Stilt and Kentish Plover accompanied by Greenshank, Wood Sandpiper and Temminck's Stint. There is a chance of both Broad-billed and Terek as well. Pratincole, Black-tailed Godwit, Little Egret, Dalmatian Pelican and a host of small birds can all be found.

To both east and west there are splendid delta areas that probably rival the main Mesolóngion lagoons and may even surpass them in terms of breeding birds. The delta of the River Évinos to the east and that of the River Akhelóös to the west are, however, difficult of access and remain little known. Most visitors work the causeway and then move quickly on to the Gulf of Árta. Will someone do a thorough job on these wetlands and let me know what they find?

SUMMER: Dalmatian Pelican, Glossy Ibis, Squacco Heron, Little Egret, Garganey, Marsh Harrier, Lesser Spotted Eagle, Black-winged Stilt, Avocet, Kentish Plover, Broad-billed Sandpiper, Marsh Sandpiper, Wood Sandpiper, Terek Sandpiper, Greenshank, Collared Pratincole, Gull-billed Tern, Black Tern, White-winged Black Tern, Little Tern, Common Tern, Mediterranean Gull, Kingfisher, Great Reed Warbler, Fan-tailed Warbler, Olive-tree Warbler, Lesser Grey Shrike, Black-eared Wheatear, Hoopoe, Red-rumped Swallow, Black-headed Wagtail.

ACCESS: Mesolóngion lies west of Athens at the mouth of the Gulf of Corinth, and is reached on the E19. From the town the causeway runs due south to the sea, where there

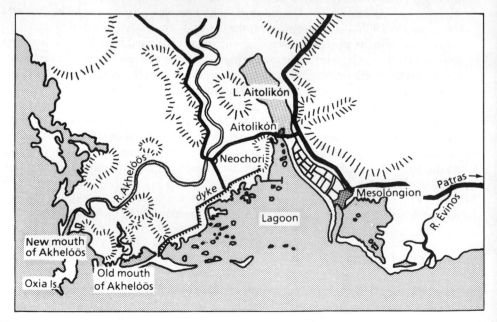

is a taverna. A walk eastward along a dusty road is also productive, with decent reedbeds and the occasional lagoon. To explore the delta areas, the villages of Krionéri (Évinos) and Oeniadae (Akhelóös) are good starting points. Indeed, from Oeniadae there is a motorable track that runs alongside a canal into the delta. This has produced some birds, including Short-toed Eagle and good passerines. Lake Aitolikón to the north of Mesolóngion is worthy of a look, but usually requires a telescope.

ROUTE: Via Athens northward on the E92, then westward.

Lake Préspa

Préspa lies, unenviably, on the borders of Greece, Yugoslavia and Albania and actually consists of two lakes, Magalí (great) and Mikrí (lesser) Préspa, separated by a narrow strip of land. Mikrí Préspa lies almost entirely in Greece and has been declared a National Park. Préspa was formerly regarded as somewhat devoid of birds and few visitors went out of their way to explore it. Many birds were, however, displaced when the Albanians drained Lake Malik and the pelicans, in particular, moved to Préspa. Today it is acknowledged as one of the most important wetlands in Greece.

Both White and Dalmatian Pelicans now breed in reasonable numbers and there are good colonies of Spoonbill, Purple and Grey Herons, Little and Great White Egrets, Glossy Ibis (30–40 pairs), Cormorant and Pygmy Cormorant and the most southerly Goosanders in Europe.

Among raptors Marsh Harriers are numerous, but the surrounding countryside holds Golden, Lesser Spotted and Imperial Eagles, and even a single pair of White-tailed Eagles breeds at the lake. In fact, if the surrounding woods and hills are included Préspa boasts a formidable list of breeding species. Migrants have not been as fully documented as the more obvious breeding birds, but a decent collection of waders and terns passes through and there is much scope for recording new species for the park, particularly among the passerines.

SPRING: Black Kite, Red-footed Falcon, Little Stint, Curlew Sandpiper, Collared Pratincole, Black Tern, White-winged Black Tern, Whiskered Tern.

SUMMER: Black-necked Grebe, Pygmy Cormorant, White Pelican, Dalmatian Pelican, Purple Heron, Great White Egret, Little Egret, Squacco Heron, Night Heron, Little Bittern, White Stork, Spoonbill, Glossy Ibis, Greylag Goose, Ferruginous Duck, Goosander, Golden Eagle, Imperial Eagle, Lesser Spotted Eagle, White-tailed Eagle, Egyptian Vulture, Booted Eagle, Short-toed Eagle, Long-legged Buzzard, Marsh Harrier, Hobby, Peregrine, Lesser Kestrel, Rock Partridge, Little Crake, Eagle Owl, Scops Owl, Alpine Swift, Bee-eater, Roller, Hoopoe, Syrian Woodpecker, Black Woodpecker, Shore Lark, Crag Martin, Red-rumped Swallow, Tawny Pipit, Lesser Grey Shrike, Alpine Accentor, Golden Oriole, Great Reed Warbler, Moustached Warbler, Marsh Warbler, Olivaceous Warbler, Barred Warbler, Orphean Warbler, Subalpine Warbler, Bonelli's Warbler, Black-eared Wheatear, Rock Thrush, Bearded Tit, Sombre Tit, Penduline Tit, Rock Nuthatch, Black-headed Bunting, Rock Bunting, Rock Sparrow.

ACCESS: Lake Préspa lies in the furthest northwest corner of Greece and is approached via the road leading northwards from Kastoría. Before reaching Agios Germanos, turn left (westward) to the isthmus that separates Mikrí from its larger neighbour. Much of the shoreline can be explored via small roads, or on foot, and the best birding areas are along the isthmus itself (tower hide); at Pyli on the western shore; along the eastern shore between the isthmus and Mikrolimni (hide); and in the south adjacent to the Albanian border. A general impression of Préspa can be obtained from hill '903' south of the isthmus on the eastern shore and from the hills beyond Krania in the southeast.

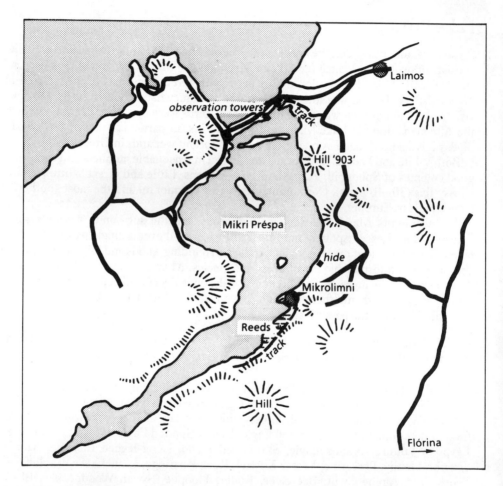

ROUTE: Via Athens.

Porto Lágo

Porto Lágo is no more than a small village, marked by a Genoese fortress, on the northeastern coast of Greece. Yet it is known throughout the birding world as one of the great spots for breeding and migrating birds and indeed is probably the best-known bird spot in the eastern Mediterranean. The village is sited on a narrow sandspit between the sea and a large lagoon called Lake Vistonís. Just east is the narrow channel through which the lake flows into the sea, while to the west lies an area of saltpans that is the main reason for Porto Lágo's reputation.

In winter Lake Vistonís has excellent numbers of duck, but in summer it holds only Black-necked Grebe, Pygmy Cormorant and Caspian Tern. The beach may be good for other terns and gulls, along with Kentish Plover and other shorebirds.

The saltpans lie south of the main coastal road and extend as far as the beach. They are of variable attraction to birds, but Avocet and Spur-winged Plover breed and passage can be simply fantastic. Among the sandpipers, Marsh is regular, Broad-billed almost so, and Terek as regular here as anywhere in Europe away from its breeding grounds. White-tailed Eagle appears from time to time and other species include White Pelican, Slender-billed Gull, Roller, Bee-eater, Collared Pratincole, Calandra Lark, Tawny Pipit and possible Cretzschmar's Bunting. There are further lagoons to the east and, taken as a whole, the Porto Lágo area offers a wide variety of habitats in a small, easily worked area — perfect for migration.

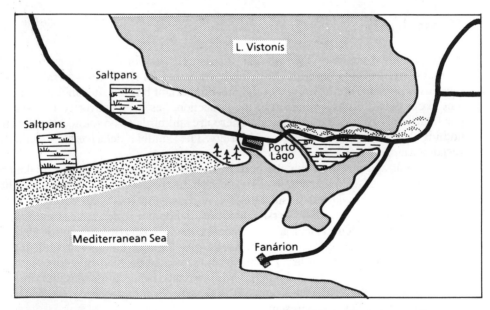

SUMMER: Black-necked Grebe, Great White Egret, Glossy Ibis, Pygmy Cormorant, Red-footed Falcon, Marsh Harrier, Montagu's Harrier, Spotted Crake, Stone-curlew, Kentish Plover, Spur-winged Plover, Avocet, Black-winged Stilt, Collared Pratincole, Caspian Tern, Slender-billed Gull, Roller, Bee-eater, Tawny Pipit, Calandra Lark, Crested Lark, Rufous Bush Chat, Great Reed Warbler, Savi's Warbler, Orphean Warbler, Sardinian Warbler, Subalpine Warbler, Black-headed Wagtail, Blue-headed Wagtail.

PASSAGE: Ruff, Greenshank, Marsh Sandpiper, Wood Sandpiper, Broad-billed Sandpiper, Terek Sandpiper.

ACCESS: Porto Lágo lies along the main road between Kaválla and the Turkish border and is easily located. The saltpans and their adjacent lagoon lie to the west of the town, between the road and the sea. They can be freely explored, but do be careful not to tread on nests during the breeding season. Lake Vistonís can be reached north of the road. The area either side of the channel connecting the lake to the sea is worthy of a full exploration. The local egrets breed on the spit of wooded land opposite the town next to the camp site. South of Mesi (follow signs to Mesi Beach) are two lagoons that may hold birds. Further east, south of Pagouria, is Lake Mitrikou together with many small pools that usually do have definite interest. Ferruginous Duck and Ruddy Shelduck, Marsh Harrier and Penduline Tit have been seen. Follow signs to Molivoli Beach, bear left, cross a bridge and turn right on a drivable track to the lagoon. Do not ignore Penduline Tit in riverside scrub en route!

ROUTE: The nearest airport is at Thessaloníki and there are decent hotels at Kaválla and Alexandroúpolis. This is not a tourist area and there are few of the usual amenities.

Thessaloníki

Within a short distance of Thessaloníki, the usual 'start' for explorations along the northeastern coast of Greece, are the deltas of several major rivers plus several areas of saltpans. Together, they form one of the most important birding sites in the country. The Axios delta, formerly the gem of the collection, has been converted to a sea of polythene and lost much of its appeal. There are still birds to be found here, but in nothing like their former abundance and variety. The Loudhias delta has been similarly reclaimed and developed.

Less spoilt and now probably the best area for birds is the delta of the Aliákmon which, southwards to Nea Agathoúpolis, is much better preserved. Further south is the excellent lagoon of Alyki with its surrounding saltpans. This is the only regular spot in Greece for Cattle Egret, while Marsh and Terek Sandpipers often appear along with Flamingo, White-tailed Eagle, Lanner and occasionally Saker. Breeding birds include a colony of 2,500 pairs of Mediterranean Gulls, plus Slender-billed Gull, Gull-billed Tern, Avocet, Stilt, Stone-curlew, Pratincole and several terns. Non-breeding summer visitors include Glossy Ibis and Spoonbill, while passage brings hosts of waders and in winter up to 20,000 duck. At this time of the year divers and grebes, egrets, harriers, Spotted Eagle and Saker are present.

Across the gulf lies the promontory of Angelohori, with more saltpans and a substantial lagoon. Here there is a collection of similar birds, including many migrant waders such as Black-tailed Godwit, Ruff, Curlew Sandpiper, Little Stint and the occasional Slender-billed Curlew. Both Black and White-winged Black Terns occur, and there are plentiful small birds including good numbers of Red-backed Shrike and Black-headed Bunting.

SUMMER: Glossy Ibis, Spoonbill, White Stork, Avocet, Black-winged Stilt, Stone-curlew, Mediterranean Gull, Slender-billed Gull, Gull-billed Tern, Common Tern, Little Tern, Calandra Lark.

PASSAGE: Pygmy Cormorant, Flamingo, Great White Egret, Little Egret, Cattle Egret, Glossy Ibis, Marsh Harrier, White-tailed Eagle, Lanner, Red-footed Falcon, Hobby, Garganey, Ferruginous Duck, Kentish Plover, Little Ringed Plover, Avocet, Black-winged Stilt, Curlew Sandpiper, Little Stint, Ruff, Marsh Sandpiper, Slender-billed Curlew, Collared Pratincole, Gull-billed Tern, Caspian Tern, Black Tern, White-winged Black Tern, Mediterranean Gull, Slender-billed Gull, Red-backed Shrike, Red-rumped Swallow, Great Reed Warbler, Icterine Warbler, Tawny Pipit, Black-headed Wagtail, Black-headed Bunting.

ACCESS: Angelohori is reached by taking the road eastward past the airport and turning right to Agios Trias, then continuing over a gradually declining road surface to a taverna. A track continues into the saltpans to the major lagoon and beach. The Axios River is between Thessaloníki and Kateríni. Access is off the road to the north, then passing under the main road southwards. This track eventually leads to the sea, then turns westward past saltpans and excellent lagoons.

The Aliákmon is best from Nea Agathoúpolis close to the E92 about 20 km (12½ miles) south of Thessaloníki. Alyki is reached via Kítros, which is 28 km (17 miles) north of Kateríni. Where the old Kateríni–Thessaloníki road crosses Kítros, turn east and follow a track to the shores of Alyki.

ROUTE: Via Thessaloníki airport.

HOLLAND

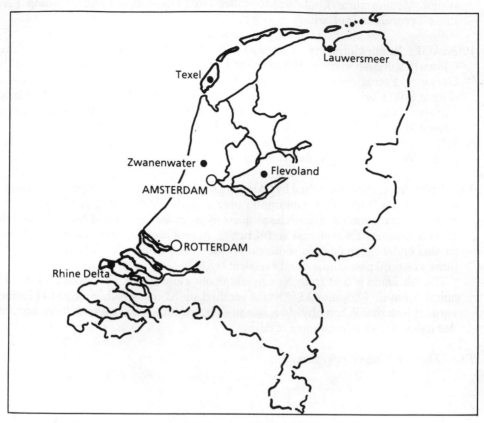

Amsterdam

Visitors to Holland with only a few hours at their disposal need not despair because they do not have the time to visit the Friesian Islands or the Polders. Some of the best Dutch birding areas are no more than a few kilometres from the city of Amsterdam and served by an excellent network of motorways. Most famous of these is the Naardermeer reserve, which should be on the itinerary of any visitor to Holland, but there are the Westzaan reserve to the north and the lakes at Botshol and Nieuwkoop to the south. Each offers splendid birding.

The Naardermeer is a totally protected area that cannot be seen from the surrounding roads. It lies 16 km (10 miles) east of the city and has been a reserve since 1906. There are Spoonbill colonies, and the surrounding reedbeds and willow thickets hold a wealth of otherwise scarce species. These include Purple Heron, Bittern, Marsh Harrier, Black Tern, Bearded Tit and various warblers.

To the south the lake at Botshol has, with the exception of Spoonbill, much the same species. It does, however, often have Red-crested Pochard as well as Little Bittern; the former is not often present at Naardermeer and the latter cannot be relied on there.

Further south still the lakes at Nieuwkoop offer similar habitat, with extensive reedbeds holding Bittern, Little Bittern and Purple Heron, plus Black Tern and warblers.

To the north of Amsterdam lies the area of Zaanstreek, often marked on maps as 'Waterland'. Here Black-tailed Godwit abound. In the west of this area is the reserve of Westzaan, with most of the Dutch specialities of meadow and marsh including Black Tern and Ruff. There are also Bittern, Snipe, Redshank and so on.

SUMMER: Cormorant, Purple Heron, Spoonbill, Bittern, Little Bittern, Garganey, Red-crested Pochard, Marsh Harrier, Hobby, Black-tailed Godwit, Ruff, Black Tern, Bearded Tit, Savi's Warbler, Great Reed Warbler.

ACCESS: It is essential to book permits for the Naardermeer reserve well in advance. Write to Vereniging tot Behoud van Natuurmonumenten, Herengradt 540, Amsterdam, giving proposed date of visit (and an alternative) and number of permits required. The reserve is reached by taking the A1 eastwards from Amsterdam and taking the exit to Muiderberg (not Muiden). Take the road to the right that runs parallel with the motorway and after 1 km (just over ½ mile) turn right to a fisherman's house called 'Visserij'.

Botshol is reached by taking the A2 southwards to its junction with the N201. Turn right (west) and then right again after 3 km (nearly 2 miles) to Botshol.

For Nieuwkoop, return to the N201 and continue westwards to the junction with the N212. Turn left (south) for 6 km (3¾ miles) then turn right to Noorden. Much of the area can be seen by turning right and viewing from the road along the northern edge.

Westzaan is reached by taking the A7 northwards to Oostzaan and forking left on the motorway to Westzaan. There is a dyke to the west along which a footpath offers good views over the reserve. Most of this area has interesting waders on the fields and other species on or around the lakes.

ROUTE: Schiphol is one of the world's busiest airports and the adjacent A9 can have you birding within a few minutes of clearing customs and hiring a car.

Flevoland

The former Zuiderzee was enclosed in 1932 to form the huge shallow inland lake the IJsselmeer. Over the years parts of this new lake have themselves been enclosed and subsequently drained to form polders. The largest and most famous of these is Flevoland. Flat, criss-crossed by dykes, rich, fertile and quite outstanding for birds at all seasons, Flevoland has become one of Europe's top birding spots. Though agriculture dominates the landscape, there are quite extensive areas of woodland, many windbreaks and several lakes and reedbeds that have been specially maintained as nature reserves. In winter Flevoland is alive with geese; in summer the meadows echo to the cries of Black-tailed Godwits.

Lelystad is a completely modern town on Flevoland itself, though most visitors prefer the more traditional delights of Harderwijk, which formerly bordered the Zuiderzee. In either case it is a simple matter to drive over fast roads to the main areas of bird interest.

Best of all is Oostvaardersplassen in the north, where huge lagoons are separated by equally huge reedbeds. Here, all of the species for which Flevoland is best known breed abundantly. There are Black-tailed Godwit, Avocet, Marsh Harrier, Bittern, Purple Heron, Bearded Tit and White-spotted Bluethroat, as well as Sedge, Great Reed, Reed, Marsh and Cetti's Warblers. Occasional summer visitors include Spoonbill and Great White Egret, while in winter this same area is excellent for duck and raptors.

A similar, though less extensive, marshland lies in the south at Harderbroek. This holds many of the same species, but is the best place for Little Bittern. The woods to the northeast have Goshawk and Honey Buzzard, while those immediately east of Oostvaardersplassen have Golden Oriole. In the southwest at Hulkesteinse is a bushy plantation area alive with Icterine and Marsh Warblers.

Winter geese are widespread, but may be difficult to locate. Bean are usually to be found in the area between Lelystad and Harderwijk, and there are usually Hen Harrier and Rough-legged Buzzard here too. Smew number 10,000 and there are thousands of other duck on the IJsselmeer at this season, with good watchpoints to the north and south of Lelystad. The bridge across the Ketelmeer is a good spot for duck and, in any case, leads to the Noordoostpolder, where the coastal road north of Urk produces both wild swans, more geese, harriers and Merlin. Further north still lies Friesland, arguably the best goose area in Europe. The area between and around Balk and Koudum is full of these birds, with totals of 20,000 Barnacles and a similar number of Whitefronts laced with other species, often including Red-breasted Goose. The coast to the west is a noted haunt of White-tailed Eagle.

SUMMER: Great Crested Grebe, Wigeon, Shoveler, Garganey, Pintail, Gadwall, Greylag Goose, Marsh Harrier, Montagu's Harrier, Buzzard, Honey Buzzard, Spoonbill, Great White Egret, Bittern, Little Bittern, Purple Heron, Water Rail, Black-tailed Godwit, Ruff, Avocet, Common Tern, Golden Oriole, Bearded Tit, Blue-headed Wagtail, Bluethroat, Savi's Warbler, Marsh Warbler, Icterine Warbler.

WINTER: Red-necked Grebe, Wigeon, Teal, Tufted Duck, Pochard, Goldeneye, Smew, Goosander, Red-breasted Merganser, Bean Goose, White-fronted Goose, Barnacle Goose, Hen Harrier, Buzzard, Rough-legged Buzzard, Goshawk, White-tailed Eagle.

ACCESS: Harderwijk is easily reached via the A28 and Lelystad is well signposted from there on the N302. This road crosses Flevoland and produces geese and raptors in winter. In Lelystad turn left along the coastal embankment to Oostvaardersplassen — a fast road with few stopping places. The eastern side of the reserve can be reached by turning left just outside Lelystad. This is quite excellent at all seasons. At the end of the marsh turn left at Torenvalk for Oriole woods and later some fine harrier scrubland.

The marsh at Harderbroek is reached by turning left as soon as the Harderhaven Bridge is crossed, and by following along this road (and aided by a local map) the Hulkesteinse area can be found. North of Lelystad is a power station-factory area with water outlets that attract winter duck, and the main A6 leads on to the Ketelmeer for duck and north to Balk in Friesland for geese. Return via the Noordoostpolder coastal road for swans.

Flevoland and Friesland both deserve exploration, and apparently aimless motoring of country roads quickly produces birds.

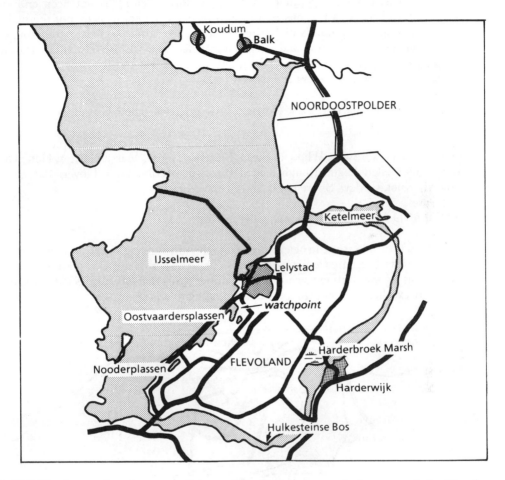

ROUTE: Amsterdam has one of the world's best connected airports and the Dutch motorway system makes travel fast and simple. Motorway restaurants and cafés are excellent.

Lauwersmeer

The Waddensee is acknowledged as the most important single intertidal area in Europe, with outstanding populations of wildfowl and waders in internationally important numbers. As with all such areas from Morecambe Bay to the Tagus estuary, there are many other birds attracted by the wildness of the landscape and some of these may have an extra appeal. The problem is how to get to grips with such a large area. As elsewhere, it is a matter of timing and placing. The best time is around high tide, and one

97

of the best places is Lauwersmeer. Until 1969 this was an estuary draining into the Waddensee south of the island of Schiermonnikoog. Then a barrage was built and drainage plans put into operation. Fortunately, this scheme has not been entirely successful and the area remains rich in wildfowl and waders. It is one of the major European wintering grounds of Bewick's Swan and Barnacle Goose, and Rough-legged Buzzard, Hen Harrier and often White-tailed Eagle can be seen at this season. Both Marsh and Hen Harriers breed and there are Godwit and Ruff as well. Passage brings a wide variety of waders and terns.

SUMMER: Marsh Harrier, Hen Harrier, Bittern, Black-tailed Godwit, Ruff, Little Gull, Black Tern.

WINTER: Bewick's Swan, Whooper Swan, Barnacle Goose, Marsh Harrier, Hen Harrier, White-tailed Eagle, Rough-legged Buzzard, Merlin, Grey Plover, Bar-tailed Godwit, Knot, Curlew, Shore Lark, Snow Bunting.

SPRING AND AUTUMN: Waders, gulls and terns.

ACCESS: The whole area can be explored from the surrounding roads, several of which overlook areas designated as nature reserves. The road across the dam to Lauwersmeer Harbour is a good starting place, while the minor roads that give access to the eastern shore are excellent. Do not ignore the surrounding woods at any season.

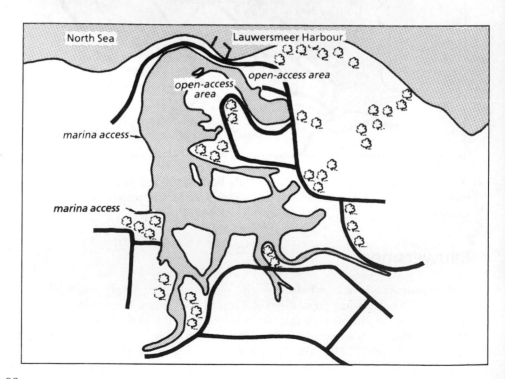

ROUTE: Take the N361 from Groningen, which is an excellent base and an attractive university town.

Rhine Delta

After the spending of a staggering amount of money and effort, the delta works at the mouth of the Rhine are now complete. The exact benefits to the economy of southern Holland (and the European Community) do not concern us here. What was once a maze of channels and mudbanks, islands and marshes has been changed by the construction of several major dams across the mouths of the various Rhine channels, effectively cutting them off from the sea. This has created a series of major lakes with marshy shorelines and some quite excellent bird habitats, some of which have, in traditional Dutch manner, been declared reserves. Whether the transformation has been beneficial or detrimental to bird populations is not the point; what is important is where to watch birds now.

Today the Rhine delta is still a major bird haunt. In winter there are vast flocks of wildfowl, including good numbers of both Barnacle and Brent Geese. Duck populations are often quite staggering and many can be approached quite closely. Off the Brouwersdam there is one of the greatest concentrations of Great Crested Grebes to be found anywhere — guesstimates talk of tens of thousands. Winter also brings a multitude of common waders, with a major high-tide roost on Duiveland on the southern shores of Schouwen. Harriers, Merlin, Peregrine and Rough-legged Buzzard are regular visitors at this season.

Passage brings excellent numbers of waders, with Little Stint, Curlew Sandpiper and Golden Plover along with almost every other wader that regularly occurs in northwestern Europe. In summer there are colonies of all the usual terns, including Arctic, plus excellent populations of Godwit, Avocet, Kentish Plover and, in the Schaelhoek reserve, Marsh Harrier, Bittern, Bearded Tit and Bluethroat.

This is an outstanding area with plenty of places to visit that has largely been ignored by foreign birders. Perhaps this account will do something to change this apparent lack of effort.

SUMMER: Great Crested Grebe, Marsh Harrier, Bittern, Shelduck, Greylag Goose, Kentish Plover, Black-tailed Godwit, Avocet, Common Tern, Arctic Tern, Sandwich Tern, Bearded Tit, Bluethroat.

WINTER: Red-throated Diver, Black-throated Diver, Red-necked Grebe, Slavonian Grebe, Great Crested Grebe, Marsh Harrier, Hen Harrier, Rough-legged Buzzard, Merlin, Peregrine, Brent Goose, Barnacle Goose, Wigeon, Gadwall, Pintail, Shoveler, Teal, Eider, Scaup, Long-tailed Duck, Scoter, Goosander, Smew, Golden Plover, Grey Plover, Knot, Curlew, Redshank, Short-eared Owl.

PASSAGE: Golden Plover, Little Stint, Curlew Sandpiper, Wood Sandpiper, Spotted Redshank, Greenshank, Black Tern.

ACCESS: There are excellent birding spots throughout the delta and a week of exploration would be very rewarding. Four major areas are outstanding and are detailed.

Brouwersdam encloses Grevelingen Lake between the islands of Goeree-Overflakkee and Schouwen-Duiveland in the north of the delta. This is superb at all seasons, but in winter has divers and duck in fine numbers plus the outstanding concentration of grebes. There are roads along the dam that make perfect vantage points. Flauwers and Weversinlagen lie on the south side of Schouwen with the excellent marshy area of Duiveland. The meadows behind the Inlagen are a major wader roost. The reserve lies west of Zierikzee and can be viewed from the road 8 km (5 miles) to the west, south of the main road to Haamstede.

Veerse Meer was one of the first arms of the delta to be cut off and forms a brackish lake with adjacent marshes. This is now an outstanding winter wildfowl haunt, with excellent passage waders and most of the good breeding birds at the reserve of Middelplaten. The whole area can be viewed from the road along the south side, but the area east of Veere is the best. This is remarkably convenient for anyone using the port of Vlissingen (Flushing), being only a few kilometres to the north.

De Scheelhoek is on the island of Goeree-Overflakkee just east of the village of Stellendam. This river, meadow and reedbed area has excellent breeding birds, but is of interest throughout the year. The whole can be seen from adjacent roads. To the west of Stellendam, close to the dyke that leads to Voorne, is Kwade Hoek, a bay with superb wader habitat and a lake behind the dunes. All can be seen from Stellendam port.

ROUTE: Excellent communications via nearby Rotterdam or via Vlissingen.

Texel

Texel (pronounced 'Tessel') is the largest and most southerly of the Friesian islands and therefore the easiest to reach and explore. This is highly fortunate, for it is also the best for birds. Being only 15 km long by 11 km wide (about 9 by 7 miles) it is relatively easy to cover, and virtually every major birding spot is a nature reserve.

In the west the coast comprises a hugh dune system, broken here and there by lagoons, slacks and inlets; here, from north to south, lie the reserves of Krim, De Slufter, Muy, Westerduinen, Bollenkamer and De Geul. In the east the shoreline is more broken, muddy and lies adjacent to the Waddensee, the most important intertidal zone in Europe; here lie (again north to south) the bird spots of Cocksdorp, Shorren, De Bol, Dijkmanshuizen and Mok. Between the two lies an island of meadows centred on Waalenburg, which is damp grazing land with abundant Black-tailed Godwit and a fine population of Ruff. There are also areas of woodland, at Dennen for example, with Golden Oriole, Icterine Warbler and Short-toed Treecreeper.

The ultimate Texel experience, however, is reserved for those who visit Muy, where there is a colony of Spoonbills together with Marsh and Montagu's Harriers. At the Slufter there are Avocet, Kentish Plover and terns, while at Geul there are more Spoonbills, plus Avocet, harriers and Godwit. A week is just long enough to visit all the reserves and other major sites and provide one of the best birding holidays to be had in northern Europe.

SUMMER: Black-necked Grebe, Bittern, Spoonbill, Garganey, Eider, Marsh Harrier, Montagu's Harrier, Water Rail, Kentish Plover, Black-tailed Godwit, Ruff, Avocet, Common Tern, Sandwich Tern, Long-eared Owl, Short-eared Owl, Grasshopper Warbler, Great Reed Warbler, Marsh Warbler, Icterine Warbler, Short-toed Tree-creeper, Golden Oriole.

ACCESS: Permits to visit the various reserves can be obtained locally or in advance. The best contact is the Tourist Office, VVV Texel, Den Burg, Texel, Netherlands, which has leaflets giving up-to-date details of access and permits. Not all the reserves are administered by the same organisation. Vereniging tot Behoud van Natuurmonumenten, Herengradt 540, Amsterdam, may also prove helpful as they administer most of the reserves in the east of Texel.

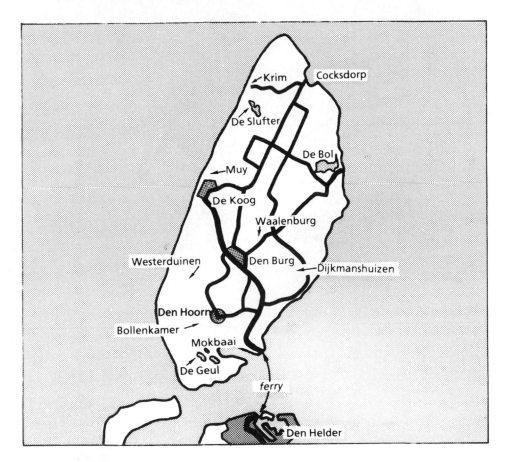

ROUTE: Texel is reached by frequent ferry from the mainland and is only a short drive from Amsterdam. Most of the villages offer some form of accommodation and there are several hotels that understand birders' proclivities.

101

Zwanenwater

This is a dune lake lying south of Den Helder that is still largely overlooked by those heading northwards to Texel. Yet its shallow waters, with their strong growth of reeds, can be compared, not unfavourably, with any other of the many marshlands of the Netherlands. Lying among the dunes near the shore, its breeding birds include Avocet and Kentish Plover. This is also the site of another Spoonbill colony and these birds can often be seen at the tiny reserve of Houdsbossche a little way south near Petten.

Spoonbills

As well as having its breeding birds, by virtue of its position the Zwanenwater is also attractive during passage periods, and terns, gulls and waders are often interesting. There are some useful pines among the dunes.

SUMMER: Spoonbill, Garganey, Hobby, Kentish Plover, Avocet, Common Tern, Long-eared Owl, Crested Lark, Reed Warbler, Marsh Warbler.

ACCESS: Via Callantsoog and minor roads. This is a reserve, but much can be seen from the adjacent dunes.

HUNGARY

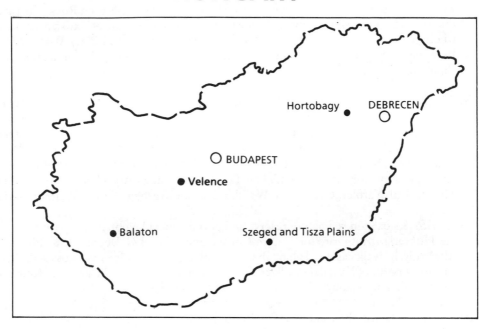

Balaton

Lake Balaton is the primary holiday resort of land-locked Hungary and most of its shoreline is not worthy of the birder's attention. There is, however, one of Europe's greatest bird reserves here, as well as various marshes and ponds nearby that attract a superb collection of birds. As with other eastern-bloc countries, such as Poland and Romania, it is difficult to understand why there are not more carloads of western birders seeking out the delights of what are usually rather better places than in the more populous west.

The gem and centrepiece of this area is the Kisbalaton reserve at the southwestern end of Balaton. Here open water has been colonised by reeds and scrub, creating the perfect environment for breeding marsh birds. Red sedge grows here and nowhere else in Europe. The outstanding bird species are the herons, with Squacco, Night and Little Egret all breeding. Spoonbill and Great White Egret also breed, though they are by no means abundant, and there are Marsh Harrier, a variety of warblers, Penduline Tit, three crakes and even the occasional Glossy Ibis. This is a splendid reserve with a great wealth of species.

Also along the shores of Balaton is Balatonelle with its series of fishponds some 6 km (3¾ miles) south of the village. These reed-fringed waters hold Little Bittern, Bearded Tit, Great Reed Warbler, the two small crakes, all three marsh terns and Ferruginous Duck on occasion.

To the north of Balaton, the western end of the Bakony Hills attracts birdwatchers based at Keszthely for Kisbalaton. These are gentle hills rising to no great height and

103

are mostly wooded, offering a chance of interesting woodland species. The beech woods around Sümeg are excellent for woodpeckers and there is even Rock Thrush at the ruined tower on the hill above the town. There is another ruin at Tatika near Bazsi, where the surrounding woods have Red-breasted Flycatcher and Black Woodpecker. Between Sümeg and Tapolca, there are fishponds on the western side of the road that should not be ignored.

SUMMER: Black-necked Grebe, White Stork, Purple Heron, Little Egret, Great White Egret, Squacco Heron, Night Heron, Little Bittern, Spoonbill, Pintail, Garganey, Ferruginous Duck, Greylag Goose, Marsh Harrier, Little Crake, Baillon's Crake, Spotted Crake, Black Tern, White-winged Black Tern, Whiskered Tern, Black Woodpecker, Syrian Woodpecker, Grey-headed Woodpecker, Rock Thrush, Golden Oriole, Lesser Grey Shrike, Penduline Tit, Red-breasted Flycatcher, Savi's Warbler, Moustached Warbler, Great Reed Warbler, Icterine Warbler, Barred Warbler, Serin.

ACCESS: Kisbalaton is a nature reserve and permits must be obtained to visit. Contact the Hungarian Authority for Nature Conservation, H-1121 Budapest, Költö u. 21. Alternatively, walk eastward along the riverbank from the bridge that crosses the Zala River just north of Kisbalaton village. The fishponds at Balatonelle lie along Route 67 southward. The Bakony Hills lie between Sümeg and Keszthely.

ROUTE: Budapest, then southwest on Route 7.

Budapest

The capital of Hungary is recognised as one of the world's most beautiful cities, a fact even acknowledged by birders. There are parks, such as the extensive Varosliget Park in the centre, that have interesting birds, but the visitor to Budapest would be well advised to look just a little further, for there are several first-class birding areas within a relatively short distance of the city.

To the north lie several areas of wooded hills extending as far as the Czechoslovakian border. Nearest are the Buda Hills, with mature oaks and a good collection of woodpeckers including Middle Spotted, Syrian and Black, together with Goshawk, Golden Oriole, Red-breasted and Collared Flycatchers and even the occasional Rock Thrush. Further north, the area around Pilis is important for breeding raptors, including Lesser Spotted Eagle, Honey Buzzard and Goshawk. Here too there are Bee-eater, Red-breasted Flycatcher and Rock Bunting.

Even further north, the Borzsony area has hills with oak and beech supporting a better raptor population, together with Black Stork, Hazelhen, White-backed Woodpecker, Rock Thrush, Red-breasted Flycatcher and Rock Bunting.

To the southwest of Budapest is the excellent Lake Velence, which is treated separately, while to the southeast is the Ócsa reserve with damp alder woodland broken by heath and reed marsh. The area of marsh and damp meadow lies on one side of the road and holds Roller, Golden Oriole, Marsh and Montagu's Harriers and Black-tailed Godwit. The forest proper is a dense jungle of vegetation and decidedly wet underfoot.

Mosquitoes find the conditions here ideal, but so do raptors. Species include Lesser Spotted Eagle, Saker and Goshawk, though the Buzzard is certainly more numerous. Syrian Woodpecker is common and River Warbler almost so.

SUMMER: Black Stork, Bittern, Spotted Eagle, Lesser Spotted Eagle, Red Kite, Black Kite, Goshawk, Marsh Harrier, Montagu's Harrier, Hazelhen, Curlew, Black-tailed Godwit, Corncrake, Great Spotted Woodpecker, Middle Spotted Woodpecker, Syrian Woodpecker, Green Woodpecker, Black Woodpecker, Golden Oriole, Roller, Bee-eater, Hoopoe, Rock Thrush, Red-breasted Flycatcher, Collared Flycatcher, River Warbler, Rock Bunting.

ACCESS: The Buda Hills lie immediately outside the city limits and can be reached by public transport. Those with their own transport would be best advised to try Pilis. Take Route 1 to Pilisvörösvár and turn right to the hills. For Borzsony, take Route 2 and then the minor roads left into the hills.
   Ócsa lies just east of Route 5. Though a reserve, there is little need to enter unless a close study of mosquitoes is intended.

ROUTE: Budapest has an international airport.

Hortobagy

The Hortobagy plain is one of Europe's most famous birding areas and it seems quite extraordinary that it is not thronged by western birders at almost all times of the year. It does, for example, have Hungary's largest heronries; a huge population of 800 pairs of

Red-footed Falcons

105

Red-footed Falcon; over 10,000 geese including Lesser Whitefronts on passage; a winter population of 25 White-tailed Eagles; and a population of 120 Great Bustards resident throughout the year. What more could any birding area offer?

The Hortobagy is an area of steppe broken by marshes, pastures, woodlands and ponds. An excellent area of steppe lies immediately east on the road to Debrecen. Here there are ponds and drying marshes with Greylag, Pratincole and Great Bustard. To the northwest, an area of fishponds bordered by roads has breeding herons and White-winged Black Terns.

Much of the area, including Hortobagy-halasto itself, is incorporated into the national park of the same name. The heron colonies here contain Great White Egret (150 pairs), Little Egret (120 pairs), Squacco Heron (130 pairs) and Spoonbill (350 pairs). There are masses of other exciting birds, including 20 pairs of Red-necked Grebe, 50 pairs of White-winged Black Tern, 300 pairs of Whiskered Tern, plus Mediterranean Gull and both small crakes.

Passage, as well as bringing the geese, also brings Crane, Black Stork, Imperial and Golden Eagles, Peregrine and Saker, along with many waders of predominantly eastern distribution.

SUMMER: Red-necked Grebe, Black-necked Grebe, White Stork, Greylag Goose, Garganey, Gadwall, Ferruginous Duck, Little Bittern, Little Egret, Great White Egret, Squacco Heron, Purple Heron, Spoonbill, Red-footed Falcon, Marsh Harrier, Little Crake, Baillon's Crake, Great Bustard, Stone-curlew, Avocet, Black-tailed Godwit, Collared Pratincole, White-winged Black Tern, Whiskered Tern, Mediterranean Gull, Golden Oriole, Hoopoe, Penduline Tit, Tawny Pipit, Short-toed Lark.

PASSAGE: Lesser White-fronted Goose, Black Stork, Crane, Imperial Eagle, Golden Eagle, Peregrine, Saker, Marsh Sandpiper.

WINTER: White-tailed Eagle.

ACCESS: Most of the area can be visited quite freely, though permission should be sought for the various areas of fishponds.

ROUTE: Budapest on Route 4 to Debrecen, which is the best base.

Szeged and the Tisza Plain

Just before it crosses the border into Yugoslavia, the River Tisza meanders over a wide plain dotted with lakes, marshes and old river courses. In some parts there are excellent reedbeds, while others have been converted to fishponds. The whole area has been recognised as an internationally important wetland and is often referred to as the Pusztaszer Conservation Area.

Within this area near Szeged is Lake Fehértó, which has been extensively modified to provide areas of fishponds, as well as lakes for extracting soda. Even today the reedbeds hold good numbers of marsh birds, including Little Bittern and Penduline Tit. There is a large colony of Black-headed Gulls here among which one or two pairs of Mediterranean can be found.

The centrepiece of the whole area is the island of Sasér, part of which forms the Martelyi Landscape Reserve, where the marshes hold one of the best heronries in Hungary. There are Great White and Little Egrets, Squacco Heron, Spoonbill, Little Bittern, and a good population of breeding waders including Avocet and Black-tailed Godwit. Stone-curlew and 40 pairs of Red-footed Falcon also breed, along with Black Stork.

SUMMER: Black-necked Grebe, Red-necked Grebe, White Stork, Black Stork, Little Bittern, Purple Heron, Little Egret, Great White Egret, Squacco Heron, Spoonbill, Ferruginous Duck, Greylag Goose, Marsh Harrier, Red-footed Falcon, Stone-curlew, Avocet, Black-tailed Godwit, Mediterranean Gull, White-winged Black Tern, Spotted Crake, Penduline Tit, Lesser Grey Shrike, Roller, Hoopoe, Barred Warbler.

ACCESS: The reserves at Lake Fehértó and Sasér can be entered with permits from the Hungarian Authority for Nature Conservation, H-1121 Budapest, Költö u. 21. A considerable amount can, however, be seen in the area without entering the reserves.

ROUTE: Southwards from Budapest towards the Yugoslavian border.

Lake Velence

This famous bird lake lies only 50 km (31 miles) southwest of Budapest and is almost as well known as Balaton. It differs, however, in being considerably smaller than that water and in offering good habitat throughout its area. Its shallow waters are fringed by reeds which form dense beds in several parts, especially at the western end. Here there are good colonies of Great White Egret and Spoonbill, but both of these, plus the other birds of Velence, can be seen at almost any point around the shoreline. The reeds also hold Purple Heron and Little Bittern, plus Savi's, Moustached and Marsh Warblers.

The main Budapest-Székesfehérvár road runs along the southern shoreline, offering excellent viewing at many points. At Dinnyes, however, the grazing marshes hold Ruff, Black-tailed Godwit and Bluethroat and offer valuable feeding grounds for many of the Velence herons. The small pond near the village is a haunt of Black Tern, as well as of Great Reed and Moustached Warblers. Together with the surrounding agricultural land, Lake Velence offers really first-class birding to anyone with a day or more to spend outside the capital.

SUMMER: White Stork, Purple Heron, Great White Egret, Spoonbill, Little Bittern, Ferruginous Duck, Garganey, Greylag Goose, Marsh Harrier, Montagu's Harrier, Little Crake, Ruff, Black-tailed Godwit, Black Tern, Quail, Roller, Bee-eater, Hoopoe, Golden Oriole, Bearded Tit, Lesser Grey Shrike, Bluethroat, Great Reed Warbler, Savi's Warbler, Moustached Warbler, Marsh Warbler, Barred Warbler.

ACCESS: There is generally free access off the main road to the lakeside, but nearby hills offer better views over the reeds. The marshes at Dinnyes can be explored from a loop track that runs from the main road near the village. Do not disturb the breeding herons at the western end.

ROUTE: Take Route 7 from Budapest. There is a pension in Gardony.

ICELAND

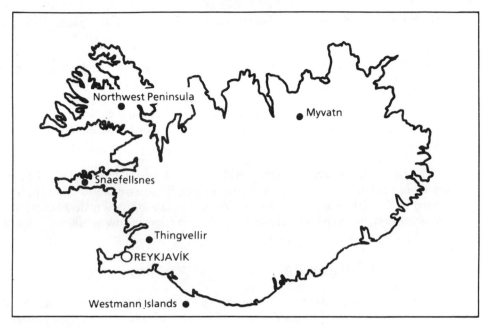

Myvatn

Myvatn — literal translation 'Lake of Flies' — is the greatest duck breeding centre in Europe and an absolute must for anyone visiting Iceland. For the birder it holds all of the special species that make the country so appealing, and for the ordinary tourist its muddy sulphur pools are an irresistible attraction.

Myvatn is some 37 km square (14¼ square miles) in area, but its coastline is so indented and broken that long-distance views are almost impossible. It varies in depth from 2 m to 4 m (6½ to 13 feet) and holds an incredible 50,000 breeding pairs of 15 species of duck. Among these are several Nearctic species that are otherwise unobtainable for the Euro-lister. Barrow's Goldeneye number some 800 pairs, while Harlequin Duck are especially numerous along the turbulent waters of the Laxa River. American Wigeon are regular, though they have not yet been proved to have bred. Great Northern Divers breed here, usually on remote upland lakes, but frequently are to be seen on Myvatn. Scoter, Long-tailed Duck, Merganser, Goosander and even non-breeding Goldeneye and Whooper Swan are all regular. Pinkfeet and Greylags breed, as do some 250 pairs of Slavonian Grebe, Red-necked Phalarope, two species of skua, Whimbrel, Redwing, Snow Bunting and Merlin.

Sandvatn lies to the northwest and has some birch scrub as well as breeding Gyrfalcon, though these birds may be seen anywhere in the area.

SUMMER: Great Northern Diver, Red-throated Diver, Slavonian Grebe, Whooper Swan, Greylag Goose, Pink-footed Goose, Teal, Gadwall, Wigeon, American Wigeon,

109

Pintail, Shoveler, Scaup, Scoter, Harlequin Duck, Long-tailed Duck, Barrow's Goldeneye, Goldeneye, Goosander, Red-breasted Merganser, Gyrfalcon, Merlin, Arctic Tern, Whimbrel, Red-necked Phalarope, Great Skua, Arctic Skua, Redwing, Wheatear, Snow Bunting.

ACCESS: The whole of Myvatn can be explored by road, and one of the best places to start is on a bridge over the Laxa River in the west where the river runs into the lake. The road northwards to the coast crosses the Laxa lower down, and here there are Harlequin and Eider. The sulphur pools lie to the east and Sandvatn to the northwest. From 15 May to 20 July all the islands, plus the shoreline in the northwest, are out of bounds. Otherwise one can explore at will.

ROUTE: Plane and bus services connect with Reykjavík several times a day. The plane takes about an hour; the bus about eight times longer. Bicycles, motorbikes and cars can be hired in Reykjahlid and there are two hotels and a wide variety of other types of accommodation, but do book in advance — even a few days in advance from Reykjavík.

Northwest Peninsula

The remote northwestern corner of Iceland is all but cut off from the rest of the country by the huge inlets of the Breidhafjördhur and Húnaflói. Its harsh landscape and sheer inaccessibility have made it the last real stronghold of Iceland's most famous birds of prey, the Gyrfalcon and the White-tailed Eagle. Both are protected even from disturbance by special fines.

The northwest has two monumental bird cliffs at Hornbjarg and Haelavikurgjarg. From the sea these two adjacent monoliths rise 500 m (1640 feet) and are packed with Guillemot, Brünnich's Guillemot, Razorbill, Puffin, Fulmar and Kittiwake. Here there are both rare raptors, but this is an incredibly awkward place to get to — foot or boat are the only alternatives. Incidentally, there are a few non-breeding Little Auks hereabouts.

Fortunately, there are roads into the northwest and these can be explored, especially along the Breidhafjördhur, where the eagle has its largest population. Naturally there are no hot spots for this bird in Iceland that can be published.

SUMMER: Great Northern Diver, Red-throated Diver, Slavonian Grebe, Whooper Swan, Eider, Long-tailed Duck, Barrow's Goldeneye, Red-necked Phalarope, Purple Sandpiper, Arctic Skua, Glaucous Gull, Guillemot, Brünnich's Guillemot, Razorbill, Puffin, Ptarmigan, Snow Bunting.

ACCESS: Isafjördhur can be reached by road and has regular bus and air services from Reykjavík. This town has hotels, guest houses and other accommodation. Thereafter it is walking, or chartering a boat and guide. Other roads can be explored, but a mixture of bus and boat may be the best method of exploring this splendid wilderness.

ROUTE: Bus or plane from Reykjavík.

Reykjavík

Reykjavík is a substantial city of 90,000 inhabitants and the obvious starting point for an exploration of Iceland. Most travellers have a day in the town at the start or end of a holiday, and birders should not neglect to take the opportunity of getting out to enjoy its rather special appeal. Lake Tjornin, in the city centre, has a small, remnant colony of Arctic Terns as well as a few Red-necked Phalaropes. In winter, the lake is a haunt of Barrow's Goldeneye, Wigeon and Eider, as well as gulls and the feral Greylag Geese. Coastal areas have waders and, together with the harbour, offer good chances of rare gulls — Glaucous in summer, Iceland in winter.

A short trip across the lava flows to Keflavik and beyond on the Reykjanes peninsula brings one to the traditional haunt of Grey Phalarope. Unfortunately these birds have declined in numbers in recent years, though they may still be seen at Midhnes, Gerdhar or Stokkseyri. The massive cliffs of Hafnarberg and Krisuvikurberg hold excellent numbers of seabirds, including Brünnich's Guillemot and Glaucous Gull, while Purple Sandpiper and Snow Bunting breed nearby. The pointed 'toe' of Reykjanes, north of Keflavik, is favoured by local birders looking for American vagrants in autumn. At the present time, two or three species a year are added to the Icelandic list.

Even totally dude birders, who would rather spend their time on the golf course, are well catered for hereabouts. The course on the Seltjarnarnes peninsula is a noted haunt of an aggressive colony of Arctic Terns, as well as of summering Glaucous Gull, Purple Sandpiper and Red-necked Phalarope.

For the ornitho-affluent, boats may be chartered to sail around the island of Eldey, with its massive gannetry. Over 16,000 pairs breed on the dramatic stack, but landing is not allowed and all but impossible anyway. The boat trip will certainly be as near as anyone will ever get to 'ticking' the Great Auk, which became extinct here in 1844.

SUMMER: Greylag Goose, Ringed Plover, Purple Sandpiper, Turnstone, Red-necked Phalarope, Grey Phalarope, Kittiwake, Glaucous Gull, Arctic Tern, Guillemot, Brünnich's Guillemot, Black Guillemot, Razorbill, Puffin, Redwing, Snow Bunting.

ACCESS: The lake, harbour and golf course are all easily found, and there is a regular bus service to Keflavik and on to the smaller villages on the Reykjanes peninsula.

ROUTE: Reykjavík has an international airport, though many planes land at Keflavik. Do not be tempted to take an (expensive) excursion to Greenland. The chances of seeing birds are decidedly slim.

Snaefellsnes Peninsula

Snaefellsnes is one of those names that at first sight seems awkward to pronounce, but which rolls off the tongues of birders with the same ease as the Camargue. Its fame rests on a single species: the White-tailed Eagle. Altogether there are some 37 pairs in Iceland, giving a total population of about 120 individuals. The recent increase is due to a solid conservation policy by the Icelandic government and strict enforcement of the 'no disturbance' rules. The Snaefellsnes peninsula has eagles on its northern shores, along with several good colonies of Glaucous Gull. The southern shores are remarkable only for really convenient Brünnich's Guillemot on the sandstone cliffs. Gyrfalcons also use the area, with the cliffs at Malarrif as good as anywhere. There are some 60 species breeding on Snaefellsnes, including Iceland's only colony of Barnacle Geese on one of the offshore islands along the north coast.

Gyrfalcon

SUMMER: Great Northern Diver, Red-throated Diver, Fulmar, Whooper Swan, Greylag Goose, White-tailed Eagle, Gyrfalcon, Merlin, Glaucous Gull, Brünnich's Guillemot, Guillemot, Razorbill, Puffin, Black Guillemot, Arctic Skua, Arctic Tern, Ptarmigan, Snow Bunting.

ACCESS: There are roads along the southern shore and to many parts of the northern shore.

ROUTE: An easy drive from Reykjavík.

Thingvellir

Some 50 km (31 miles) east of Reykjavík, in a landscape of lava flows, volcanoes and grassy meadows, lies Iceland's largest lake and the seat of the country's 'Parliament'.

The meadows are reminiscent of Europe and it is not surprising to find breeding Black-tailed Godwit here, though this is their furthest north. Thingvallavatn is not so good as Myvatn (too deep), but it is much easier to get to, has a good hotel and can offer several specialities. Gyrfalcon is reasonably regular and Great Northern Diver breeds in small numbers. The River Oxara has Harlequin, and Barrow's Goldeneye occurs in autumn.

SUMMER: Great Northern Diver, Goosander, Harlequin, Tufted Duck, Scaup, Gyrfalcon, Merlin, Whimbrel, Black-tailed Godwit, Arctic Tern, Lesser Black-backed Gull, Snow Bunting.

ACCESS: A well-signposted drive of 50 km (31 miles) from the capital, with frequent bus services. Good roads to the west, north and particularly the eastern (best) side.

ROUTE: Via Reykjavík.

Westmann Islands

These islands lie off the southwest coast of Iceland and have a worldwide reputation for their seabird colonies. The group consists of 15 islands, only one of which, Heimaey, is inhabited. The second largest island is Surtsey, which emerged from the sea as a result of volcanic activity between 1963 and 1967, and which is now the home of a few Black Guillemots and Fulmars.

Four of the smaller islands hold gannetries, but Heimaey has five species of breeding auk, including Brünnich's Guillemot, here hugely outnumbered by their common cousins. Altogether 15 species of seabird breed, the most numerous of which is probably the Puffin.

Manx Shearwater and both Leach's and Storm Petrels breed, though they are difficult to locate because of their nocturnal habits. Shearwaters can, however, often be seen gathering offshore in the late afternoon. Heimaey has all the birds and some of the most spectacular cliff colonies in the world.

SUMMER: Manx Shearwater, Fulmar, Storm Petrel, Leach's Petrel, Gannet, Cormorant, Shag, Guillemot, Brünnich's Guillemot, Black Guillemot, Razorbill, Puffin, Glaucous Gull, Kittiwake, Great Skua.

ACCESS: The islands can be reached by daily ferry from Thorlakshofn, itself in contact with the capital by a regular bus service, or by daily flights from Reykjavík which usually pass over Surtsey. If you take a 'day' trip, take all your luggage as services are often held up somewhat. You are also advised to avoid the first week of August, when a festival ensures that everything is full up.

ROUTE: Via Reykjavík.

IRELAND

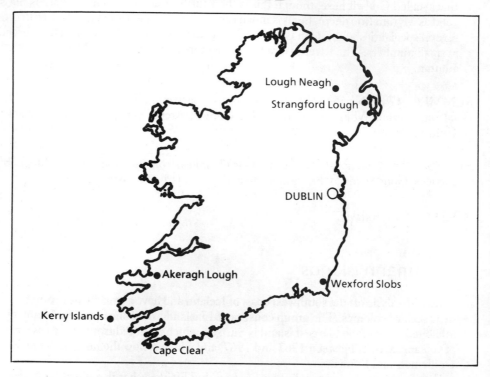

Akeragh Lough

Akeragh Lough is the only stretch of permanent fresh water in northern Kerry, but this by itself does not mean very much. What it does mean is that it is also one of the nearest stretches of fresh water to North America. Akeragh Lough lies behind the sand-dune beach at the head of Ballyheighe Bay to the south of Kerry Head. It is a shallow water of 2.4–2.8 ha (6–7 acres) normally, but sometimes almost dries up in the summer. It is set in a flat landscape and a slight change in water level affects its size considerably. Its marshy surrounds are grassy and typical of those favoured by Ruff, while there are also considerable areas of reeds. It is noted as the Irish stronghold of Gadwall, and other duck occur according to the water level. It is, however, its position 'across the sea' from America that has brought Akeragh ornithological fame as the eastern 'home' of Nearctic waders. Pectoral Sandpipers are annual visitors, and others have included Killdeer, Lesser Golden Plover, dowitchers, Least Sandpiper, Baird's Sandpiper, White-rumped Sandpiper and Western Sandpiper. American duck sometimes turn up as well.

AUTUMN: Ruff, Little Stint, Greenshank, rarities.

ACCESS: Akeragh Lough, which is private property, lies south of Ballyheighe village and can be best looked over from Route 105 which passes it on the landward side.

114

ROUTE: Via Dublin, which has an international airport.

Cape Clear Island

First established as a bird observatory in 1959, Clear was in the forefront of the seawatching mania of the 1960s and remains an outstanding site for these birds today. Situated at the southwestern corner of Ireland, it is ideally placed for watching birds that have been blown inshore by the southwesterly gales of late summer. It is equally well placed to receive American birds that find their first European landfall here. Over the years Clear has had its fair share of rarities, and it is surprising that it has not received more attention from rarity-hunters, especially as Scilly is becoming so overcrowded during the October peak.

Though Clear has a few interesting breeding birds, it is the migration seasons that offer most to the adventurous birder who comes here. August to October is best and seawatchers can expect most of the specials that regularly occur in Europe. Passerines definitely merit more attention than they have so far received. Go for an autumn week and see what turns up.

AUTUMN: Great Shearwater, Cory's Shearwater, Sooty Shearwater, Manx Shearwater, Storm Petrel, Leach's Petrel, Gannet, Great Skua, passerines.

SUMMER: Black Guillemot, Chough.

ACCESS: By far the best way of arranging a week (or more!) on Clear is to write to the Bird Observatory. Contact Beech Grove, Tring, Hertfordshire, England, for current details of bookings. The observatory will provide up-to-date details of its own arrangements for accommodation, which are hostel/self-catering type for up to ten people, and can also put prospective visitors in touch with locals offering accommodation elsewhere on the island.

ROUTE: The mailboat sails daily from Baltimore, Co. Cork, at 2.15 p.m. . . . more or less.

Kerry Islands

The westernmost points of Ireland are a collection of small, largely uninhabited islands off the coast of County Kerry. They lie in three groups as continuations of the peninsulas separated by Dingle Bay and the Kenmare River. Nobody can tell you how many birds there are here, but all species of breeding British seabirds are found.

The islands have romantic-sounding names, and part of their attraction lies in the manner of reaching them by fishing boat from the charming western Ireland fishing villages. The islands and their birds are:

Inishtooskert: Storm Petrel, Manx Shearwater.

115

Inishtearaght: large colonies of Storm Petrel, Manx Shearwater, Puffin.
Inishabro: Storm Petrel, Manx Shearwater, Fulmar.
Inishvickillane: large colonies of Storm Petrel, Manx Shearwater, Fulmar, Puffin, Razorbill.
Puffin Island: 20,000 Manx Shearwater, Fulmar, Puffin.
Little Skellig: 22,000 Gannet.
Great Skellig: Storm Petrel, Manx Shearwater.
Bull Rock (actually in Co. Cork): 500 Gannet, Kittiwake, Razorbill.

ACCESS: It is possible to charter boats from the adjacent fishing villages, price by negotiation. Remember that petrels and shearwaters are only about at night and that, unless you intend to camp and stay for several days, it is as well to choose an island where birds, such as auks and Gannets, can be seen during the day. Landing is difficult and really unnecessary, but this can make for a marvellous holiday for birders who organise thoroughly. Camping on the Blaskets is prohibited, except on Great Blasket.

ROUTE: Via Dublin.

Lough Neagh

This is the large, empty rectangle shown on so many bird-distribution maps of Ireland. It is a huge wetland of about 40,000 ha (nearly 100,000 acres) and measuring 25 km by 17 km (15½ by 10½ miles). Lying only a short drive to the west of Belfast, it attracts considerable attention from both resident and visiting birders, particularly in winter when it harbours more duck than any other Irish site.

Lough Neagh is shallow and reed-fringed, offering feeding opportunities to a wide variety of species. Outstanding are the flocks of diving duck, with Pochard and Tufted regularly reaching a combined total of 40,000 birds. Several other species reach four-figure totals and all three swans find a major stronghold here. Because of its size, Lough Neagh is seldom accurately censused and may, sometimes, prove disappointing to visitors. There is, however, an adjacent water called Lough Beg, which is much smaller, shallower, and offers rich feeding to many wildfowl. It also has the habit of attracting passage waders, including the odd Nearctic species.

In summer there is a good population of breeding birds that includes 1,000 pairs of Tufted and the occasional Garganey. Goldeneye regularly summer here.

WINTER: Mallard, Teal, Wigeon, Pintail, Shoveler, Tufted Duck, Pochard, Scaup, Goldeneye, Mute Swan, Bewick's Swan, Whooper Swan.

SUMMER: Great Crested Grebe, Teal, Shoveler, Garganey, Tufted Duck, Goldeneye, Red-breasted Merganser, Scoter, Common Tern.

ACCESS: Lough Neagh is easily viewed at many points around its perimeter from public roads. Birds often congregate in the lee shore. Lough Beg is private, but may be approached via public roads from the west.

ROUTE: Easily reached westwards from Belfast.

Strangford Lough

This is a virtually land-locked sea lough to the southeast of Belfast which acts as a magnet to local watchers. At low tide it exposes a huge area of intertidal mud that attracts large numbers of wintering and passage waders. The northern shore has many low islands that form important high-tide roosts. These regularly attract Knot (10,000), Bar-tailed Godwit (1,700), Dunlin (10,000), plus large numbers of Curlew, Oyster-catcher and Redshank. Wildfowl are equally impressive, with over half the Irish population of Brent Goose (10,000) wintering along with huge flocks of Wigeon. Whooper Swan, Pintail and Merganser all reach three figures.

The only river to enter the lough has been dammed as part of a flood-control scheme and now forms a freshwater pool known as the Quoile Pondage, a National Nature Reserve. This is always worth a look.

On passage a wide variety of waders and other species put in an appearance and, as elsewhere in Ireland, there is every chance of an American wader or two in the autumn. Breeding birds include terns and gulls, along with Merganser.

WINTER: Brent Goose, Shelduck, Wigeon, Pintail, Red-breasted Merganser, Whooper Swan, Curlew, Bar-tailed Godwit, Knot, Dunlin.

SUMMER: Red-breasted Merganser, Shelduck, Arctic Tern.

ACCESS: Although birds can be found along the whole shoreline, the largest concentrations are usually in the northwest, north of Mahee Island. There are several shoreline refuges as well as island sanctuaries, though, in general, the whole area can be explored via public roads and pathways.

ROUTE: Easily reached southeastwards from Belfast.

Wexford Slobs

Long famous as the major wintering ground of wildfowl in Ireland, the Slobs have changed quite dramatically since the first *Where to Watch Birds* appeared. Much of the North Slob has been put to the plough, while the South Slob has changed from a region of grazing to one of mowing. Fortunately, though breeding birds have undoubtedly suffered, the appeal to winter enthusiasts remains the same, while rarity-watchers have the same chances as ever.

About half of the world population of Greenland Whitefronts winter here, along with several hundred Brent. Many duck reach numbers in excess of 1,000 and for Lapwing and Golden Plover the damp fields offer a refuge when Britain is ice-bound. Black-tailed Godwits are particularly important in winter, while during passage periods the Slobs become a major staging post to a wide variety of waders.

117

As this is one of the major wetlands in Ireland, American birds do have a habit of appearing here. Snow Geese are more or less regular, presumably having arrived with the Greenland geese, and transatlantic waders appear every autumn.

Pectoral Sandpiper

WINTER: Slavonian Grebe, Bewick's Swan, Brent Goose, White-fronted Goose, Pink-footed Goose, Barnacle Goose, Teal, Pintail, Scaup, Golden Plover, Black-tailed Godwit.

PASSAGE: Whimbrel, Spotted Redshank, transatlantic waders, Little Gull.

ACCESS: The South Slob is reached from Route 8 south of Wexford. Turn left to Rosslare, past Killinick, and continue to Burrow.

ROUTE: Dublin international airport.

ISRAEL

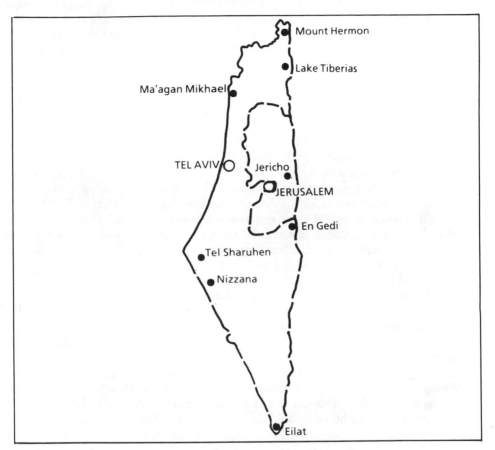

Mount Hermon

Lake Tiberias

Ma'agan Mikhael

TEL AVIV

Jericho

JERUSALEM

En Gedi

Tel Sharuhen

Nizzana

Eilat

Eilat

Eilat is Israel's port on the Red Sea and is strategically situated to receive migrants on their way to and from Africa. At first it was regarded simply as a splendid place to watch for raptors, especially in the spring, when over three-quarters of a million birds of prey have been counted moving northwards. This figure is ten times the number to be counted over the Bosporus and five times as many as over the Straits of Gibraltar. Such a dramatic passage inevitably attracted a considerable number of enthusiasts, and it is their work, coupled with that of the local Society for the Protection of Nature in Israel (SPNI), that has publicised Eilat's other attractions.

Migrants of a wide variety of species find refuge among the various habitats in what is otherwise a decidedly inhospitable landscape. The buildings and their gardens offer shelter to small migrants, as do the intensively farmed kibbutz to the north of the town. Such birds include hordes of the common visitors to northern Europe, as well as the more exotic Red-throated Pipit, Thrush Nightingale, Rufous Bush Chat, Black-eared

119

Wheatear, Olivaceous and Bonelli's Warblers, Masked Shrike and Cretzschmar's Bunting. Waders pour through, mostly concentrating on the saltpans that lie immediately east of the airport. The sewage canal attracts crakes and rails, while there are common migrants such as Pied and Collared Flycatchers and Wrynecks virtually everywhere. There are even records of the latter frequenting a traffic roundabout.

The massive passage of raptors and small migrants would certainly be enough to attract birders from all over Europe, but Eilat's geographical position gives it one more major attraction. As it is on the Red Sea, there is a chance of several seabirds that are otherwise not to be found in the Western Palearctic. Brown Booby and Western Reef Heron fall into this category, along with various gulls and terns that could include Lesser Crested and Bridled Terns and even White-eyed Gull. Eilat is also an 'oasis' for desert birds that live in the surrounding area, and various species of sandgrouse, larks, chats and finches occur that are both decidedly southern and definitely desert-dwelling.

With good international transport links, a variety of accommodation, easy (if expensive) car hire, absolutely superb birding and good local contacts, it is surprising that Eilat is not inundated by birders every spring and autumn. One word of warning: as with other desert areas, the peaks of bird activity are in the early morning and late afternoon. Apart from waders and seabirds, most species simply disappear during the heat of the day and it is unwise to chase around after them. Heat stroke and dehydration can be very serious and most visitors avoid the sun during midday and afternoon. Birders usually gather at the seawatch point to exchange information.

PASSAGE: Brown Booby, Western Reef Heron, Night Heron, Squacco Heron, Cattle Egret, Little Egret, Great White Egret, White Stork, Black Kite, Egyptian Vulture, Lappet-faced Vulture, Short-toed Eagle, Steppe Eagle, Honey Buzzard, Buzzard, Long-legged Buzzard, Pallid Harrier, Levant Sparrowhawk, Osprey, Barbary Falcon, Sand Partridge, Spur-winged Plover, Marsh Sandpiper, Broad-billed Sandpiper, Collared Pratincole, Cream-coloured Courser, Slender-billed Gull, Gull-billed Tern, Whiskered Tern, Lichtenstein's Sandgrouse, Crowned Sandgrouse, Eagle Owl, Bee-eater, Blue-cheeked Bee-eater, Little Green Bee-eater, Masked Shrike, Bifasciated Lark, Bar-tailed Desert Lark, Pale Crag Martin, Citrine Wagtail, Red-throated Pipit, Yellow-vented Bulbul, Arabian Babbler, Rufous Bush Chat, Hooded Wheatear, White-crowned Black Wheatear, Thrush Nightingale, Blackstart, Graceful Warbler, Scrub Warbler, Arabian Warbler, Desert Finch, Dead Sea Sparrow, Trumpeter Finch, Sinai Rosefinch, House Bunting, Tristram's Grackle, Brown-necked Raven.

ACCESS: Eilat lies mainly on the western shore of the Gulf of Aquaba, with an area of hotels around the lagoon (marina) on the North Beach. The main birding areas lie to the north between the main road northwards and the Jordanian border. A good introduction to this area is to join one of the free guided birding tours in English that start at the Marina Bridge every Sunday, Tuesday and Thursday at 8.30 a.m. This lasts about three hours and takes in the major wetland and migrant areas.

The saltpans are reached via the drivable track up the western side of the sewage canal — Flamingo, waders and Dead Sea Sparrow. The railway station and the Kibbutz Fields — Namaqua Dove, Little Green Bee-eater, Desert Finch — are approached by driving up the eastern side of the canal, past a palm plantation, and eventually ending up at a pumping station on the main north road. The small pond here regularly attracts desert species to drink, including early-morning Crowned Sandgrouse. Just before the pumping station, there is a turning on the right leading to the Northern Fields. These are good for small birds such as Pale Rock Sparrow and Bimaculated Lark.

The North Beach itself is the regular seawatch and afternoon-meeting place. Gather at the mouth of the sewage canal. The football field lies to the west and is reached by taking the turning opposite the airport-terminal buildings. Turn left at the second intersection and then take the first right into Jerusalem Street. Watch for a dome on the left-hand side and, as the road swings left, take the track on the right. Just over the rise the water-sprinklers keep the pitch in prime condition and attract huge numbers of migrants. Further along the track, the water-pumping station has a small pool that attracts Trumpeter Finch and House Bunting. At dusk, Lichtenstein's Sandgrouse come to drink. The secret is to park a car about 20 m away facing the pool. Turning headlights on is now banned. Access at dusk is restricted to two nights per week.

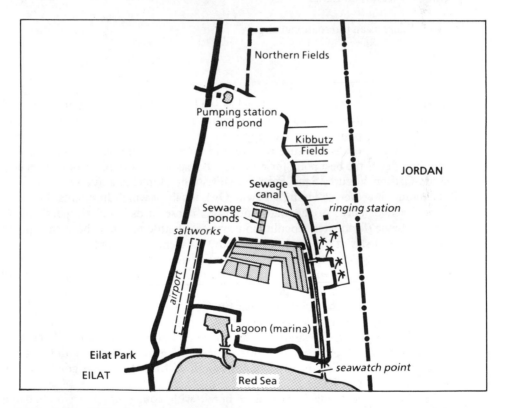

The Moon Valley Mountains are the best spot for raptor-watching, though migrating birds can be seen throughout the area. About 13 km (8 miles) north of Eilat, the Be'er Ora area is good for Courser and Bifasciated and Bar-tailed Desert Larks. Though there is no reason to suppose that these birds do not occur throughout this area, a stop at kilometre post 32 gives a chance of Lappet-faced Vulture soaring over the hills to the west at about 7 a.m. There is only the one pair in Israel. Desert birds are best to the east of the road.

Returning towards Eilat, watch for kilometre post 20 and a track westward signposted 'Amrans Pillars'. Drive along and take a right-hand fork at 5 km (3 miles) to a parking area. Sinai Rosefinch winters here until the third week of March (sometimes into April), frequenting the rubbish bins. Desert Lark and White-crowned Black Wheatear are also regularly seen here.

Yotvata is an area of bushy scrub just beyond kilometre post 45 on the north road out of Eilat. There is a petrol station and café on the right-hand side of the road, behind which is a rubbish dump among the acacia trees. This is good for migrants and specialities such as Arabian Warbler — an Orphean-type bird with a completely black tail, which is continuously cocked, and a rounded bulbul-type head. Also found here are Scrub Warbler, Olivaceous Warbler and Little Green Bee-eater. To the south, at kilometre post 45, the area west of the road holds similar species, plus possible Temminck's Horned Lark.

ROUTE: Eilat has an international airport.

En Gedi

The Dead Sea lies 394 m (1292 feet) below sea level and is the lowest place on earth. Its waters are highly saline and virtually devoid of life. The most famous birding here is centred on the oasis of En Gedi approximately half way along the western shore. The main wadi here is a nature reserve and is excellent for small migrants, while along the ridge is the best point for watching the passage of raptors. Local specialities include Griffon Vulture, Sand Partridge, Tristram's Grackle and Arabian Babbler. Outstanding, however, is Hume's Tawny Owl, a pair of which frequents the area of the field school north of the wadi entrance. These birds regularly perch on the boundary fence (fortunately floodlit) and can, with a little patience, be seen superbly. It is possible to stay at the field centre or the adjacent youth hostel.

Unfortunately, the wadi reserve does not open until 9 a.m., so early-morning walkers tend to concentrate their attention on the trees and bushes on the south side of the wadi — excellent for migrants.

All of the wadis to the south between En Gedi and Masada are worth exploring. They hold a good variety of species, including both ravens, Blackstart, Scrub Warbler and Trumpeter Finch. Two in particular, Wadi en Zafzafa and Wadi n Ze'elim, are noted as haunts of Lammergeier, while the latter is also a possible Hume's site. A further wadi about 3 km (nearly 2 miles) south of Masada is also good for these species plus Bonelli's Eagle.

The En Gedi Kibbutz is run as a hotel, with cottage-style accommodation, swimming pool etc, and is one of the nicer places to stay. The bushes on the right-hand side of the road are a wintering ground of Cyprus Warbler.

PASSAGE: Lammergeier, Griffon Vulture, Short-toed Eagle, Steppe Eagle, Bonelli's Eagle, Buzzard, Long-legged Buzzard, Honey Buzzard, Barbary Falcon, Sand

Partridge, Hume's Tawny Owl, Bee-eater, Pale Crag Martin, Masked Shrike, Desert Lark, Arabian Babbler, White-crowned Black Wheatear, Hooded Wheatear, Thrush Nightingale, Blackstart, Scrub Warbler, Cyprus Warbler, Trumpeter Finch, House Bunting, Cretzschmar's Bunting, Tristram's Grackle, Fan-tailed Raven, Brown-necked Raven.

ACCESS: The wadi reserve is easily found, with the field school and youth hostel at the entrance. Hume's Tawny Owl can be seen after dark on the perimeter fence. North of the field centre is an amphitheatre, beyond which is a gate through the fence leading up a path to a raptor-watching spot. The reserve is open at about 9 a.m., but may still be worth visiting. The area south of the wadi is good for migrants.

The wadis to the south (see above) should all be explored to and beyond Masada — good for culture vultures (perhaps literally). There are no restrictions on access.

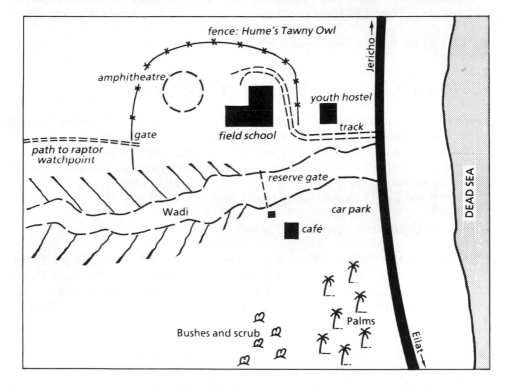

ROUTE: En Gedi is an hour from Jerusalem and three times that from Eilat.

Jericho

The area around Jericho southwards to the Dead Sea makes an ideal 'day off' for anyone with time on their hands either in Jericho or Jerusalem. To the south of the town, the road crosses the large Wadi Quilt. On the south side of the bridge, a track leads westwards along the rim of the wadi to a monastery and the canyon. This is an excellent spot for a variety of species, including the elusive Hooded Wheatear and Bonelli's Eagle.

Further south, on the Dead Sea road, the Qayla Fishponds are on the right-hand side of the road about 0.5 km (550 yards) before the right-hand turn to Qayla. These ponds have Clamorous Reed Warbler, as well as Little Crake and other wetland species.

SUMMER: Bonelli's Eagle, Black Francolin, Sand Partridge, Little Crake, Pale Crag Martin, Desert Lark, Arabian Babbler, Hooded Wheatear, Tristram's Grackle, Rock Sparrow, Cinereous Bunting.

ACCESS: Wadi Quilt is easily found between Jericho and the Jerusalem–Dead Sea road. Qayla Fishponds are nearer the Dead Sea. For both, follow instructions above.

ROUTE: Less than an hour by road from Jerusalem to Jericho.

Ma'agan Mikhael and Hadera Fishponds

These two areas of fishponds lie adjacent to the Mediterranean coast and only a short drive north from Tel Aviv. They are, therefore, an excellent place for those with only a day free for birding. The first-named attracts those with more time by virtue of being a wintering (late-spring?) haunt of Great Black-headed Gull. Other regular species include Flamingo, Greater Sand Plover, Spur-winged Plover, Glossy Ibis, Smyrna and Lesser Pied Kingfishers and Slender-billed Gull.

WINTER: Great Black-headed Gull, Slender-billed Gull.

SUMMER: White Pelican, White Stork, Glossy Ibis, Little Egret, Night Heron, Squacco Heron, Great White Egret, Spur-winged Plover, Greater Sand Plover, Black-winged Stilt, Slender-billed Gull, Water Rail, Little Crake, Baillon's Crake, Smyrna Kingfisher, Lesser Pied Kingfisher, Clamorous Reed Warbler, Rüppell's Warbler.

ACCESS: Ma'agan Mikhael is reached on the old road north of Tel Aviv (not the motorway) after 50 km (31 miles). Turn left (signposted) and then right opposite the football pitch. After 200 m (220 yards) turn right to the cemetery, where a rocky area to the north holds Rüppell's and other warblers. Return and continue northwards along the road to the 'No Entry' sign. Park and continue on foot, turning left to the beach then north again, checking all the gulls. There is another entrance off the main road north of the fishponds.

The fishponds can be explored on foot by returning to the football pitch and turning right (west) towards the sea. There are ponds to left and right. At the coast, turn right and watch over a marshy ditch for crakes.

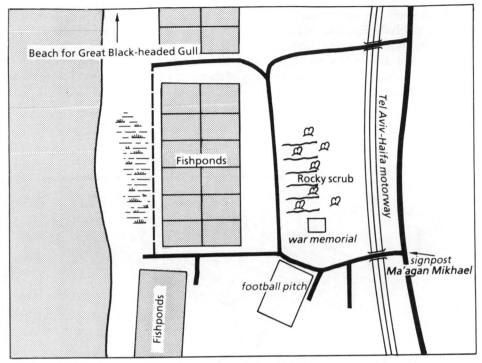

Hadera fishponds lie north of Tel Aviv, a little way north of the town of Hadera to the east of the main road. They offer similar species to the more famous Ma'agan Mikhael area, while lacking some of the specialities. A ditch running along the southern edge of the ponds may sometimes hold Painted Snipe.

ROUTE: About an hour's drive northward from Ben Gurion airport.

Mount Hermon and the Golan Heights

The Golan Heights are etched on the memory of anyone with even the slightest awareness of Israel's history. Strategically of critical significance, the area is now settled and developed into a holiday area for skiing. It is also remarkably good for birds, with several species that are otherwise almost impossible to find within the country's borders. This is an alpine area with woods, meadows and high screes, where snow is regular and may still fall as late as April. Warm protective clothing is essential at all times.

At the top of Mount Hermon, Crimson-winged Finch is the speciality. Lower down, species such as Syrian Serin, Rock Sparrow, Sombre Tit and Orphean Warbler are found around the area of the ski-lift base station, as well as along the approach road. The serin also occurs as low as Majdal Shams, and there are also Rock Nuthatch, Black-eared Wheatear, Rüppell's and Upcher's Warblers and Cretzschmar's Bunting.

125

Lower still, on the approach road south of Masada, are Calandra and Bimaculated Larks and Isabelline Wheatear. Even Finsch's Wheatear may be seen here, and in late summer White-throated Robin occurs. Raptors, including Griffon and Egyptian Vultures and Bonelli's and Short-toed Eagles, are present throughout the area. Anyone wishing to see as wide a variety of species as possible in Israel cannot afford to miss this area.

Bimaculated Lark

SUMMER: Griffon Vulture, Egyptian Vulture, Short-toed Eagle, Bonelli's Eagle, Long-legged Buzzard, Little Swift, Rock Nuthatch, Calandra Lark, Bimaculated Lark, Short-toed Lark, Woodlark, Sombre Tit, Rock Thrush, Black-eared Wheatear, Finsch's Wheatear, Isabelline Wheatear, White-throated Robin, Orphean Warbler, Rüppell's Warbler, Upcher's Warbler, Syrian Serin, Crimson-winged Finch, Rock Sparrow, Pale Rock Sparrow.

ACCESS: There is an army check-point on the final approach to Mount Hermon that does not permit access until 9.30 a.m. Continue northwards after this time to the end of the road at the ski-lift base station. Check that you are allowed out at the top; it is pointless to waste money and time if you are not. Crimson-winged Finch is the only reason for going so high.

The area around the base station is good, especially the rubbish tip, and, on the drive down, a small lake on the right has two mounds with Rock Nuthatch, Rock Sparrow and Rock Thrush. Lower still, a car park with a monument on the right has similar birds. Below this, there is a one-way system below Majdal Shams. At the T-junction turn right, and watch for a car park with a wrecked coach on the left after a few hundred metres. Syrian Serin, Sombre Tit, Cretzschmar's Bunting and Rüppell's and Upcher's Warblers can be found in the area north and south of the road. Just south of Masada, soon after the turning to Bu'Qata, there are some tin sheds to the right of the road. A track alongside them leads into a stony area for three larks and Isabelline Wheatear.

If time permits, the area of Caeserea Philippi will produce Griffon Vulture and other raptors, Rock Thrush and Little Swift.

ROUTE: Northwards from Tiberias through Rosh Pinna to Majdal Shams.

Nizzana

The old castle of Nizzana lies right against the Egyptian border in the Negev Desert, south of Beersheba. It takes little knowledge of recent history to realise that this is a highly sensitive area, full of military, armed to the teeth with tanks and personnel-carriers. Birders have been asked to leave the area, had their films confiscated and even been detained and interrogated. It is for each to calculate whether or not it is worthwhile to explore what is the only area in the country that may produce Houbara Bustard and Temminck's Horned Lark.

The approach is via Beersheba southwards; the old road to Nizzana ia closed, so an up-to-date map is essential. Beyond the Zeelim turn-off, the area of pools at Ashalim has three species of sandgrouse soon after dawn; but beware, for they are often dry by mid-April. A wadi here has produced Houbara, Cream-coloured Courser and Lesser Short-toed Lark.

About 15–20 km (9–12½ miles) further, a balloon will appear on the left with garage and café just beyond. Past this is a garrison area, then after 2 km (1¼ miles) a bridge across a wadi with a ridge just beyond. North of the road, the wadi may produce Houbara, Spotted Sandgrouse and Temminck's. The ridge has Bar-tailed Desert Lark, while the area to the south holds Desert Wheatear, Desert Lark and Lesser Short-toed.

Continuing southwards, a flat plain is noted for Bifasciated and Lesser Short-toed Larks and possible Houbara. A turning to the left leads to the castle itself, where Desert Wheatear, Courser and Pin-tailed and Spotted Sandgrouse have been seen. The whole area is worth exploring — but discreetly.

SUMMER: Lanner, Long-legged Buzzard, Houbara Bustard, Black-bellied Sand-
grouse, Pin-tailed Sandgrouse, Spotted Sandgrouse, Cream-coloured Courser,
Bifasciated Lark, Desert Lark, Lesser Short-toed Lark, Temminck's Horned Lark,
Desert Wheatear, Desert Finch, Trumpeter Finch.

ACCESS: Take the new Nizzana road southwards from Beersheba and watch for the
roadside pools and adjacent ridge after the turning (right) to Ashalim. Some
15–20 km (9–12½ miles) further and you are in the Nizzana area — directions
above.

ROUTE: Beersheba can be reached from Tel Aviv or Jerusalem in a day.

Tel Sharuhen and Wadi Besor

These two adjacent areas lie within the Nahal Habosar Nature Reserve on the edge of the Negev Desert. Wadi Besor is a huge affair extending from the desert right to the coast, while the Tel is an obvious, rounded hill with a deep quarry on its southern side. Though much of the surroundings is dry and arid, irrigation has converted large areas to agriculture. There are some trees and bushes that hold Scops Owl and Syrian Woodpecker, while the fields have Courser, Stone-curlew and Pin-tailed Sandgrouse. Raptors are often present and include Imperial Eagle, Pallid Harrier and Lanner, but above all there is an excellent Eagle Owl spot in the quarry on the Tel.

In winter the area around Urim has Sociable Plover, while to the south, nearer the border, the area around Yevul and Deqel is a haunt of Houbara Bustard.

To the east, between this area and Ofaqim, the area between Maslul and Hippushit has been little explored, but it shows considerable promise. Imperial Eagle, Saker, Courser, various larks and sandgrouse have been seen.

SUMMER: Imperial Eagle, Long-legged Buzzard, Pallid Harrier, Lanner, Chukar, Stone-curlew, Cream-coloured Courser, Eagle Owl, Hume's Tawny Owl, Pin-tailed Sandgrouse, Bifasciated Lark, Calandra Lark.

WINTER: Sociable Plover, Dotterel, Little Bustard, Houbara Bustard, Pin-tailed Sandgrouse.

ACCESS: Leave Beersheba northwards and turn left for Ofaqim. Some 18 km (11 miles) further, there is a car park on the left-hand side of the road just before Wadi Besor. Walk down the western side of the wadi to the Tel. At dusk, Eagle Owl may be seen from the southern edge of the hill. Examine fields and wadi for other species.

East of Ofaqim, watch for a minor turning to Maslul on the north side of the road. Opposite this is a track. Motor about 2 km (1¼ miles) to a line of pylons and explore. Continue south toward Hippushit.

ROUTE: Beersheba can be reached from Tel Aviv and Jerusalem in a day.

Lake Tiberias

Tiberias makes a first-class base for exploring several places for a wide variety of species. In particular there are two areas of fishponds, a marshland nature reserve, many wadis and a handy mountain area. Altogether, it is a splendid area ranking with any in Israel, except, of course, Eilat.

To the north of Tiberias, on the road to Qiryat Shemona, lies the Huleh reserve. This is approached via a track eastwards off the main road which passes an area of fishponds before arriving at the car park. Three otherwise rather difficult species can be seen, both at the ponds and in the reserve: White Pelican, Marbled Teal and Clamorous Reed Warbler. Dead Sea Sparrow may be here, and there are always herons and egrets as well as Smyrna and Lesser Pied Kingfishers on the reserve. Penduline Tit, Moustached

Warbler and small crakes can usually be seen. Additionally, the area to the north of the reserve, where the swamp has been drained, is a regular wintering ground of Spotted Eagle. Raptors come to roost within the reserve at dusk.

To the south, westwards off the main road, is Wadi Amud, a wadi that leads into a deep canyon with some very good birds. Eagle Owl is found throughout the year and Little Swift and Blue Rock Thrush both breed. Syrian Woodpecker may be found, and this is one of the spots for Long-billed Pipit. On the way check Lake Tiberias at its northwestern corner, which is good for kingfishers.

Smyrna Kingfisher

Just a little way to the south there is a road to Maghar where, just south of the town, is another canyon leading into Arbel Mountain. This has Alpine Accentor and Wall-creeper, and has produced Finsch's Wheatear in the past.

Along the eastern shore of the lake is Wadi Sumakh. This is the only site in this book for Brown Fish Owl and a special trek is required even for a chance of this bird. Access is along the wadi, which lies 750 m (nearly ½ mile) north of the turning to Ramat Mogshimm, for about an hour. Despite bushes and thickets, stay close to the stream and look for an obvious rock in the middle covered with crab shells and droppings. Some have said that the rock is not obvious! Having located the rock, settle down for a long wait, or return at dusk. This is the owl's feeding post. When it is quite clear that the bird is present, point a powerful torch skywards, turn it on and slowly bring it down to point at the rock. Good luck is needed, for the bird is decidedly erratic even here.

Southwards from Tiberias, there are fishponds north of Bet She'an on the left-hand side of the road. Take a left and park after 100 m. These ponds cover a substantial area, but should produce Barbary Falcon, Clamorous Reed Warbler, Penduline Tit and possible Great Snipe.

SUMMER: White Pelican, White Stork, Glossy Ibis, Night Heron, Purple Heron,

129

Squacco Heron, Cattle Egret, Little Bittern, Barbary Falcon, Griffon Vulture, Marbled Teal, Little Crake, Black-winged Stilt, Great Snipe, Brown Fish Owl, Eagle Owl, Little Swift, Alpine Accentor, Wallcreeper, Syrian Woodpecker, Long-billed Pipit, Penduline Tit, Blue Rock Thrush, Finsch's Wheatear, Moustached Warbler, Clamorous Reed Warbler, Orange-tufted Sunbird, Dead Sea Sparrow, Rock Bunting.

WINTER: Spotted Eagle.

ACCESS: The Huleh Swamp is reached 10 km (6¼ miles) north of Rosh Pinna, beyond Yesud Hama'ala. The track to the fishponds and reserve is on the right, but poorly signposted.

For Wadi Amud, leave Tiberias northward and take the small turning left to Huqoq. After a further 6–7 km (4 miles) a large wadi, with a bridged river, runs beneath the road. There is a car park, with a footpath leading northwards (right) along the wadi and canyon. Take this until the canyon becomes less steep and it is possible to scramble up the left-hand side to the top. Eagle Owls start calling before dusk. Long-billed Pipit is found in grass-covered areas broken by gorse bushes. Syrian Woodpecker haunts the trees on the western side of the wadi on the south side (left) of the road.

For Arbel Mountain, take the Maghar road, which is closer to Tiberias than the Huqoq road above. Just before Maghar, turn left into a deep gorge with cliffs holding Wallcreeper and (possible) Finsch's Wheatear.

The Fish Owl site is well detailed above.

ROUTE: Tiberias is easily reached by road from the south. Hotels are a little simple, but decidedly cheap.

ITALY

Gran Paradiso
○ MILAN
● Po Delta and Venice
FLORENCE
○
Orbetello
● ROME
Circeo
Gargano
○ NAPLES
● Sardinia
River Tellaro

Circeo National Park

While most Italian national parks are centred on the high mountains of the Alps and the Appennines, Circeo is a coastal wilderness on the west coast half way between Rome and Naples. It is, inevitably, something of a playground for city-dwellers, but the extensive forests of evergreen oaks together with coastal lagoons and marshes swallow them up and have plenty of fine sites for birding. The breeding birds include White Stork, Great Spotted Cuckoo and Golden Oriole, but on passage and in winter there may be impressive gatherings of birds of a wide range of species. Glossy Ibis, Spotted Eagle and Red-footed Falcon may be enough to whet the appetite, but Marsh Sandpiper and Audouin's Gull are among other reasonably regular birds here.

Winter brings some wildfowl, including Ferruginous Duck, but the park is said to be a good Wallcreeper spot at this time of the year. Flamingo also frequently put in an appearance.

131

SUMMER: White Stork, Great Spotted Cuckoo, Golden Oriole, Subalpine Warbler, Sardinian Warbler.

WINTER: Black-throated Diver, Great White Egret, Flamingo, Ferruginous Duck, Sandwich Tern, Wallcreeper.

PASSAGE: Glossy Ibis, Osprey, Red-footed Falcon, Crane, Marsh Sandpiper, Collared Pratincole, Audouin's Gull, Caspian Tern, Whiskered Tern, Woodchat Shrike.

ACCESS: The coastal road southwards between Latina and Sabaudia and beyond passes the main lagoons and gives access to the major areas of woodland.

ROUTE: Southwards along the main coastal road from Rome.

Gargano

The Gargano peninsula forms the spur of the boot of Italy on the Adriatic coast, and is an excellent area offering a wide range of different habitats within a short distance of the town of Manfredonia. To the south lies Brindisi, with its ferries offering an alternative route to Greece, and several crews have stopped off for a day or two in the Gargano area.

The mountains of Gargano are limestone and relatively bare on their lower slopes. Higher up there are extensive forests of beech and oak, and it is among these that both White-backed and Black Woodpeckers occur. Here too are Short-toed Eagle, Saker and Long-legged Buzzard.

To the north, the lagoons of Varano and Lesina have good winter wildfowl populations, with regular Bean and White-fronted Geese. They are certainly worth exploring during passage periods, and in summer the reedbeds hold both bitterns, Great Reed Warbler and probably Marsh Harrier. Lesina is best at all seasons and is generally easier to work than Varano.

To the south, the coastline between Zapponeta and Margherita is backed by extensive saltpans which may produce good gatherings of passage waders. Though there are no available records of unusual eastern species here, they must surely occur.

SUMMER: Bittern, Little Bittern, Little Egret, Short-toed Eagle, Honey Buzzard, Long-legged Buzzard, Hobby, Saker, Marsh Harrier, Scops Owl, Black Woodpecker, White-backed Woodpecker, Penduline Tit, Lesser Grey Shrike, Woodchat Shrike, Red-backed Shrike, Melodious Warbler, Orphean Warbler, Fan-tailed Warbler, Black-eared Wheatear, Rock Bunting, Black-headed Bunting.

PASSAGE: Black-winged Stilt, Wood Sandpiper, Greenshank, Spotted Redshank, Curlew Sandpiper, Little Stint, Ruff, Black Tern.

WINTER: Bean Goose, White-fronted Goose, Scoter, Velvet Scoter, Eider, Goldeneye, Red-breasted Merganser.

ACCESS: The best route into Gargano is from Vico del Gargano southwards on Provincial Route 528, but all the mountain roads are worthy of exploration. The woods, as well as the high tops and passes, should be explored.

Lake Lesina has its largest reedbeds at the eastern end, but is generally awkward to work. Fishermen might be persuaded to take one out; try the pumping station at the eastern end off the Torre Mileto–Sannicandro road. Beware weekend shooting. Lake Varano can be seen from the road along the isthmus, but Lesina is a much better bet.

The saltpans at Margherita may be viewed from the coast road and from a small road signposted to Trinitapoli on the northwestern outskirts of Margherita. A similarly signposted track extends from the southeastern outskirts of Zapponeta.

ROUTE: Naples is the nearest major airport, with a good road to Foggia.

Gran Paradiso

The Gran Paradiso National Park lies against the French border in northwestern Italy and covers 60,000 ha (150,000 acres) of high mountain. There are 57 glaciers and some 60 lakes, surrounded by forests of fir and larch, and over three-quarters of the park lies above the 3000-m (9850-foot) contour. The actual park boundary also follows the contours, thus excluding most of the deep valleys and meadows. This is an area of superb scenery with many typical alpine birds, including Golden Eagle, Ptarmigan, Alpine Accentor, Snow Finch and Alpine Chough. It is, however, best explored at a leisurely pace with considerable walking, preferably from one refuge to the next.

Across the French border lies the Vanoise National Park, offering the same sort of landscape and similar birds. The whole area is best known for its ibex, but those prepared to spend time among the peaks and forests may be rewarded with some of the best birding in Italy.

SUMMER: Golden Eagle, Ptarmigan, Black Grouse, Hazelhen, Eagle Owl, Tengmalm's Owl, Black Woodpecker, Three-toed Woodpecker, Alpine Swift, Crag Martin, Alpine Accentor, Ring Ouzel, Crested Tit, Snow Finch, Citril Finch, Nutcracker, Alpine Chough.

ACCESS: Aosta is a pleasant town that makes an excellent base. The valley has several camp sites and a variety of accommodation. From the road that runs between Aosta and the Mont Blanc Tunnel, several minor roads lead southward into the park. The villages of Cogne and Valnontay are the starting points of several paths toward refuges, but do not ignore the roads on the way. Other areas worth exploring are from Degioz towards Alpe Djuan and from Cretaz towards Pousset. In the southeast of the park, the road through the Col di Nivolet is a little rough, but well worth the effort.

ROUTE: South of the main road between Mont Blanc and Milan.

Orbetello

Mount Argentario is a substantial rocky promontory along the western coast of Italy, to the north of Rome, best known for its picturesque sixteenth-century Spanish forts. It is joined to the mainland by three sandbars that enclose two large lagoons, Burano and Orbetello. Though these are popular beachside resorts, the WWF has now converted 2600 ha (6400 acres) of Orbetello into a nature reserve and dramatically increased the population of breeding birds. Here the combination of marshy edges, open water, scrub and pine woods holds a good variety of Mediterranean species, including Montagu's Harrier, Stilt, Stone-curlew and Bee-eater. Not so long ago, one could find only a few Kentish Plovers trying to hatch out their eggs among the topless beauties.

Passage birds, arriving out of season, always fared rather better, but Ferruginous Duck, Crane, Osprey and Marsh Sandpiper are now regular, indicating the possibilities of other considerably scarcer species that might reasonably be expected to pass through. As this is a winter haven, the lack of shooting over the reserve has significantly affected the variety and number of birds that can be expected. Reasonably regular species include Spoonbill, Great White Egret, Greylag Goose, duck and Moustached Warbler. All in all, the Orbetello area has been converted from a good place where something might appear to a regular haunt of a splendid variety of Italian birds. It is the prime example of what can be achieved with control and protection. Flamingoes are now non-breeding visitors.

SUMMER: Montagu's Harrier, Kentish Plover, Black-winged Stilt, Stone-curlew, Hoopoe, Bee-eater, Short-toed Lark, Reed Warbler, Cetti's Warbler, Melodious Warbler, Sardinian Warbler.

PASSAGE: Ferruginous Duck, Osprey, Crane, Flamingo, Marsh Sandpiper, Red-necked Phalarope, Black Tern, White-winged Black Tern, Bluethroat.

WINTER: Black-throated Diver, Shelduck, Pintail, Long-tailed Duck, Smew, Eider, Greylag Goose, Spoonbill, Great White Egret, Sandwich Tern, Moustached Warbler.

ACCESS: Much of the lagoon can be seen from the road along the isthmus that holds the town of Orbetello. The WWF reserve may be entered by permit, for which there is a small charge. Contact the WWF for current details prior to departure.

ROUTE: Orbetello is 148 km (92 miles) north of Rome on the Via Aurelia.

Po Delta and Venice

The River Po reaches the sea in northern Italy between Venice and Ravenna and a glance at a map should be sufficient to convince anyone that this is a good birding area. In fact, the whole of the coastline from the Yugoslavian border is broken by lagoons and marshes, though those in the south are generally regarded as the best. Thus the Venetian lagoons, the Valli di Comacchio and the delta itself are treated here as one huge birding centre.

Everyone, they say, should see Venice before they die; and it is the most beautiful place, despite shark-like gondoliers, rip-off restaurants and far too many tourists. It is also nice for the family birder to be able to lace culture with some excellent birding. Venice stands on an island on the landward side of a huge lagoon, almost cut off from the sea by sandbars. Regular boat services connect the various islands with the city and the main beach resorts, and offer easy access to many of the better spots, plus the chance of viewing passage Black Tern. Much can, however, be seen from the network of surrounding roads.

This is still a major staging post for duck, with Garganey often abundant in spring, and a large and varied wintering population. Waders too are regular migrants, though breeding birds suffer from excessive disturbance.

To the south, the Po delta is a huge maze of channels, islands and marshes and one of the most important wildfowl wintering grounds in Europe. Some areas have been given reserve status, but there are no restrictions on access save to the private fishing reserves. In 1981 Pygmy Cormorants bred, but the more usual breeding population includes Bittern, Avocet, Stilt, Little Gull and Caspian Tern. A wide variety of species occurs on passage, including Spoonbill, Lesser Spotted Eagle and Terek and Marsh Sandpipers, though there is no information about the regularity (or otherwise) of the eagle. Winter brings divers, Great White Egret and a splendid and varied duck population. The delta can be penetrated by various routes, via Porto Talle, Bonelli, Goro and Pila Contarina. Boat exploration (easily rented) is recommended, though personally I have always found boats a frustrating form of birding transport.

Further south, the Valli di Comacchio is a huge, salty-brackish lagoon surrounded by marshes and smaller waters. It is a primary resort of duck, and regularly attracts a good collection of passage waders and terns. In summer, there are Stilts, Avocets and Pratincoles here. The lake can be worked from the road between Ostellato and Porto Garibaldi, and southwards off this from the road that crosses the lagoon from Spina to Alfonsine.

There are so many marshes and lakes along this coast that the whole area would repay an intensive survey. Full checklists for any site would be most welcome.

SUMMER: Bittern, Avocet, Black-winged Stilt, Collared Pratincole, Little Gull, Mediterranean Gull, Common Tern, Caspian Tern, Whiskered Tern.

WINTER: Red-throated Diver, Black-throated Diver, Great White Egret, Wigeon, Pintail, Shoveler, Pochard, Tufted Duck, Ferruginous Duck, Scaup, Eider, Golden-eye, Red-breasted Merganser.

PASSAGE: White Stork, Spoonbill, Garganey, Osprey, Lesser Spotted Eagle, Spotted Redshank, Terek Sandpiper, Marsh Sandpiper, Ruff, Temminck's Stint, Jack Snipe, Stone-curlew, Grasshopper Warbler, Aquatic Warbler, Bluethroat.

ACCESS: As detailed above under individual sections. Outside Venice, accommodation is available at reasonable prices.

ROUTE: Venice airport or package holidays to the Lido.

Sardinia

Sardinia may be a Mediterranean island, but it should not be imagined that a week at a single resort is sufficient for a thorough exploration. This is a big island and one that should not be taken lightly. There are some splendid marshes and saltpans, some excellent mountain areas and some rocky coasts that deserve more attention than they get. Though much of the recent holiday development on Sardinia has taken place in the northeast, the main airport and capital lies in the south at Cagliari. In many ways this is fortunate, for it is the southern half of Sardinia that holds the best birds.

Oristano, on the west coast 92 km (57 miles) north of Cagliari, is an old town with some really excellent wetlands nearby. There are lagoons and saltpans at Cabras, which is handily reached from the coast at Marina di Torre Grande — the ideal base. Avocet, Stilt and wildfowl make this an internationally important wetland, and there are even Purple Gallinule and White-headed Duck. Passage brings a wider variety of species, including good numbers of waders, Eleonora's Falcon, Flamingo and Spoonbill, while in winter White-tailed Eagle and Peregrine are more or less regular.

Inland, there are two major areas of interest: the Giara di Gesturi and Monti del Gennargentu. The latter is the highest point of Sardinia and has Griffon and Egyptian Vultures and Golden and Bonelli's Eagles, while the former is a plateau with wild ponies and Little Bustard.

Visitors to Sardinia will, inevitably, hope for those two Mediterranean island specialities, Marmora's Warbler and Eleonora's Falcon. There are some 200–300 pairs of falcons grouped into two main sites: in the east around the Capo di M. Santu and in the south near Carbonia. The latter is easiest of access, with good colonies on the isle of San Pietro. This large island is, in fact, worthy of more than a cursory once-over. It has huge sea cliffs and a hinterland of scrub with considerable areas of pine woodland. Eleonora's Falcon is easily found, but there are also Bonelli's Eagle and Peregrine here, along with Audouin's Gull, Marmora's Warbler and Storm Petrel. The more widespread Scops Owl, Alpine Swift, Woodchat Shrike, Spectacled Warbler and Blue Rock Thrush make San Pietro a highly desirable holiday base. In any case, the lagoons and saltpans at the head of the Golfo di Palmas are good for marsh birds, including Flamingo.

One of the very best areas of Sardinia is, however, centred on Cagliari itself. Here, within a few kilometres of the airport and town, are extensive areas of saltpans to the west and the remarkable pool of Molentargius to the east. The latter covers some 500 ha (1235 acres) of reed marsh and open water and has been recognised as a wetland of international importance. As a result, hunting is banned, and both Cattle Egret and Glossy Ibis bred in 1986. Flamingo, Purple Gallinule, Stilt, Avocet, Slender-billed Gull, Pratincole and a variety of warblers all occur. There are often arriving and departing Eleonora's here, and in winter Spotted Eagle is not unknown.

Eleonora's Falcon

Sardinia has some of the best birding places in Italy and is certainly worthy of more attention than it has received to date.

SUMMER: Storm Petrel, Flamingo, Little Egret, Purple Heron, Glossy Ibis, Purple Gallinule, Griffon Vulture, Egyptian Vulture, Golden Eagle, Bonelli's Eagle, Short-toed Eagle, Eleonora's Falcon, Peregrine, Avocet, Black-winged Stilt, Kentish Plover, Collared Pratincole, Slender-billed Gull, Audouin's Gull, Scops Owl, Bee-eater, Hoopoe, Pallid Swift, Alpine Swift, Blue Rock Thrush, Marmora's Warbler, Sardinian Warbler, Cetti's Warbler, Great Reed Warbler, Cirl Bunting, Citril Finch, Spanish Sparrow.

WINTER: Flamingo, White-tailed Eagle, Spotted Eagle, Osprey, Moustached Warbler.

PASSAGE: White Stork, Spoonbill, Ruddy Shelduck, Red-crested Pochard, Ferruginous Duck, Osprey, Pallid Harrier, Red-footed Falcon, Eleonora's Falcon, Crane, Caspian Tern.

ACCESS: Oristano is 92 km (57 miles) northwest of Cagliari on Route 131. A minor road leaves to Cabras and to Marina di Torre Grande. The lagoons and saltpans can be seen from the road between the two.

Golfo di Palmas lies south of Carbonia to the east of the road to San Antioco. The lagoons and saltpans are adjacent. Local exploration to the isle of San Pietro for Eleonora's Falcon etc via the ferry between Calasetta and Carloforte. Cagliari is the main town of Sardinia, and there are lagoons and saltpans to the west viewed from the main coast road towards Pula. The pool of Molentargius is reached via a footpath near the IP petrol station in Cagliari, or along the drainage canal adjacent to Quartu S. Elena.

Giara di Gesturi is reached by turning eastwards off the A131 south of Oristano at Uras. Continue through Ales to Escovedu and Senis. Gennargentu is found by

137

continuing eastwards after Gesturi to Laconi and then turning northward. After several kilometres turn right on to Route 295 to Aritzo, then exploring to the south (right).

Monte Limbara, in the northeast, can be reached via roads toward the radar station. It holds many altitude birds including Blue Rock Thrush and Cirl Bunting, as well as Marmora's Warbler.

ROUTE: Sardinia has regular international flights, plus many ferries from mainland Italy.

River Tellaro

Sicily, even more than the rest of Italy, has been largely ignored by birders. At first sight this may not seem so surprising. The idea of wasting a holiday looking for non-existent birds being pursued by shotgun-toting mafiosi does not have a great deal of appeal. Yet Sicily is rugged, mountainous country, with large unfrequented areas of countryside, and is on a known migration route, particularly of birds of prey.

Fortunately, one area of the island has been worked in spring and produced a good collection of both local and migrant species. The River Tellaro rises in the mountains and reaches the sea at the southeast corner of Sicily on the Gulf of Noto. For the last kilometres of its length it is fringed with reeds, while at the mouth there are a few small pools used by migrant waders in the mornings before the nude bathers arrive. Behind the beach are areas of scrub and stony fields, with some olive and almond groves further inland.

Squacco and Purple Herons regularly use the river, while Little Egret, Spoonbill and Little Bittern also occur. If you are lucky, a flock of Glossy Ibis that have wintered in Tunisia may pass through. Raptors vary day by day, but harriers are regular and other species do occur. Waders are regular in small numbers (perhaps the lagoons 10 km/6 miles south might produce more?), while gulls include regular Little and terns regular Sandwich. Warblers and chats pass through and local species include Cetti's, Sardinian, Fan-tailed and Nightingale.

Elsewhere in Sicily there are still Lanners, but no longer Black Vulture.

SPRING: Cory's Shearwater, Little Bittern, Squacco Heron, Little Egret, Purple Heron, Glossy Ibis, Spoonbill, Garganey, Marsh Harrier, Black Kite, Montagu's Harrier, Osprey, Little Ringed Plover, Kentish Plover, Little Stint, Green Sandpiper, Wood Sandpiper, Common Sandpiper, Little Gull, Sandwich Tern, Common Tern, Pallid Swift, Hoopoe, Short-toed Lark, Crested Lark, Tree Pipit, Red-throated Pipit, Woodchat Shrike, Hooded Crow, Cetti's Warbler, Great Reed Warbler, Sardinian Warbler, Subalpine Warbler, Fan-tailed Warbler, Black-eared Wheatear, Nightingale, Short-toed Treecreeper, Serin, Cirl Bunting.

ACCESS: A road runs southward from Avola as far as the Hotel Eloro, then turns inland to join the Pachino road. A path leads from the Eloro to the mouth of the Tellaro where the wader pools are located. Walk inland along the river, with tracks to the right through scrub, fields and groves.

ROUTE: Catania, to the north, has an airport.

MOROCCO

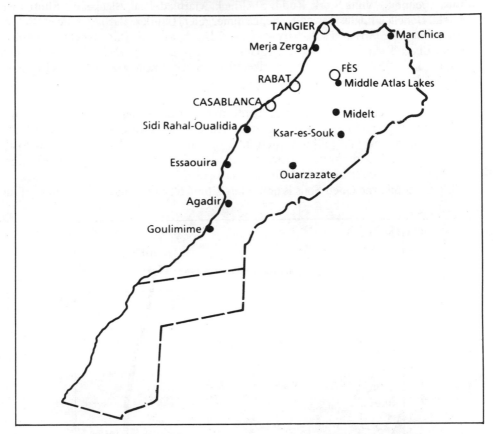

Agadir

Devastated by an earthquake, Agadir has been rebuilt as a modern city, with beach hotels offering holidays to the sun-worshippers of northern Europe. Fortunately, there are several excellent birding areas within comfortable reach of the city and many south Moroccan specialities can be located. Without leaving Agadir, it is possible to see Little Swift, Bulbul, Moussier's Redstart and House Bunting, but excursions northwards to Cap Rhir and the Tamri estuary, inland to Taroudannt, and southwards to the Oued Sous and the Oued Massa will all prove highly rewarding.

Likely species include Lanner and Barbary Falcon, Flamingo, Audouin's Gull, Ruddy Shelduck, plus hosts of waders and warblers and the chance of Chanting Goshawk, Black-headed Bush Shrike and Red-necked Nightjar.

For those who do not mind long journeys in search of their birds, a drive inland to Aoulouz brings one to one of the few remaining colonies of Bald Ibis left in the world. To the north lies the rugged Tizi-n-Test pass, with Lammergeier, Long-legged Buzzard and Short-toed Eagle.

139

SUMMER: Cory's Shearwater, Flamingo, Little Egret, Cattle Egret, Glossy Ibis, Bald Ibis, Spoonbill, White Stork, Ruddy Shelduck, Marbled Teal, Black Kite, Short-toed Eagle, Bonelli's Eagle, Tawny Eagle, Lammergeier, Lanner, Barbary Falcon, Peregrine, Chanting Goshawk, Barbary Partridge, Black-winged Stilt, Avocet, Audouin's Gull, Black Tern, Roller, Bee-eater, Common Bulbul, Little Swift, Brown-throated Sand Martin, Black-headed Bush Shrike, Black-eared Wheatear, Moussier's Redstart, House Bunting.

ACCESS: The road northwards from Agadir to Cap Rhir passes several small beaches where the gulls and terns should be examined with some care — Audouin's Gull is regular. Cap Rhir may produce interesting seabirds and the Tamri estuary is easily viewed from the road: egrets, waders, more Audouin's, Moussier's and possible Lanner or Barbary Falcon. It is only an hour back to Agadir.

   To the south, the Oued Sous is only a few kilometres away and is the estuary of the

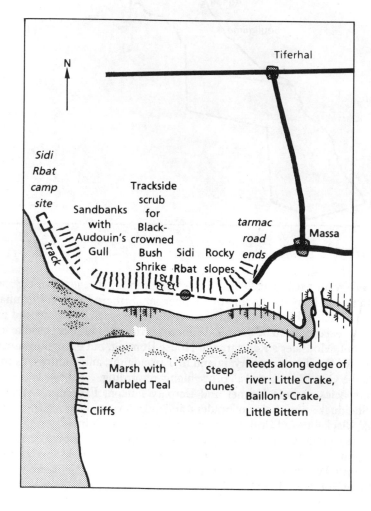

Sous River which runs inland to Taroudannt and beyond. Flamingo, Spoonbill and waders are good here, and Brown-throated Sand Martin and Bush Shrike can be found. About 1 km (just over ½ mile) south of the airport, there is a track which leads to Hotel Pyramid and the estuary. About 30 km (18½ miles) to the south is the Oued Massa, a large lagoon adjacent to the sea, which has gained an extraordinary reputation for its ability to build a big bird list. Ruddy Shelduck, Marbled Teal, Bonelli's Eagle, Flamingo, Spotted Crake, Black-bellied Sandgrouse and masses of waders are among the attractions, with Bush Shrike among the adjacent eucalyptus. The approach is via the main road, turning right towards Massa village at Tiferhal and continuing along the valley to the sea.

Inland, the grove-like countryside around Taroudannt is the most reliable area for Chanting Goshawk, as well as a possible one for Tawny Eagle. Some 5 km (3 miles) south of Taroudannt, the main road crosses the Oued Sous. Soon after this a track leads left past a rubbish tip, and after 1.5 km (1 mile) a row of trees on the left has Red-necked Nightjar and Bush Shrike. Continue for 80 km (50 miles) to Aoulouz for Bald Ibis, Lanner and Barbary Falcon. Stop at the bridge and walk northwards along the western edge of the gorge for 2 km (1¼ miles) to the colony of Bald Ibis. Alternatively, turn left 30 km (18½ miles) earlier to Tizi-n-Test for mountain species.

ROUTE: Agadir airport.

Essaouira

Under colonial rule Essaouira was called Mogador, and the long, low island offshore is still generally referred to as Mogador Island. This island has long been famous as the only non-Mediterranean breeding site of Eleonora's Falcon, though another colony has now been discovered further south along the Moroccan coast. From May to October, the birds can be seen hawking over the island from the mainland coast. Boat trips can be arranged . . . but let's try to discourage the practice. In any case, the falcons regularly frequent a wadi just south of the town where they bathe among the mass of gulls that loaf in the area.

This wadi is actually a little gem, with open water and muddy edges encouraging a good variety of waders to pause on passage, along with egrets and the occasional Spoonbill. In the upper parts of the wadi there are areas of dense thorn scrub, and here are many warblers plus Rufous Bush Chat and Black-crowned Bush Shrike. Another area for this latter species is 12 km (7½ miles) north of the town on the main road.

AUTUMN: Little Egret, Spoonbill, Eleonora's Falcon, Osprey, Barbary Partridge, Little Ringed Plover, Green Sandpiper, Greenshank, Little Stint, Mediterranean Gull, Black Tern, Crested Lark, Red-rumped Swallow, Little Swift, Rufous Bush Chat, Hoopoe, Great Grey Shrike, Woodchat Shrike, Black-crowned Bush Shrike, Cetti's Warbler, Melodious Warbler, Pied Flycatcher, Serin, House Bunting.

ACCESS: Essaouira lies on the main coast road 192 km (120 miles) north of Agadir. The old town is picturesque and, from the quay, views of Mogador Island (and falcons) can be had. The wadi lies 2 km (1¼ miles) south of the town and is easily found on tracks leading to the beach.

ROUTE: Agadir airport.

Goulimime and the South

Beyond Goulimime (Guelmine), the landscape gets progressively more arid and the roads more treacherous and ill-maintained. At Tan-Tan Plage it reaches the sea, and then sticks close to it until reaching Tarfaya and the border with Spanish Sahara. Though a border crossing is indicated on maps, the Spanish Sahara is not a country that one can enter easily and simply turning up is unlikely to do much good. Road conditions apart, there is no problem in motoring south as far as Puerto Cansado; indeed, there is much to recommend it. Here there are decent birds that are otherwise decidedly awkward. The typical larks include Bar-tailed Desert, Thick-billed, Bifasciated and Temminck's Horned, while the wheatears include Desert, Black and Red-rumped. The only other area for many of these birds lies east of Ouarzazate. Sandgrouse of three species, Cream-coloured Courser, Trumpeter Finch, Brown-necked Raven and the highly elusive Scrub Warbler await the intrepid in this area.

There are also two fine wetlands, the Oued Chebeika and the lagoon of Puerto Cansado, that offer a wide variety of wetland birds at all seasons. The latter is particularly important for waders, with over 100,000 birds in winter including huge flocks of Knot, Dunlin and Redshank together with a staggering 8,000 Little Stints; it also holds the largest known flock (500–800) of Slender-billed Curlews. Oued Chebeika too holds many wintering waders, but is also known as the stronghold of Flamingo and Scrub Warbler.

PASSAGE: Sooty Shearwater, Little Egret, Flamingo, Bonelli's Eagle, Long-legged Buzzard, Osprey, Lanner, Whimbrel, Slender-billed Curlew, Black-tailed Godwit, Wood Sandpiper, Spotted Redshank, Little Stint, Curlew Sandpiper, Ruff, Avocet, Collared Pratincole, Cream-coloured Courser, Audouin's Gull, Slender-billed Gull, Caspian Tern, Pin-tailed Sandgrouse, Black-bellied Sandgrouse, Spotted Sandgrouse, Bar-tailed Desert Lark, Thekla Lark, Bifasciated Lark, Thick-billed Lark, Brown-necked Raven, Desert Wheatear, Red-rumped Wheatear, Black Wheatear, Scrub Warbler, Fan-tailed Warbler, Trumpeter Finch, House Bunting.

ACCESS: The road from Bou-Izakarn southward produces desert birds, with best numbers over the long stretch (120 km/75 miles) between Goulimime and Tan-Tan. For sandgrouse, larks and wheatears there are no particular places, but Brown-necked Raven is often on the Goulimime rubbish tip and Coursers are most frequently seen around this town. Scrub Warbler is a Chebeika speciality, though it has been found elsewhere, while the waders and seabirds are confined to the two wetland areas.

ROUTE: The nearest airport is Agadir, and it is quite possible to drive to Puerto Cansado in a day. However, this is desert country and it is foolhardy to go ill-prepared and ill-equipped. Some birders have done the Chebeika estuary in a family saloon with camping equipment; it would seem a better idea to take a 4 × 4 drive and preferably two vehicles. Camping is essential, and food, water and spare petrol should be carried.

Ksar-es-Souk and the South

Ksar-es-Souk is a major crossroads, with main roads leading to the four major points of the compass. Birders on the grand Moroccan tour inevitably pass through, for to the north lies Midelt with Dupont's Lark; to the west lies Boulmane and all the larks and chats; to the south lies Erfoud with real desert species; while the road to the east to Boudenib remains unexplored. It is the road into the desert with which we are concerned here. This route follows the line of a major wadi, with palms and occasional oases. Throughout the area there are most of the larks, chats, birds of prey, sandgrouse and so on, but the really intrepid drive southwards through Erfoud to Rissani and on to Merzouga. This oasis is really quite impossible to find without a guide; hire one in Erfoud. Even then, there is no guarantee that your vehicle will not end up bogged down in sand. Surprisingly enough, there is a hotel at the end of the trek — Hotel Merzouga.

SUMMER: Houbara Bustard, Arabian Bustard, Eagle Owl, Egyptian Nightjar, Blue-cheeked Bee-eater, Bar-tailed Desert Lark, Bifasciated Lark, Fulvous Babbler, Desert Wheatear, White-crowned Black Wheatear, Desert Warbler, Scrub Warbler, Desert Sparrow.

ACCESS: Along the way south from Ksar-es-Souk, watch for Brown-necked Raven, Fulvous Babbler (at Source Bleue de Meski), Mourning Wheatear and Blue-cheeked Bee-eater. Beyond Erfoud a road leads westward to Jorf, and 10 km (6¼ miles) beyond this passes through an area of heavily broken, scrub-covered land. This has Desert and White-crowned Black Wheatears, Bar-tailed Desert and Bifasciated Larks, Scrub and Desert Warblers plus Houbara Bustard and Eagle Owl. Also starting at Erfoud is the track direct to Merzouga running alongside the dunes. Strange as it may seem, the first café among the dunes has a birders' log which, according to one group, is 'a gripping read'. This is one site for Desert Sparrow. There are also irregular sites for this high-value species 300 m (330 yards) north of Merzouga (there are two villages — try them both), and another in an isolated palm 1 km (1000 yards) east of the road, 7 km (4¼ miles) north of Merzouga. Desert Warbler may be found where the tarmac road ends between Erfoud and Merzouga, and two other high-value species — Egyptian Nightjar and Arabian Bustard (as well as Houbara) — are also worth the searching. The nightjar is best located in headlights at night, while the bustards just require searching and luck. Even if the specialities do not appear, the town is excellent for migrants and has been thoroughly enjoyed by all who have braved the trek.

ROUTE: Via Ksar-es-Souk or from Tinedad on Route 3451.

Mar Chica and Oued Moulouya

Mar Chica is a large lagoon, virtually separated from the sea, on the Mediterranean coast not too far from the Algerian border. The Oued Moulouya reaches the same coast about 70 km (43 miles) to the east, after rising high in the Middle Atlas. Between the two is a virtual desert of sandy scrub that is difficult to penetrate and which remains largely unexplored by birders. The resort town of Nador lies on the Mar Chica and is an excellent base for exploration of the whole area.

The Mar Chica attracts gulls, terns and waders and is a regular stop-over for a number of Ospreys. All the species that one would expect to pass through the Mediterranean on passage appear, often in good numbers. Stilts are often the dominant wader, closely followed by Black-tailed Godwit, Greenshank, Wood Sandpiper and Little Stint. Black and Caspian Terns also appear regularly. At the eastern end of Chica lies an area of saltpans at Arkmane, where all of these species can be found.

The mouth of the Oued Moulouya is marked by a series of lagoons with reeds, making a freshwater complement to the saline habitats of Chica. Here Purple Heron and Little Bittern can be added to the list, along with Purple Gallinule, Marbled Teal and a good selection of warblers. Just offshore lie the Chafarinas Islands, a noted breeding site of Audouin's Gull. These birds are regular along the adjacent beach.

PASSAGE: Purple Heron, Little Egret, Little Bittern, Marbled Teal, Pintail, Shoveler, Marsh Harrier, Osprey, Water Rail, Purple Gallinule, Bar-tailed Godwit, Black-tailed Godwit, Wood Sandpiper, Spotted Redshank, Greenshank, Ruff, Little Stint, Curlew Sandpiper, Black-winged Stilt, Audouin's Gull, Slender-billed Gull, Black Tern, Caspian Tern, Kingfisher, Great Grey Shrike, Common Bulbul, Rufous Bush Chat, Cetti's Warbler, Fan-tailed Warbler.

ACCESS: Birds such as the terns and Osprey can be seen from Nador itself. About 6 km (nearly 4 miles) south of the town, a road to the left leads to Kariet-Arkmane and the saltpans. From here, a track leads eastward for 40 km (25 miles) to Ras-el-Mar, opposite the Chafarinas Islands. This track may or may not be passable; indeed, it may even now be a proper road. In any case, it is a simple matter to detour via Selouane to the mouth of the Oued Moulouya.

ROUTE: Melilla airport is near Nador and there are ferry connections to Málaga and Almería in Spain.

Merja Zerga

Merja Zerga is a large shallow lagoon surrounded by damp grassland and marshes on the Moroccan coast between Tangier and Rabat. It is connected to the sea via a narrow channel through the dunes at the resort of Moulay-Bou-Selham, and lies at the very heart of the seasonally flooded area of the Rharb. Though these seasonal wetlands are noted mainly for their concentration of wildfowl and waders, Merja Zerga is attractive at all seasons. It has a wide range of breeding birds, though these are as yet little worked, it is exciting during migration, and it even has other outstanding sites within striking distance. Not surprisingly, it is a compulsory stop for all visiting birders. Egrets, storks and Flamingo are regular, and the variety and number of waders can be outstanding: 5,000 Black-tailed Godwit, 1,000 Little Stint, 400 Greenshank, 250 Spotted Redshank, 50 Wood Sandpiper plus thousands of the more common species all on a single autumn day indicates the possibilities here. Terns regularly include Lesser Crested and Caspian, with both sometimes into double figures. Slender-billed Curlews do occur and may reach quite decent numbers in winter.

To the north, beyond Larache, is an area of cork groves covering rolling countryside where Black-winged Kite is regularly seen, along with other species typical of that habitat. African Marsh Owl has even been seen in this area.

To the south, beyond Mehdiya Plage, lies the small coastal lagoon of Sidi Bourhaba. As well as being a haunt of Marsh Owl, Marbled Teal and Crested Coot, this delightful water regularly collects a good number of migrants and should not be missed.

PASSAGE: Little Egret, Cattle Egret, White Stork, Glossy Ibis, Flamingo, Shoveler, Pintail, Marbled Teal, Black-winged Kite, Long-legged Buzzard, Osprey, Hobby, Little Ringed Plover, Kentish Plover, Slender-billed Curlew, Black-tailed Godwit, Wood Sandpiper, Spotted Redshank, Greenshank, Ruff, Little Stint, Temminck's Stint, Curlew Sandpiper, Black-winged Stilt, Avocet, Little Gull, Black Tern, Whiskered Tern, Gull-billed Tern, Caspian Tern, Lesser Crested Tern, Fan-tailed Warbler, Subalpine Warbler, Short-toed Lark.

ACCESS: Moulay-Bou-Selham is a good base, and gives access to the north side of the lagoon and the river exit to the sea. Boats can be taken out into the lagoon, but are seldom rewarding. There is a road inland and a turn right (south) towards Kénitra, both of which give access to marshes. Continuing southwards, a village with a line of tall trees appears on the right-hand side. A sharp right leads into this and continues on a track to the southern side of the lagoon and probably the best viewpoints. Drive through the village without stopping — everyone claims to be the warden and in need of financial assistance.

The cork woods north of Larache are best watched where the road rises about 20–23 km (12–14 miles) north of the town. The Lac de Sidi Bourhaba lies on the coast south of Mehdiya Plage, itself just west of Kénitra. There is a causeway across the marsh at the northern end of the lake. This is the spot to watch for Marsh Owl at dusk.

ROUTE: Rabat has an airport, but Tangier is nearer.

Middle Atlas Lakes

To the northeast of Ifrane lies a series of mainly small, shallow lakes with a narrow growth of emergent vegetation sufficient to give shelter to a number of breeding birds. They also attract an interesting population of duck on passage and in winter, along with good numbers of waders and terns. Outstanding are the small numbers of Crested Coot that breed here, though they are often difficult to locate among thousands of their more

145

common relatives. Ruddy Shelduck and Marbled Teal are both more numerous and can usually be located without too much difficulty. The main lakes are Dayet Aaoua, Dayet Hachlaf with its reedbeds, and Dayet Afourgan. There are others in the same area, but these are the most generally visited. Demoiselle Crane is a speciality here, though decidedly difficult to locate.

The best lake of all, however, is much further north just west of Fès at Douyiet. This excellent water has all the attributes of the others, but has the advantage of being very near a major city. Fès itself is notable for the huge colony of Alpine Swifts that nest in the walls of the old city: tens of thousands (?) at dusk.

PASSAGE: Great Crested Grebe, Black-necked Grebe, Purple Heron, Cattle Egret, Little Egret, Night Heron, Ruddy Shelduck, Marbled Teal, Marsh Harrier, Barbary Partridge, Crested Coot, Demoiselle Crane, Little Ringed Plover, Black-tailed Godwit, Greenshank, Black-winged Stilt, Avocet, Black Tern, Whiskered Tern, Alpine Swift, Levaillant's Woodpecker, Woodlark, Bluethroat, Fan-tailed Warbler, Spanish Sparrow, Raven.

ACCESS: Leave Fès on the Meknès road and stop at Douyiet after 20 km (12½ miles). The other lakes are best worked from Ifrane; all are passed by roads. If short of time, Dayet Aaoua is conveniently situated off the main road (P24) towards Fès. Turn right at the junction with Route 4630 and then right again beside the lake. The rows of trees

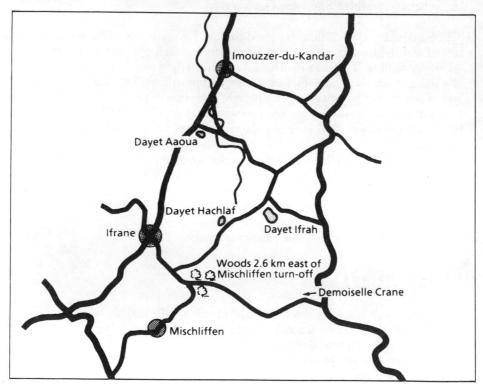

along this track and the woods to the right have Levaillant's Woodpecker. This bird can also be seen in the woods around Mischliffen.

The Demoiselle area lies between the P20 and Route S309 southeast of Ifrane, but many fail to find them.

ROUTE: Fès has an airport, but the area is usually worked on the way to or from the area south of the Atlas via Gorges du Ziz. See Midelt.

Midelt

Midelt is no more than a convenient centre for access to a number of specific bird spots that do not, in themselves, merit separate entries. These places are, however, far from unimportant; they are simply highly specific. To the south lies the Tizi-n-Talrhenit, the pass leading to Ksar-es-Souk. Tristram's Warbler can be seen 2 km (1¼ miles) north of the summit, along with Crimson-winged Finch. Most will explore this on their way, rather than make a specific excursion from Midelt, but it should not be ignored. Here there are Lammergeier, Lanner, Long-legged Buzzard, Chough, Moussier's Redstart and others.

To the west is the spectacular Cirque de Jaffar, with a strangely north European type of fauna that includes Woodpigeon, Great Spotted Woodpecker, Woodlark, Magpie, Jay and Robin. Here too, however, is a concentration of Moussier's Redstart and Tristram's Warbler. Among others there are often good flocks of Rock Sparrow.

To the north of Midelt, the countryside becomes a gently rolling steppe with large

Moussier's Redstart

clumps of halfa grass. Here on the Plateau de l'Arid is the best spot for Dupont's Lark. The technique is to sit in a vehicle and watch carefully for the walking bird. In despair, some have walked (run?) up the hillside to catch a glimpse of this elusive species. Try kilometre stone 26 or the track running westwards signposted to Ait Illousen 3 km (nearly 2 miles) south of Zeida. About 1 km (just over ½ mile) down this track is a quarry. Turn south and wait. Cream-coloured Courser and sandgrouse, Red-rumped Wheatear and Thick-billed Lark are also possibilities here.

Further north still, the road to Azrou leads through the Col du Zad — worth a stop — before passing along the Foum Kheneg toward Timhadite. This is another of the few spots for Bald Ibis, though here, as elsewhere, the recent decline may have put an end to the colony.

SUMMER: Lammergeier, Red Kite, Long-legged Buzzard, Lanner, Black-bellied Sandgrouse, Bald Ibis, Thekla Lark, Woodlark, Lesser Short-toed Lark, Dupont's Lark, Great Grey Shrike, Moussier's Redstart, Tristram's Warbler, Tawny Pipit, Serin, Crimson-winged Finch, Rock Sparrow.

ACCESS: All of the areas are easily found along the roads in the directions indicated, except the Cirque de Jaffar which lies southwest of Midelt on a well-marked minor road. Dupont's can be looked for anywhere about 26 km (16 miles) north of Midelt, but patience is a necessity.

ROUTE: The area lies on the road between Ifrane and Ksar-es-Souk. It is thus somewhat artificially divided from the lakes of the Middle Atlas near Ifrane.

Ouarzazate and the South

Ouarzazate is a large 'oasis' town south of the High Atlas and an excellent headquarters for exploring the arid lands along the northern edge of the Sahara. There are good roads in several directions, giving access to a wide range of habitats and offering the chance of finding many species typical of the area. For our purposes, the most important areas lie to the southeast, east and northwest along the roads to Zagora, Tinehir and Marrakech. All three can be worked from Ouarzazate, though the distances are significant. Many of the species here are widespread and easily found throughout the area: Desert Lark, Bar-tailed Desert Lark, Mourning Wheatear, White-crowned Black Wheatear, Black Wheatear and House Bunting can all be found without difficulty. Other species are more localised and must be more definitely sought after.

The main areas to visit are Tizi-n-Tichka, the high pass through which the Ouarzazate–Marrakech road winds its way and where Lammergeier is a possibility; Zagora, where the huge dunes of the northern Sahara can be seen and where the riverside palms hold Fulvous Babbler and Scrub Warbler; Boulmane, where sand-grouse and wheatears abound and where there is access to Houbara Bustard country; and the Gorge du Todra, which has Pale Crag Martin among its specialities. Ouarzazate itself has areas of tamarisk and a rubbish tip, neither of which should be ignored.

Though the breeding birds of the area and the possibilities of seeing all the wheatears

Little Swifts

and larks are the main attraction, the passage of warblers and chats through the area cannot be ignored in either spring or autumn.

SUMMER: Cattle Egret, Black Kite, Long-legged Buzzard, Booted Eagle, Egyptian Vulture, Lammergeier, Lanner, Houbara Bustard, Cream-coloured Courser, Coronetted Sandgrouse, Rock Dove, Little Swift, Bee-eater, Blue-cheeked Bee-eater, Roller, Hoopoe, Shore Lark, Temminck's Horned Lark, Bifasciated Lark, Short-toed Lark, Lesser Short-toed Lark, Desert Lark, Bar-tailed Desert Lark, Thick-billed Lark, Thekla Lark, Pale Crag Martin, Common Bulbul, Scrub Warbler, Blue Rock Thrush, Wheatear (including Seebohm's), Desert Wheatear, Black-eared Wheatear, Mourning Wheatear, Red-rumped Wheatear, White-crowned Black Wheatear, Black Wheatear, Moussier's Redstart, Rufous Bush Chat, Fulvous Babbler, House Bunting, Rock Bunting, Trumpeter Finch, Chough, Alpine Chough, Raven.

ACCESS: The Tizi-n-Tichka is the major pass across the High Atlas. Just below the pass on the southern side, a road leads eastward to Telouet, which is a beautiful valley replete with palace and frequented by tourists. Bald Ibis has been recorded and White Storks breed. Lammergeier, Chough and Alpine Chough, Blue Rock Thrush and Shore Lark may be seen on or near the pass. North of the pass there is a cluster of shops, with a hairpin bend a further 400 m (¼ mile) beyond. Walk left along the ridge for Crimson-winged Finch.

Zagora and the Drâa valley are easily reached, and a good exploration of the Agdz area should produce Babbler, Bulbul, Scrub Warbler and Blue-cheeked Bee-eater.

Boulmane lies east. Beyond the town and just past a garage there is a track which leads southward towards Tagdilt. After a few kilometres there is a major fork. The land between the arms of the fork holds the major concentration of Red-rumped Wheatear, Temminck's Horned Lark and Coronetted Sandgrouse. Continue southwards on the

149

left-hand track for 25 km (15½ miles) in the search for Houbara. Along the way, stop at a small oasis for Trumpeter Finch. A further Houbara area lies 20 km (12½ miles) west of El Kelaa (west of Boulmane) at telegraph pole no. 1421, where the wadi should be explored.

Gorge du Todra lies above Tinehir in a steep escarpment. It can be driven (by the intrepid), and the palm groves and rocky cliffs hold a good variety of species including Pale Crag Martin, Rock Dove, Black Wheatear and Grey Wagtail. Higher up, the road crosses the river from right to left. Some 2.5 km (1½ miles) further is an area of scrub for Tristram's Warbler, as well as Bonelli's Eagle and Lanner.

Several of the specialities are awkward to find and have not yet been mentioned under specific places. Of these, Trumpeter Finch and Thick-billed and Bifasciated Larks will be found by stopping a few kilometres east of Ouarzazate and simply walking out in a large loop over the surrounding plains and broken wadis. Of the three, Thick-billed often proves the most elusive. Moussier's Redstart can be found along the road between Tichka and Ouarzazate, and Lanner and Long-legged Buzzard are often seen between Boulmane and Tinehir.

ROUTE: The airport at Agadir is the gateway to the south of the Atlas, though Marrakech is nearer and has the advantage of a direct route into the Tizi-n-Tichka.

Sidi Rahal — Oualidia

Between El Jadida and Cap Beddouza, the coastline runs straight and true from the northeast to the southwest. Here huge dune beaches have been built up, broken here and there by rocky outcrops. These dune systems have cut off an almost continuous stretch of marshland between Sidi Rahal and Oualidia, an area that for some reason has escaped receiving a common birders' name. Over the years these marshes have been converted to rough grazing and saltpans, though in the north and the south the sea maintains access and two intertidal lagoons have developed. Thus, the landscape varies from virtually dry fields intersected by reed-lined dykes to open shoreline.

This huge area is one of Morocco's outstanding wetlands, offering a vast range of species to those prepared to explore thoroughly. There are egrets, storks, waders and terns, as well as many warblers and chats. Among the regular species are Slender-billed Curlew. This bird is, of course, one of the scarcest of species, and is found here only during the late autumn and winter. Even then this is not their major Moroccan haunt and numbers are small. Probably the best and easiest area for this bird is at the mouth of the river at Azemmour, where a scrub-dune area south of the river mouth is excellent for migrants of all types. Though seabirds can often be seen resting on the embankments between the saltpans, most tend to roost either on the beach or on the sandy spits found at the two saltwater inlets. Gulls and terns are often good, with Audouin's Gull and Royal and Lesser Crested Terns present in small numbers. Skuas of several species are often seen in autumn, and there are sometimes good flocks of large shearwaters feeding close inshore. In fact, all the regular shearwaters, terns and skuas may be seen in a single good day.

South of the main area lies Cap Beddouza, a rocky headland that has proved a fine seawatching site. Barbary Falcon is regular and, in autumn, the large shearwaters may be present in substantial flocks.

PASSAGE: Black-necked Grebe, Cory's Shearwater, Great Shearwater, Sooty Shearwater, Balearic Shearwater, Gannet, Purple Heron, Little Egret, White Stork, Spoonbill, Flamingo, Long-legged Buzzard, Marsh Harrier, Montagu's Harrier, Peregrine, Lanner, Barbary Falcon, Slender-billed Curlew, Black-tailed Godwit, Little Stint, Curlew Sandpiper, Ruff, Avocet, Black-winged Stilt, Collared Pratincole, Long-tailed Skua, Audouin's Gull, Royal Tern, Lesser Crested Tern, Black Tern, Hoopoe, Crested Lark, Fan-tailed Warbler, Melodious Warbler, Spotless Starling, Serin.

ACCESS: The coast road south of El Jadida runs alongside this splendid area and gives views over many of the marshes and saltpans. The first major area is at Sidi Moussa, with saltpans to the north and an intertidal inlet to the south. Both can be easily explored on foot.

Southwards, there are various marshes and lagoons that should be investigated before reaching the Oualidia area. Here the marsh extends for several kilometres north to another large area of saltpans, the whole forming probably the best site along the whole coast. Oualidia itself is a small resort situated on the second intertidal lagoon. At the mouth of this the rocks are an excellent seawatch site. The whole area is worth a thorough exploration, and there are even reports of Andalusian Hemipode here. Cap Beddouza lies straight along the coast road southwards.

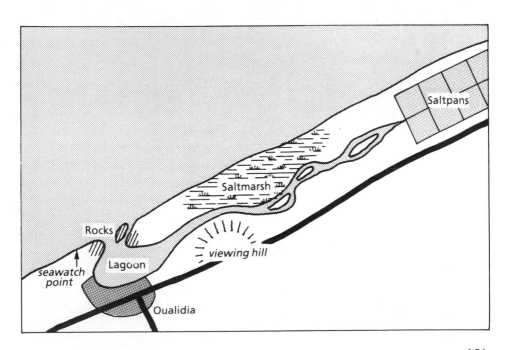

To the north, at Azemmour, take a track that leads towards the beach south of the town and river. This excellent scrub-covered area and estuary has Slender-billed Curlew in season and has produced Lesser Crested Tern.

ROUTE: Casablanca and its airport are only 130 km or so (80 miles) to the north.

NORWAY

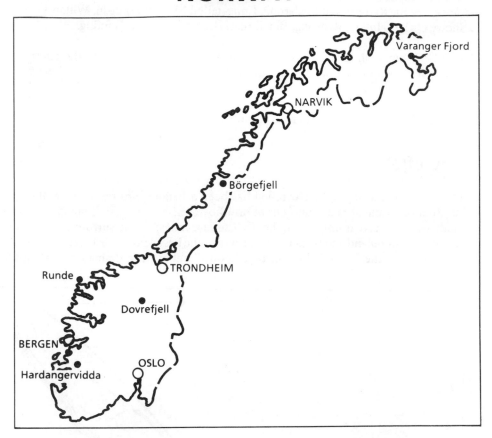

Börgefjell

This large national park lies on the border of the provinces of Nordland and Nord-Tröndelag, approximately half way between Trondheim and Narvik. The main base is Fellingfors, but there are plenty of villages and huts offering accommodation in all parts of the area. This is a mountainous landscape with cascading rivers, lakes, marshes, forests and large areas of birch scrub. The birds are typical of northern Scandinavia, with Pied Flycatcher and Bluethroat among the scrub, Phalarope and Temminck's Stint on the marshes, Goldeneye and Goosander on the pine-surrounded lakes and Snow Bunting and Ptarmigan on the open tops. There are Bean and Lesser White-fronted Geese here, though they may take a bit of tracking down, and raptors include Rough-legged Buzzard. To the north is Rössvatn, a huge water with Black-throated Diver and Scoter. This is a remote area, and visitors should be prepared to walk for their birds and treat the mountains with appropriate respect.

SUMMER: Black-throated Diver, Bean Goose, Lesser White-fronted Goose, Long-

153

tailed Duck, Scoter, Goldeneye, Goosander, Rough-legged Buzzard, Dotterel, Temminck's Stint, Red-necked Phalarope, Long-tailed Skua, Ptarmigan, Willow Grouse, Snowy Owl, Fieldfare, Redwing, Bluethroat, Brambling, Snow Bunting.

ACCESS: From Fellingfors a road leads eastward, with Börgefjell to the south and Rössvatn to the north. Smaller roads facilitate exploration, but be prepared to walk to get the best out of this beautiful area.

ROUTE: The main north–south road of Norway runs through Fellingfors.

Dovrefjell

The Fokstua reserve on the Dovrefjell has been a famous bird resort for well over a hundred years and attracts hundreds of ornitho-tourists every year. Though relatively small — the reserve is only 7.5 sq. km (2.9 square miles) — the surrounding areas of fjell, marsh, woodland and lakes make this one of the best-known bird areas in Europe. Over the years the Dovrefjell has changed considerably, most dramatically when the

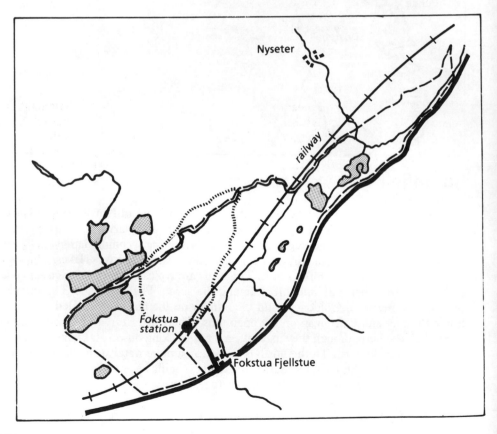

Dovre railway was constructed in 1916–17 through the best area of the marsh. Some species have abandoned the area only to return later, while others have colonised for the first time. Today, the Crane is no longer the regular breeder it once was, though it does still breed in most years. Temminck's Stint, Whimbrel and even Lesser White-fronted Goose have bred, along with a fine cross-section of birds usually found much further to the north.

On higher ground Snow Bunting, Shore Lark and Purple Sandpiper breed, while Rough-legged Buzzard usually does. This is an excellent, easy-to-explore area, worthy of a short holiday rather than an overnight stop on the way elsewhere.

SUMMER: Red-throated Diver, Crane, Hen Harrier, Peregrine, Rough-legged Buzzard, Dotterel, Whimbrel, Temminck's Stint, Ruff, Purple Sandpiper, Great Snipe, Red-necked Phalarope, Great Grey Shrike, Dipper, Ring Ouzel, Fieldfare, Bluethroat, Shore Lark, Brambling, Siskin, Redpoll, Snow Bunting, Lapland Bunting.

ACCESS: Permits for the Fokstua reserve may be obtained from the warden near the railway station. Much, however, can be seen from walking the boundary without penetrating the reserve at all. Dombås, to the south, offers a reasonable range of accommodation and is used as a base by most visitors.

ROUTE: By road or rail from Oslo or Trondheim to Fokstua station.

Hardangervidda

The Hardangervidda is a popular holiday area for the people of Oslo and Bergen in both summer and winter. Though it reaches no great altitude, the hills and marshes, the forests and meadows hold a variety of species more typical of land considerably further north. Indeed, for a number of Arctic birds Hardanger represents their furthest point south. Dotterel, Purple Sandpiper and Temminck's Stint are cases in point. Here too there are Tengmalm's and Pygmy Owls, both present and both elusive. Bluethroat, Brambling and Fieldfare are widespread and there is often a good population of raptors, though numbers vary according to the lemming population. As elsewhere in Norway, there is an excellent series of huts offering overnight accommodation and meals. They are reached via tracks and well-marked paths and, though they require a certain degree of fitness, they are used by all ages. Hill-walking is something of a passion with the Norwegians. Altogether, the woods, hills and lakes here are among the most accessible sites for northern birds.

SUMMER: Golden Eagle, Osprey, Merlin, Scaup, Goldeneye, Velvet Scoter, Dotterel, Greenshank, Whimbrel, Wood Sandpiper, Purple Sandpiper, Temminck's Stint, Pygmy Owl, Tengmalm's Owl, Three-toed Woodpecker, Black Woodpecker, Fieldfare, Bluethroat, Brambling, Redpoll, Crossbill.

ACCESS: Dyranut has a hostel and is a good base from which to explore the Bjoreidal valley and then head southwards to Randhellern on Lake Langesjöen, Sandhang on Lake Normannslågen and Hadlasker to the northwest.

ROUTE: Dyranut is on the main Oslo–Bergen road.

Runde

The island of Runde (Rundöy) lies in the southern part of Norway's fjord coastline not far from Ålesund. It is a rugged land with fearsome cliffs that hold huge numbers of seabirds and the country's largest gannetry. Fortunately, it also has a good human population centred on the villages of Runde and Goksöyr, so that access is relatively straightforward and accommodation can be obtained. Kittiwake and Puffin are the most numerous species, with largest concentrations at Rundebranden near Goksöyr. The Gannets nest at Storebranden and have increased steadily in numbers since their first colonisation in 1946; by 1974 there were nearly 500 pairs. These seabird cliffs are among the best in Europe, but Runde is also home to White-tailed Eagle and Eagle Owl.

White-tailed Eagle

SUMMER: Fulmar, Gannet, Shag, Eider, Peregrine, White-tailed Eagle, Curlew, Oystercatcher, Kittiwake, Puffin, Guillemot, Razorbill, Eagle Owl.

ACCESS: There are regular ferry sailings from Ålesund to Runde, where accommoda-

156

tion may be obtained in private homes. Fishermen are usually willing to sail around the island under the seabird cliffs.

ROUTE: By air or steamer from Bergen, or by train from Oslo.

Varanger Fjord

Varanger is the most northeasterly part of the European mainland outside the Soviet Union. Opening eastwards into the Arctic Ocean, it receives far less benefit from the warming effects of the Gulf Stream and is consequently both cold and barren. The result is that several species can be found only here, or further to the east. The White-billed Diver is more common than the Great Northern, and this is the only European site for both Steller's and King Eiders. It is also the only place outside Iceland for Brünnich's Guillemot.

Though these species may be the 'stars' of Varanger from a twitcher's angle, there is much more top-rate birding hereabouts. The surrounding fjells and marshes are full of breeding waders, and this is really the only accessible spot in 'Siberia'. Red-necked Phalarope, Purple Sandpiper, Turnstone, Bar-tailed Godwit and both stints can be seen, along with skuas, Glaucous Gull, Red-throated Pipit, Snow Bunting and Arctic Redpoll. All in all it is a unique piece of Europe.

Exploration is relatively straightforward along the road that clings tenaciously to the northern shore. Conditions do, however, become progressively more severe as one proceeds eastward, and several crews have found that an increasing number of sweaters are required as they progress from Varangerbotn at the head of the fjord to Vardö at the mouth and Hamningberg around the corner on the Arctic Ocean.

SUMMER: White-billed Diver, Red-throated Diver, Black-throated Diver, Long-tailed Duck, Velvet Scoter, Eider, King Eider, Steller's Eider, Gyrfalcon, Dotterel, Bar-tailed Godwit, Temminck's Stint, Little Stint, Purple Sandpiper, Red-necked Phalarope, Arctic Tern, Glaucous Gull, Arctic Skua, Long-tailed Skua, Snowy Owl, Bluethroat, Arctic Warbler, Shore Lark, Red-throated Pipit, Lapland Bunting, Snow Bunting, Arctic Redpoll, Mealy Redpoll.

ACCESS: The main areas to visit are the following.

Varangerbotn has a muddy area at the head of the fjord for waders, including summer-plumage Knot and Godwit, and the chance of Arctic Warbler.

Nesseby has a quaint church and adjacent wader pool which is noted for Red-necked Phalarope. From the promontory there is a good chance of King Eider, which occurs from here eastwards.

Vadsö is the main town, with shops and a hotel, and a rubbish dump on an offshore island reached by a motorable bridge. This is a good spot for odd gulls, including late or early Arctic species, as well as both stints.

Ekkeröy is a prime seawatching spot where all the specialities of Varanger can be seen. Ekkeröy Island, connected to the mainland via a causeway, has good seabird cliffs in the south, pools in the interior and a sandy shore in the north. This is the spot for masses of stints, Red-throated Pipit, Lapland Bunting and Shore Lark. Steller's are often seen from here.

Falkefjell lies inland from Ekkeröy and is worth a walk for scrub-dwelling Arctic Redpoll, Bluethroat and Red-throated Pipit. There are also good wader pools, and Dotterel, skuas and even Snowy Owl on the higher slopes.

Vardö is an unpleasant, fish-based town on an offshore island reached by car ferry. An offshore islet has five species of auk and a seawatch may produce many of Varanger's specials.

Hamningberg is a splendid climax to the drive along the fjord, with spectacular scenery, snow down to sea level, even in summer, and many Arctic birds.

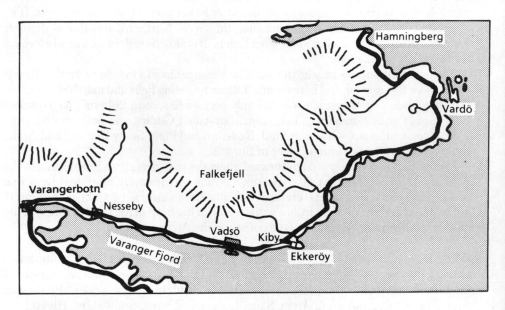

Pasvik valley is not often visited because it lies on the southern shore in an extension of Norway southwards between Finland and the Soviet Union. The only route is via Kirkenes southwards to Nyrud. The scrub, pools and marshes hold a fine collection of waders, including Bar-tailed Godwit, plus Arctic Redpoll, Bean Goose and other scarce species.

ROUTE: By air to Vadsö, or by road. The best time is late June and early July, when birding 24 hours a day is available.

POLAND

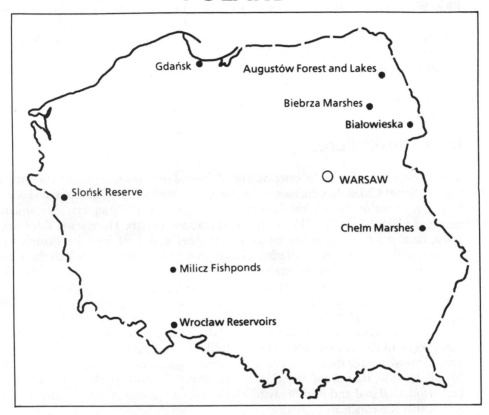

Gdańsk

Augustów Forest and Lakes

Biebrza Marshes

Białowieska

○ WARSAW

Słońsk Reserve

Chełm Marshes

Milicz Fishponds

Wrocław Reservoirs

Augustów Forest and Lakes

This area lies close to the Soviet border in eastern Poland and could be regarded as a northward extension of the Biebrza Marshes to the south. Certainly, any birders getting as far as this should explore both. The present area is, if anything, even more daunting than Biebrza, but there are several lakes around Augustów that can be reached by road and the Augustów Canal runs conveniently through the area, offering splendid birding from boats. The area is basically wet forest with lakes and marshes, and certainly deserves a thorough exploration.

Among a host of species are Lesser Spotted and Short-toed Eagles, Crane, Black Stork, Eagle Owl, White-backed and Three-toed Woodpeckers, as well as Goldeneye and both Goosander and Merganser.

For those lacking time in this part of the country, a canal trip offers the best chance of making contact with some of these special birds.

SUMMER: Little Bittern, White Stork, Black Stork, Goldeneye, Red-breasted Merganser, Goosander, Goshawk, Red Kite, Lesser Spotted Eagle, Short-toed Eagle, Hen

159

Harrier, Crane, Eagle Owl, White-backed Woodpecker, Three-toed Woodpecker, River Warbler, Great Reed Warbler, Scarlet Rosefinch.

ACCESS: Wigry Lake and Serwy Lake are just two of many waters worthy of exploration in this area. The best method of exploration, however, is to take one of the tourist boats that ply the Augustów Canal.

ROUTE: Augustów can be reached by train from Warsaw.

Białowieska Forest

This famous forest lies in the extreme east of Poland and continues across the border into the Soviet Union. It is the home of the only wild herd of European bison and is the largest remnant of the original European forest; it covers 580 sq. km (224 square miles), of which 47.5 sq. km (18 square miles) is a national park. Hornbeam, alder, oak, birch, lime, maple and pine are the dominant trees, and there are open glades, wet marshes and park-like areas, offering a home to over 200 species. Though there are eagles, owls, woodpeckers and cranes here, the visitor is unlikely to see many of the more exotic species — and that includes the bison. Lesser Spotted Eagle is common, but Short-toed is scarce. There are Eagle, Tengmalm's and Pygmy Owls, but all are highly elusive, though the latter is said to be fairly common. Hazelhen are definitely here but are, as elsewhere, difficult to locate. Woodpeckers are, in contrast, easy to locate, but difficult to see. Grey-headed, Black, Middle Spotted, White-backed and Three-toed all breed, though their numbers vary. Thrush Nightingale is common, as are River, Marsh, Icterine, Barred and Wood Warblers, while Greenish breeds in smaller numbers. Both Collared and Red-breasted Flycatchers are common, and Golden Oriole and Scarlet Rosefinch are regularly seen.

Fortunately the Park Palacowy, which lies a short distance from the reserve entrance and also holds the main hotel, is excellent for most of the smaller birds. The reserve can be visited and it is worth watching out for nestboxes with Collared Flycatchers. The best bet for seeing the scarcer birds, however, is to contact one of the local ornithologists and get him to show you birds at known nests. Such a tactic may produce woodpeckers, owls and conceivably Hazelhen.

The River Narewka can be walked on both banks, though only for 1 km (just over ½ mile) on the east bank. There are good forest areas to the southwest of the town, plus a good track to the northwest to a wet forest area. Białowieska is a fine area that would repay the efforts of those with a little time to spare. It is quite unsuited to a mad thrash.

SUMMER: White Stork, Black Stork, Crane, Honey Buzzard, Black Kite, Goshawk, Booted Eagle, Lesser Spotted Eagle, Spotted Eagle, Short-toed Eagle, Hazelhen, Capercaillie, Corncrake, Crane, Green Sandpiper, Tengmalm's Owl, Pygmy Owl, Nightjar, Wryneck, Grey-headed Woodpecker, Three-toed Woodpecker, Black Woodpecker, Middle Spotted Woodpecker, White-backed Woodpecker, Thrush Nightingale, Bluethroat, River Warbler, Marsh Warbler, Great Reed Warbler, Icterine Warbler, Barred Warbler, Greenish Warbler, Wood Warbler, Red-breasted Flycatcher, Collared Flycatcher, Pied Flycatcher, Golden Oriole, Red-backed Shrike, Serin, Scarlet Rosefinch, Ortolan Bunting.

ACCESS: The Hotel Iwa is situated in the grounds of the Palace Park, where many of the small birds can be seen. The reserve entrance is along the road leading due north, and the scientific staff live in flats in the next street to the east. There is a good track running westwards just north of the River Narewka. Permits can be obtained at the Białowieska Tourist Office.

ROUTE: Train from Warsaw to Białystok and then on to Białowieska. The hotel is only a short walk from the station.

Biebrza Marshes

These great marshes extend along the River Biebrza between Augustów and Łomza to the northwest of Warsaw near Białystok. Here, the meandering river has created a network of channels, backwaters and floods, with islands, lakes and huge marshes. There are areas of woodland and some considerable forests, but the area is thinly inhabited. There is a reserve at Czerwone Bagno, but the whole is worthy of exploration.

The variety of habitats is demonstrated by the wealth of species that can be found here, though even today there is some doubt about what does and what does not breed. Osprey, Red and Black Kites, Goshawk, Spotted and Lesser Spotted Eagles, Golden and White-tailed Eagles, Marsh, Hen and Montagu's Harriers and Hobby make a formidable list of raptors, but all were seen in a recent three-day visit. Wetland birds

Great Snipe

include Bittern and Little Bittern, Crane, Spotted and Little Crakes, Great Snipe at a significant-sized lek, Jack Snipe and Little Gull, and Black and White-winged Black Terns. Aquatic Warbler is common, and Bearded and Penduline Tits both breed.

SUMMER: Bittern, Little Bittern, White Stork, Black Stork, Garganey, Ferruginous Duck, Osprey, Red Kite, Black Kite, Goshawk, Spotted Eagle, Lesser Spotted Eagle, Golden Eagle, White-tailed Eagle, Short-toed Eagle, Hen Harrier, Montagu's Harrier, Marsh Harrier, Hobby, Black Grouse, Crane, Water Rail, Spotted Crake, Little Crake, Ruff, Black-tailed Godwit, Great Snipe, Jack Snipe, Little Gull, Black Tern, White-winged Black Tern, Eagle Owl, Tengmalm's Owl, Barred Warbler, Icterine Warbler, Savi's Warbler, Aquatic Warbler, River Warbler, Great Reed Warbler, Bearded Tit, Penduline Tit, Great Grey Shrike, Nutcracker, Scarlet Rosefinch.

ACCESS: The best area extends from Wizna to Goniadz and can be explored via minor roads and tracks on the eastern side. At the centre of this area lies the tiny (three houses) village of Budy, which has access in most directions and even two observation towers within walking distance. This is a wet area with poor roads, so wellies are essential. The

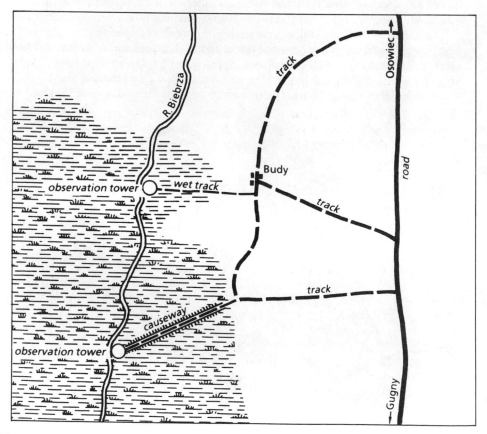

best Great Snipe area is from a causeway 2 km (1¼ miles) south of Budy, but continue to the observation tower. The terns breed at a small lake just north of Goniadz. There is a hotel in Lomza and a restaurant at Goniadz. Camping at Budy is possible, but take food and mosquito repellent — not necessarily in that order.

ROUTE: Take a bus from the PKS Bus Station, Piwnica na Wojtowskiej, Lomza. Change to bus to Trzciama and get off at Gugny and walk. Alternatively hire a car, but remember that petrol stations are not numerous. Also remember that this is one of the greatest raptor spots in Europe, and may well be worth all the effort of getting there.

Chełm Marshes

To the north and east of Chełm, between the town and the Soviet border, lies an extensive area of peat bogs and wet meadows some 900 ha (2220 acres) of which are protected as a reserve. This wetland holds a wealth of breeding species, including some specialities such as Crane, Bittern, Hen Harrier, Bluethroat and Penduline Tit. There are woods with Black Grouse and many of the 'eastern' specials that one would expect to see in this part of central Europe. Most attractive of all are breeding White-winged Black Tern and Aquatic Warbler.

SUMMER: Bittern, White Stork, Black Kite, Goshawk, Hen Harrier, Marsh Harrier, Black Grouse, Crane, Water Rail, White-winged Black Tern, Thrush Nightingale, Barred Warbler, Icterine Warbler, Aquatic Warbler, Penduline Tit, Scarlet Rosefinch.

ACCESS: There are no restrictions on access to the area, which can be explored by road from Chełm. The marshes lie to the north, northeast and east of the town. Contact Jaroslaw Krogulec, Zaklad Ochrony Przyrody, Instytut Biologii, ul. Akademicka 19, 20-003 Lublin.

ROUTE: Chełm can be reached by train from Lublin.

Gdańsk

Gdańsk lies on the shores of the Baltic near the mouth of the River Vistula and forms an admirable base for exploring this exceptionally bird-rich shoreline. Generations of migrant-watchers have counted and ringed the millions of birds that annually pass along this coast, and the variety that put in an appearance here is quite remarkable. Gdańsk is, however, not just a migration place, for the whole of northern Poland is rich in lakes, and only a short distance to the west is an area of water, marshes and woods around Kartuzy. Here breeding birds include White-tailed Eagle, Black Stork, Little Bittern, Thrush Nightingale, Red-breasted Flycatcher and River Warbler. It is, however, in autumn that this region becomes internationally important.

Mierzeja Helska is a narrow sandy peninsula that separates the Bay of Puck from the open sea. It has huge beaches and some quite extensive pine forests, together with areas

163

of meadows, ponds and a handy sewage farm. In spring and autumn there is a ringing station near Chalupy, though the area around Jastarnia has a reputation for producing the largest number of rare birds in Poland. Spring brings Citrine Wagtail and Red-throated Pipit, while in autumn there are Broad-billed Sandpiper, Richard's and Olive-backed Pipits and the real chance of a new species for the country.

On the south side of the Bay of Puck the River Reda joins the Baltic north of Rewa. The marshes here are excellent for waders, especially in autumn. This area is, however, overshadowed by the area of the mouth of the Vistula east of Gdańsk, which is generally recognised as the best wader-tern-gull site in Poland. Caspian Tern is numerous, and waders include regular Broad-billed and Terek Sandpipers and Red-necked Phalarope. This area is continually being transformed by deposition and storms, and there are lagoons, islands and marshes to explore. In summer, this is the only Polish breeding site of Arctic and Sandwich Terns. Finally, Druzno Lake lies to the southeast beyond Elblag, and is a shallow, reed-fringed water surrounded by marshes. Although less than 1 m (3¼ feet) deep, there are still areas of open water separating floating islands of reed and sedge. The wealth of breeding species here is impressive by any standards, and includes Night Heron, Ferruginous Duck, Lesser Spotted Eagle, Crane, Little Gull, Black Tern, River Warbler and Scarlet Rosefinch.

SUMMER: Red-necked Grebe, Black-necked Grebe, White Stork, Black Stork, Night Heron, Little Bittern, Bittern, Ferruginous Duck, Goshawk, Hen Harrier, Marsh Harrier, Lesser Spotted Eagle, White-tailed Eagle, Crane, Little Crake, Ruff, Little Gull, Sandwich Tern, Arctic Tern, Black Tern, Golden Oriole, Thrush Nightingale, Bluethroat, Icterine Warbler, River Warbler, Great Reed Warbler, Marsh Warbler, Barred Warbler, Red-breasted Flycatcher, Scarlet Rosefinch, Ortolan Bunting.

AUTUMN: Black-throated Diver, Velvet Scoter, Eider, Smew, White-fronted Goose, Bean Goose, Whooper Swan, White-tailed Eagle, Rough-legged Buzzard, Honey Buzzard, Broad-billed Sandpiper, Terek Sandpiper, Purple Sandpiper, Curlew Sandpiper, Little Gull, Caspian Tern, Citrine Wagtail, Red-throated Pipit.

ACCESS: Kartuzy is 30 km (18½ miles) west of Gdańsk, and the best lakes are Reduńskie, Kiodno and Ostrzyckie to the southwest. There is a good network of roads and the area can be reached by train and bus.

Mierzeja Helska can be reached by train from Gdynia to Jastarnia, the best spot on the peninsula. Rewa, to the south, is reached by road from the same town. The Vistula mouth is reached by taking a bus from Gdańsk railway station to Swinbo and then proceeding on foot to the river mouth.

Druzno Lake can be reached via Elblag, which has a good bus service from Gdańsk. Contact the Ornithological Station, ul. Nadwislanska 108, 80-680 Gdańsk 40.

ROUTE: Gdańsk can be reached by road or rail from Warsaw in a day; or by air in about an hour.

Milicz Fishponds

The fishponds at Milicz lie in the flat valley of the River Barycz, itself a tributary of the Oder, in southern Poland near Wrocław. The ponds were created by Cistercian monks in the fourteenth century, and have been largely preserved to the present day. The annual crop of carp is huge, but involves draining a number of ponds each autumn. These ponds vary enormously, from over 400 ha (990 acres) down to tiny 'village' type ponds. They are surrounded by marshes, grazing land and extensive woods that offer a home to a wide variety of species. Though generally shallow with a considerable growth of emergent vegetation, the open water is maintained for both fish and birds: an effective conservation.

The ponds hold good populations of grebes, harriers, Greylag Goose and Mute Swan, duck and a fine variety of warblers. Outstanding species include White-tailed Eagle and Poland's only breeding Purple Herons. The best areas of water are, from west to east, Radziqdz, Ruda Sulowska, Milicz, Krosnice and Potasznia. The surrounding meadows hold Black-tailed Godwit, Garganey and Grasshopper Warbler, while the margins between ponds and meadows have Penduline Tit.

South of Milicz the Trzebnica hills near Żmigród are covered with mixed deciduous woodland, offering a home to White-tailed Eagle, Black Stork, Roller, various woodpeckers plus Red-breasted Flycatcher.

In autumn, the area is a major staging post for geese and duck and the eagles may then be quite numerous.

SUMMER: Red-necked Grebe, Black-necked Grebe, Purple Heron, Little Bittern, Bittern, Black Stork, Ferruginous Duck, Greylag Goose, Red Kite, Black Kite, White-tailed Eagle, Honey Buzzard, Marsh Harrier, Crane, Little Crake, Black-tailed

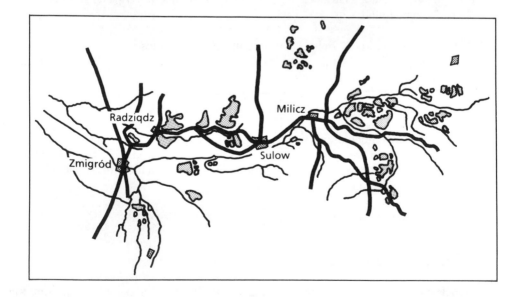

Godwit, Roller, Grey-headed Woodpecker, White-backed Woodpecker, Middle Spotted Woodpecker, Black Woodpecker, Golden Oriole, Penduline Tit, Bluethroat, River Warbler, Great Reed Warbler, Savi's Warbler, Barred Warbler, Red-breasted Flycatcher, Great Grey Shrike, Serin.

ACCESS: The main pond areas extend east and west along the Barycz valley from Milicz, and can be explored by minor roads. There is, however, a bird station and visitors are well advised to make contact to find the whereabouts of special birds and of local 'hot spots'. Contact Jozef Witkowski, Ornithological Station, Ruda Milicz, 56-300 Milicz, on arrival.

ROUTE: Milicz lies no great distance north of Wrocław and may be reached by train or bus. The ornithological station is a 4-km (2½-mile) walk to the east at Ruda Milicz, and it will issue permits for the ponds that are included in a nature reserve.

Słońsk Reserve

This great wetland reserve lies at the confluence of the Rivers Warta and Odra on the German DR border south of Szczecin. Over 500 ha (1235 acres) are flooded and, with numerous shallow lakes and splashy pastures, the whole forms the most important wetland in western Poland. The area is particularly significant to migratory waders and wildfowl, and is noted as the wintering ground of thousands of Bean and White-fronted Geese together with hundreds of Whooper Swan. All are outnumbered several times over by surface-feeding duck.

In summer the breeding birds include a wide variety of species, among which White-tailed Eagle is perhaps the star, though Shelduck are far from common in Poland. Duck include Gadwall and Shoveler, while both River Warbler and Penduline Tit can also be found.

SUMMER: Red-necked Grebe, Cormorant, Greylag Goose, Shelduck, Gadwall, Shoveler, White-tailed Eagle, Marsh Harrier, Water Rail, Barred Warbler, Icterine Warbler, River Warbler, Penduline Tit.

WINTER: Whooper Swan, Mute Swan, Bean Goose, White-fronted Goose.

ACCESS: Though much of this wetland can be seen from roads leading eastward from Kostrzyn, the main area and reserve is situated at Słońsk on the Kostrzyn Reservoir. Permits can be obtained from Przemyslaw Majewski, Station of Polish Hunting Association, 64-020 Czempin.

ROUTE: By train from Poznań to Kostrzyn, then by bus to Słońsk.

Wrocław Reservoirs

Wrocław lies in southern Poland, and makes an ideal starting point for exploring the border country as well as the famous fishpond area of Milicz in the Barycz valley. To the south and the southeast two huge reservoirs have been constructed and these, together with the surrounding land, have become the subject of considerable attention from local birders. They are, however, virtually unknown outside Poland.

The Nysa Reservoir lies west of the town of the same name very near the Czech border. This lake covers some 20 km square (8 square miles) and is at its most attractive in late summer and autumn when the water level is at its lowest, exposing huge areas of mud along the margins. Over the years, it has become the single most important inland stop-over place for migrant waders in Poland. Almost all the species one could reasonably expect to see in this region have occurred, many in really substantial numbers. Marsh and Broad-billed Sandpipers are regular, as is Red-necked Phalarope, and rarities are recorded annually. There are also, of course, good concentrations of wildfowl.

Turawa Reservoir lies immediately east of Opole and is similarly best in autumn, when the water level is at its lowest. It too attracts large numbers of waders and wildfowl, including the specialities also found at Nysa. Great White Egret is, however, also regular at this site.

Though primarily migration spots, the two areas also hold many of the species that one would expect to see in central Europe, even if they are not in full song in autumn. These include Penduline Tit and Scarlet Rosefinch.

AUTUMN: Black-necked Grebe, White Stork, Pintail, Black Kite, Osprey, Black-tailed Godwit, Green Sandpiper, Marsh Sandpiper, Broad-billed Sandpiper, Wood Sandpiper, Curlew Sandpiper, Little Stint, Temminck's Stint, Common Tern, Black Tern, Bluethroat, Barred Warbler, Icterine Warbler, Tawny Pipit, Great Grey Shrike, Penduline Tit, Scarlet Rosefinch.

ACCESS: Nysa Reservoir can be seen from the surrounding public roads, and is best along the southern and western shoreline off the Otmuchow–Paczków road west of Nysa. Turawa Reservoir is best in the east, and can be viewed via Szczedrzyk.

ROUTE: Both reservoirs enjoy easy access from Wrocław. Nysa and Opole can be reached by both train and bus and thereafter by bus to Siestrzechowice (Nysa) or Szczedrzyk (Turawa).

PORTUGAL

Aveiro Lagoons

LISBON Tagus Estuary

Alentejo

Sado Estuary and
Setúbal

Santo André Lagoon

Sagres and
Cape St Vincent   Faro   Rio Guadiana

Alentejo

The Alentejo is a land of vast rolling plains broken here and there by rocky outcrops, cork and pine forests and by a network of small rivers. These plains stretch from Montemor in the west to Elvas and the Spanish border in the east; indeed, they extend across the border to Badajoz and beyond. Vast cornfields dominate, but there are still areas of traditional grazing with tall thin grass that makes perfect cover for nesting birds. Little Bustard is widespread throughout this region and any open, unploughed area is likely to hold flocks of these birds. Great Bustard too is as common in this area as anywhere else, but always needs some searching. The best area of all is between Elvas and the Spanish border, as well as in adjacent Spain. Two species of sandgrouse, hordes of larks, shrikes along the roadside, Lesser Kestrel in the towns and many more widespread birds make this area one of the best places for birds in Iberia.

168

SUMMER: White Stork, Lesser Kestrel, Montagu's Harrier, Great Bustard, Little Bustard, Black-bellied Sandgrouse, Pin-tailed Sandgrouse, Hoopoe, Crested Lark, Thekla Lark, Golden Oriole, Bee-eater, Quail, Woodchat Shrike, Great Grey Shrike, Black-eared Wheatear, Fan-tailed Warbler.

ACCESS: The N4 between Montemor and Elvas gives access to typical landscape and to a maze of minor roads worth exploring. Évora is an attractive town with both bustards nearby and, near the border, there are tracks and small roads heading northwestward from Elvas that are probably the best bet for Great Bustard.

ROUTE: Lisbon and the N10 to junction with N4.

Aveiro Lagoons

South of Porto, the sea has built up a huge sandy beach that has all but cut off the Rivers Vouga and Agueda from the sea. In fact, these and several other smaller waters have created a huge lagoon system around Aveiro, to the west of which lies a single narrow channel to the Atlantic. The lagoons, together with their low-lying surroundings, are rich in birds, particularly during passage periods.

Aveiro itself lies on the landward side of the lagoons and is a sort of Portuguese Venice: canals with picturesque buildings etc. It is not a difficult area to work, yet has been strangely neglected by non-Portuguese birders.

In the summer there are egrets, harriers, Black Kite, Avocet and Stilt, plus a good selection of southern European birds. During the spring and autumn, these species are joined by many waders and reasonably regular Flamingo. Seabirds may prove interesting and should certainly include Gannet, skuas, plus several of those species breeding on the Berlenga Islands to the south.

SUMMER: White Stork, Cattle Egret, Little Egret, Black Kite, Marsh Harrier, Kentish Plover, Black-winged Stilt, Avocet, Crested Lark, Red-rumped Swallow, Tawny Pipit, Great Grey Shrike, Woodchat Shrike, Great Reed Warbler, Fan-tailed Warbler, Bonelli's Warbler, Black-eared Wheatear.

PASSAGE: Cory's Shearwater, Gannet, Shag, Flamingo, Black-winged Stilt, Avocet, Little Stint, Greenshank, Wood Sandpiper, Arctic Skua.

ACCESS: The road along the shoreline from Ovar, in the north, to San Jacinto overlooks the northern arm of the lagoon, and there is even a pousada with bedrooms perfectly sited for viewing. The bridge between Bestida and Torreira crosses the lagoon.

From Aveiro, a road runs westward across the lagoon to Barra and then southward along the beach. This road passes areas of saltpans which should be investigated.

The inland marshes can be reached at several points, including several off the road to Bestida. There are many tracks, and those with time should investigate in the hope of coming across a little gem.

ROUTE: Porto has an international airport and is only a brief drive away.

Faro

Faro is the largest town on the Algarve, has an international airport and offers arguably the best birding in southern Portugal. The city lies sheltered behind a complex dune system that extends east as far as Tavira, and which has effectively sealed off a number of lagoons and created a bird-rich habitat that starts immediately west of the town. Despite its proximity, several teams have found it a difficult area to work properly, though those that have succeeded have been well rewarded.

Passage waders are excellent in season, with a good variety of the species one would expect to see along this coastline. Local breeding birds are, however, not to be missed. They include Cattle Egret, Night Heron, Little Bittern, Red-crested Pochard and Purple Gallinule. The latter is a speciality of the best location in the Faro area, the lagoon adjacent to the salinas at the western end of the Faro airport. It can often be seen when taking off into a westerly wind — but by then you are on your way home! The adjacent woods have Azure-winged Magpie and there are often Waxbills in the area. Caspian Tern and Mediterranean Gull are regular outside the breeding season.

SUMMER: White Stork, Cattle Egret, Little Egret, Night Heron, Little Bittern, Red-crested Pochard, Black Kite, Purple Gallinule, Little Bustard, Kentish Plover, Black-

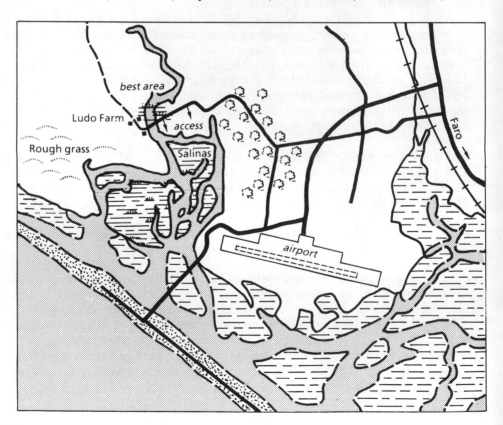

winged Stilt, Avocet, Pratincole, Hoopoe, Bee-eater, Woodchat Shrike, Great Grey Shrike, Azure-winged Magpie, Waxbill.

PASSAGE: Whimbrel, Black-tailed Godwit, Wood Sandpiper, Curlew Sandpiper, Little Stint, Sanderling, Avocet, Caspian Tern, Mediterranean Gull.

ACCESS: Leave Faro on the main Portimão road and turn left for the airport. Follow signs for 'Praia de Faro' and explore the beach and the connecting causeway. Return to the airport and take the first left after leaving it. Pass through woods and turn right at a T-junction. At the next junction, turn left through more woods to the salinas. Continue until the lagoon (with Purple Gallinule) appears on the right.

ROUTE: Faro airport and walk if necessary!

Guadiana River

The Guadiana forms the boundary between Portugal and Spain and is crossed by a regular car-ferry service at Ayamonte. The Portuguese bank is particularly interesting at its mouth near Vila Real and Castro Marim, where a considerable area of saltpans has been created. Together with the pines that line the coastal dunes and the adjacent groves, they form a good area with a wide variety of species. The salinas are excellent during passage periods, with good numbers of the more common species of waders, terns and gulls. There is a good chance of Slender-billed Gull, plus reasonably regular Caspian, Gull-billed and Whiskered Terns. Flamingo and Spoonbill put in appearances, while in summer the variety of breeding birds includes good numbers of White Stork together with Little Bustard and a variety of larks and warblers.

A short distance northwards are further areas of saltpans where similar species may be found, while around the village of Azinhal the woods hold Azure-winged Magpie.

The breakwater at the mouth of the Guadiana may produce a few seabirds, including Balearic and Cory's Shearwaters, as well as the more regular terns, gulls and waders.

SUMMER: White Stork, Flamingo, Spoonbill, Cattle Egret, Little Egret, Black Kite, Booted Eagle, Griffon Vulture, Montagu's Harrier, Lesser Kestrel, Little Bustard, Kentish Plover, Black-winged Stilt, Little Tern, Short-toed Lark, Lesser Short-toed Lark, Calandra Lark, Crested Lark, Thekla Lark, Hoopoe, Red-rumped Swallow, Black-eared Wheatear, Spectacled Warbler, Short-toed Treecreeper, Azure-winged Magpie, Great Grey Shrike, Woodchat Shrike, Serin.

PASSAGE: Cory's Shearwater, Balearic Shearwater, Gannet, Spotted Redshank, Ruff, Black-tailed Godwit, Slender-billed Gull, Caspian Tern, Gull-billed Tern, Whiskered Tern, Black Redstart, Red-throated Pipit.

ACCESS: The pines can be explored directly west of Vila Real where a road runs parallel to the coast. Northwards off this road, the road to Castro Marim crosses a river bridge and after a short distance an access track leads left to the salinas.

There are storks in the orchard here. Permission should be obtained to explore the pans, though there seem to be no problems with access.

ROUTE: Faro, with its international airport, is a little over an hour's drive away, and Monte Gordo is a rather unattractive resort town 5 km (3 miles) west.

Sado Estuary and Setúbal Peninsula

The Sado estuary lies only a short distance from Lisbon and the estuary of the Tagus, and it is quite possible to sandwich a brief exploration of both into a single day. That would, however, be to miss the delights of each. The Sado is quite different in character from the Tagus, with larger areas of saltings and considerably more exposed mud. It is far less developed and, as a result, is much more awkward so far as access is concerned. There are areas of saltpans in the north, to the east of Setúbal, and along the Sado itself as far as Alcacer do Sal. Other parts of the valleys are given over to rice cultivation. Three main areas deserve exploration: in the north, the saltpans and saltings east of Setúbal; in the south, the dune coastline around Comporta; and, in the east, the saltpans around Alcacer. Here waders abound both in winter and on passage, with Grey Plover reaching substantial numbers. Stilt, Avocet and Kentish Plover breed and most of the villages have White Stork. Around Alcacer, there are large groves of cork oaks with Azure-winged Magpie, Woodchat, Wryneck and many warblers.

Azure-winged Magpie

The Setúbul peninsula is, in contrast, a beautiful rugged landscape, with the Sierra da Arrabida falling, in places, almost directly to the sea. Here Peregrine, Golden Oriole and typical scrub warblers can be found, while in the far west Cabo Espichel is a first-class seawatch spot. Gannet, Cory's Shearwater and Manx Shearwater, skuas and

172

terns can all be seen at appropriate seasons, and small migrants should certainly not be ignored. A little to the north lies the Lagoa de Albufeira, which continues to prove a disappointment to visiting birders, though the surrounding land does have a good selection of widespread birds.

SUMMER: Gannet, White Stork, Little Egret, Cattle Egret, Black Kite, Marsh Harrier, Peregrine, Kentish Plover, Avocet, Black-winged Stilt, Great Grey Shrike, Woodchat Shrike, Dartford Warbler, Sardinian Warbler, Orphean Warbler, Melodious Warbler, Bonelli's Warbler, Azure-winged Magpie, Golden Oriole, Raven.

PASSAGE: Cory's Shearwater, Manx Shearwater, Grey Plover, Ringed Plover, Little Stint, Curlew Sandpiper, Greenshank, Arctic Skua.

ACCESS: Comporta and the road to the mouth of the estuary on the southern shore is a long drive south to Alcacer and on to Grândola. Here take the N261.1 and join the N261 at Comporta. There is, however, a regular ferry at the mouth. This is pretty spectacular scenery — if you like dunes. At Alcacer a small track follows the northern bank of the Sado westward through the saltpans: expect to get lost, but it is possible to emerge at Palma, back on the N5.

The northern shore of the Sado is found by leaving Setúbal eastwards along the shoreline. Many have failed to find the correct track, but always fork right and there should be no difficulty. At high tide there are huge numbers of waders, but the saltings are extensive.

ROUTE: Lisbon and the autoroute southward to Setúbal.

Sagres and Cape St Vincent

Anyone wishing to start a new bird observatory in Iberia would glance at a map and immediately head for Cape St Vincent. This furthest, southwest point of Portugal sticks out into the Atlantic and has great gathering power. It has a lighthouse and some splendid cliffs, but is rather devoid of good cover and is too high for effective seawatching. It is also thronged by tourists (just like Lands End), and the best areas lie away from the point of the cape itself. Migrant passerines include Melodious and Bonelli's Warblers, Tawny Pipit, Pied Flycatcher and all the more usual stuff. So far it has had little opportunity to produce the rarities that would undoubtedly appear. Seawatching too has produced no more than Cory's and Balearic Shearwaters, Gannet, skuas and terns; yet we know that there are Wilson's Petrel, Sabine's Gull and Great Shearwater offshore. Enthusiasts have joined fishing expeditions or 'hitched' a day out in a local fishing boat to find these species, plus Madeiran and Trinidade Petrels. In fact, all it needs is a good westerly gale to produce these birds off the cape.

Local birds should not be ignored. They include Little Bustard, Stone-curlew and quite definite Thekla Lark (there are said to be no Crested here), as well as a good assortment of typical warblers. Sagres has its own cape, complete with lighthouse, and makes an excellent base for working the area. A few seabirds frequent the fishing harbour and there are Chough and Peregrine on the cliffs.

SUMMER: Peregrine, Quail, Little Bustard, Stone-curlew, Woodlark, Thekla Lark, Black Redstart, Spectacled Warbler, Sardinian Warbler, Fan-tailed Warbler, Blue Rock Thrush, Woodchat Shrike, Chough.

PASSAGE: Balearic Shearwater, Cory's Shearwater, Wilson's Petrel, Storm Petrel, Gannet, Arctic Skua, Woodchat Shrike, Pied Flycatcher, Bonelli's Warbler, Melodious Warbler, Tawny Pipit.

ACCESS: Cape St Vincent and Punta de Sagres are both easily found. The road between the two has a number of rough tracks leading inland among grassy fields for Stone-curlew and Little Bustard. There are some areas of pines and it is these that hold grounded migrants.

ROUTE: Faro and its international airport are a drivable distance to the east. There are several hotels, including a modern pousada.

Santo André Lagoon

The difficulties of keeping a guide of this sort up to date are epitomised by the Lagoon of Santo André. In an earlier edition this lagoon was treated under the heading of 'Sines', a delightful little coastal town that I visited in the late 1960s. In 1979, a correspondent wrote: 'Sines must have lost a great deal of its attraction because of the gigantic oil and ore terminal of which Sines is the centre.' As a result of this construction work, an autoroute leads from the town northwards to the Santo André Lagoon and almost resulted in this super site being banished from the book. As it is, however, a nature reserve, it has managed to keep both its status and its appeal. Both Santo André and its northerly neighbour, the Lagoon of Melides, are joined to the sea by narrow entrances almost closed by the build-up of dunes along this part of the coast. Though the surrounding land holds a good selection of species, including Tawny Pipit, Stone-curlew, Great Spotted Cuckoo, Orphean Warbler and so on, the lagoons themselves are best during passage periods. Seabirds may include Gannet, skuas, terns and oddities such as Scoter. Waders are often interesting and passerines are worthy of attention, though the adjacent woodland does, if anything, offer too much cover.

SUMMER: Little Egret, Kentish Plover, Stone-curlew, Great Spotted Cuckoo, Great Grey Shrike, Woodchat Shrike, Hoopoe, Bee-eater, Crested Lark, Short-toed Lark, Sardinian Warbler, Orphean Warbler, Cetti's Warbler, Fan-tailed Warbler.

PASSAGE: Gannet, Spoonbill, Kentish Plover, Little Stint, Sanderling, Sandwich Tern, Gull-billed Tern, Arctic Skua.

ACCESS: Leave the N120 near Grândola on the N261.2 to Melides. Both lagoons can be reached by road from this town. The surrounding land and the ground between the two is worth exploring.

ROUTE: Southwards from Lisbon via Setúbal.

174

Tagus Estuary

From Lisbon, one can look eastwards over one of the best birding areas in Portugal and one of the most important of European wetlands. The Tagus estuary is a vast complex of creeks, marshes and saltings, yet it is only a shadow of its former self. Many marshes have been converted to grazing, even more to saltpans, but these in themselves are attractive to birds and together with the intertidal areas are home to a wide variety of species. Immediately to the east lie the plains of the Alentejo. At first these are covered with rich woodlands of pine and cork oak; later they are more open, with grassland beloved of bustards. The whole area offers some splendid birding in a fine cross-section of habitats.

The Tagus itself is a major wintering ground of waders, with Avocet particularly numerous. Passage brings a wider range of species, and at this time the saltpans at Alcochete and Montijo are particularly attractive. Apart from the resident Waxbill, Stilt, Little Stint, Ruff, Greenshank, Wood Sandpiper and, indeed, most of the regular European waders pass through. Gulls and terns are always worth a look here, and there are egrets and harriers too. Better for these latter species is the area at the head of the estuary between the Tagus and the tributary the Samora. Known as Lezerias Land, this was formerly open grassland with grazing cattle. Today much has been converted to arable, though there are still areas of reed and water where Cattle and Little Egrets, Marsh Harrier, Black Kite, Roller, Great Grey Shrike and others can be found.

The area between the Tagus and the road that loops around from Vila Franca to Marateca and Setúbal, the N10, lies in the western part of the Alentejo. The cork oaks here are full of birds, with Azure-winged Magpie, Wryneck, Hoopoe, Golden Oriole and much more. Though not open enough for Great Bustard, the Little Bustard can be found even among the cork groves. There are also some substantial colonies of White Stork, and Cattle Egrets are widespread.

SUMMER: White Stork, Little Bittern, Bittern, Cattle Egret, Little Egret, Purple Heron, Marsh Harrier, Montagu's Harrier, Black Kite, Kentish Plover, Avocet, Black-winged Stilt, Collared Pratincole, Hoopoe, Roller, Bee-eater, Crested Lark, Great Grey Shrike, Woodchat Shrike, Wryneck, Azure-winged Magpie, Black-eared Wheatear, Orphean Warbler, Serin, Hawfinch, Waxbill.

PASSAGE: Kentish Plover, Little Ringed Plover, Whimbrel, Black-tailed Godwit, Little Stint, Curlew Sandpiper, Wood Sandpiper, Greenshank, Ruff.

ACCESS: Lezerias, in the north, is reached via Vila Franca de Xira and the autoroute northwards from Lisbon. Turn eastward on the N10 and watch for a small road on the right to Ponta da Erva. Follow this to the end. Continue eastwards on the N10, stopping to explore the Alentejo woodlands. Beyond Marateca, take a turning into the network of roads leading to Barreiro and Alcochete for the saltpans. The autoroute from Setúbal to Lisbon makes for a speedy return and a complete lap of the area in a day.

ROUTE: Lisbon airport, and a good range of accommodation to south and west.

ROMANIA

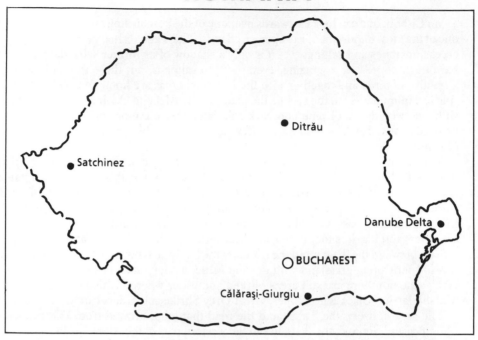

Călăraşi-Giurgiu Floodland

The River Danube floods twice each season, covering a huge area that remains wet and marshy throughout the year. On the Romanian side these floods are particularly extensive and considerable areas of open water remain, forming shallow lakes at almost all times. The area between Călăraşi and Giurgiu is full of such waters, including the large Lake Călăraşi, which is heavily overgrown with reeds and *Salix*, and the similar Lake Greaca above Olteniţa. Just a little way downstream, though on the other bank, is Lake Oltina near Băneasa.

Throughout this huge stretch of countryside the marshes hold the most extraordinary variety of birds, including most of those found in the Danube delta, plus others that are absent from that famous wetland. Though they do not breed here, White Pelicans are regular visitors. Glossy Ibis, most of the herons and egrets, Pygmy Cormorant, Spoonbill, the three marsh terns, and Savi's, Moustached and Great Reed Warblers all breed. Raptors are decidedly more abundant than in the delta, and there is a good chance of Spotted, Lesser Spotted and White-tailed Eagles, Hen and Marsh Harriers, Saker and Red-footed Falcon. Add to this the more widespread smaller birds and the potential for list-building here is outstanding.

Some of the hot spots are the northern end of Lake Oltina, with its Purple and Squacco Herons and Glossy Ibis; the rock outcrops to the east of Băneasa, with Eagle Owl and Pied Wheatear; the southern edges of Lake Călăraşi and its subsidiary lakes Melcu and Rotundu, with Glossy Ibis, Little Egret and Night and Squacco Herons; nearby

176

Lake Derfu, with a colony of Spoonbills; Lake Greaca, with more heronries; and the adjacent Comana Forest and Lake Mostistea.

These wetlands, together with the surrounding forests and agricultural land, are simply outstanding.

SUMMER: Black-necked Grebe, Dalmatian Pelican, White Pelican, Bittern, Little Bittern, Purple Heron, Night Heron, Squacco Heron, Glossy Ibis, Spoonbill, Garganey, Corncrake, Spotted Crake, Little Crake, Honey Buzzard, Lesser Spotted Eagle, White-tailed Eagle, Hen Harrier, Marsh Harrier, Short-toed Eagle, Booted Eagle, Saker, Hobby, Goshawk, Black Tern, White-winged Black Tern, Whiskered Tern, Eagle Owl, Alpine Swift, Bee-eater, Roller, Golden Oriole, Hoopoe, Lesser Grey Shrike, Great Grey Shrike, Red-backed Shrike, Olivaceous Warbler, Icterine Warbler, Savi's Warbler, Moustached Warbler, Great Reed Warbler, Thrush Nightingale, Pied Wheatear, Ortolan Bunting, Spanish Sparrow.

ACCESS: Since the first *Where to Watch Birds in Britain and Europe* picked out these areas of the Danube as the outstanding bird haunt that they obviously are, comparatively few birders have made the effort to explore them. There are a number of reasons for this, including the difficulties of finding reliable and quick transport, other than a car, in Romania and more importantly the actual difficulties of access. One correspondent told me of his three-day-long wrangle to be allowed to walk through the Băneasa area following a cursory turnback at Călăraşi. This involved a journey to Constanţa to obtain a permit, only to be told that one was not required to watch birds. Clearly the border area is sensitive, and with armed police posts scattered here and there it is sensible to be well prepared. There is no established formula for dealing with this problem, so I suggest that anyone thinking of working this area should write to the Romanian Embassy asking for a permit to watch birds in the areas concerned. When the letter saying that no permit is required is received, keep it as if it were a permit! If you can get a Romanian translation (try the Tourist Board), so much the better. If this seems too much to go birding, I can only quote my correspondent again: 'All the hassle', he wrote, 'was completely worthwhile since within one hour I saw Lesser Spotted Eagle, Booted Eagle, Red-footed Falcon and Short-toed Eagle. The woods echoed to the calls of Golden Oriole and Hoopoes, Bee-eaters and Rollers are all relatively common.' (Thanks again Alistair!)

Access (with the letter!) is along the riverbanks and minor roads with the aid of the best map you can find.

ROUTE: Bucharest is no distance from Olteniţa, which is a good starting point. Constanţa, on the Black Sea coast, has charter flights from several parts of Europe serving package holidays at Mamaia.

Danube Delta

The Danube forms one of the three great European deltas, the others being the

Camargue in France and the Coto Doñana in Spain. Yet while the others have become famous birding resorts, the Danube delta has remained quietly on most people's dream list of places to visit. There are several reasons why this should be, but mostly it is the daunting scale of this great eastern wetland and the fact that there is no tourist infrastructure to support individual journeys.

The Danube delta is huge. It covers 3000 sq. km (1160 square miles) of marsh, lake, reedbeds, swamps and forest, all built up by the millions of tons of silt that the river dumps at its mouth every year. At 100 km (62 miles) from its mouth, the Danube divides into three major channels, the Chilia, Sulina and St Gheorghe. Thereafter there is a maze of waterways, connected and interconnected, known only to local boatmen. Roads and tracks are few or non-existent, and the settlements are mostly on islands, so that waterborne birding is the norm. This is a slow and leisurely process and a complete contrast to the modern drive-tick-drive school of listing crews. It can, however, provide a unique experience, with great flocks of White Pelicans at close range and Pygmy Cormorant and Glossy Ibis in view at all times. Frankly, I think the Danube to be worth all the effort required to explore.

Pygmy Cormorant

The other drawback is the general uniformity of the delta. Vast reedbeds broken by open waters and a scattering of willows occupy over 90 per cent of the landscape. To this can be added the riverine forests along the main channels, a little agricultural land, the villages and the shoreline, and that is that. Thus, it is not a huge logistical problem to explore the delta habitats as such.

178

To the south there are two huge open lakes, Razelm (Razim) and Sinoe, which are shallow and full of birds. Here Ruddy Shelduck have a European toehold, but there are masses of herons, egrets, waders and duck, plus substantial breeding colonies of Collared Pratincole, Gull-billed Tern and many small birds in the surrounding dry countryside. In fact, a visit to the southern point of Sinoe produces a huge range of species in vast numbers. Migrant waders are often abundant here, and the area is certainly worth more than a single stop.

The delta proper can be explored from Tulcea, from where a system of regular ferry services operates downstream. These slow-moving boats stop frequently to take on and put down passengers, and offer excellent birding opportunities. Birds likely to be seen include White and Dalmatian Pelicans, Glossy Ibis, Pygmy Cormorant, Little and Great White Egrets and Spoonbill. The first recommended stop is Maliuc, where there is a hotel catering for tourists. Try to get a front-facing room to avoid the noisy generator at the rear. From Maliuc, it is possible to hire a boatman for a day's outing to Lake Fortuna and thereabouts, but start before dawn for the best results. Here, there are Ferruginous Duck, Whiskered Tern, Roller, Penduline Tit, Thrush Nightingale, Moustached Warbler and Bluethroat.

Further downstream, Crisan is worth a stop to explore along the embankment that runs to the south. This, at least, is *terra firma* and, therefore, makes the use of a telescope a possibility. There are several reserves around here, but permits seem almost impossible to obtain and are not necessary anyway.

Near the mouth lies the fishing port of Sulina, and here there is more chance of finding accommodation and of exploring on dry land. It is not, of course, geared up to birding tourists.

SUMMER: Red-necked Grebe, Black-necked Grebe, White Pelican, Dalmatian Pelican, Pygmy Cormorant, Purple Heron, Great White Egret, Little Egret, Squacco Heron, Night Heron, Little Bittern, Bittern, Spoonbill, Glossy Ibis, White Stork, Greylag Goose, Ruddy Shelduck, Garganey, Red-crested Pochard, Ferruginous Duck, Honey Buzzard, Black Kite, Marsh Harrier, Montagu's Harrier, Lesser Spotted Eagle, Booted Eagle, Hobby, Collared Pratincole, Little Gull, Mediterranean Gull, Gull-billed Tern, Caspian Tern, White-winged Black Tern, Black Tern, Whiskered Tern, Roller, Bee-eater, Syrian Woodpecker, Calandra Lark, Tawny Pipit, River Warbler, Moustached Warbler, Great Reed Warbler, Icterine Warbler, Olivaceous Warbler, Collared Flycatcher, Red-breasted Flycatcher, Bearded Tit, Penduline Tit, Golden Oriole, Rose-coloured Starling.

ACCESS: There is a network of reasonable roads around and among Lakes Razelm and Sinoe, both of which are easily reached from Mamaia, the package-holiday resort. In the south of the delta proper the village of Murighiol is welcoming, offering meals and rowboat excursions into the marshes. The starting point for the delta ferry boats is Tulcea, which has a hotel. Maliuc, in the delta, has a hotel which should be booked in advance. Elsewhere, see where the ferries lead and explore on foot or with a local boatman. This is no place for those on tight schedules.

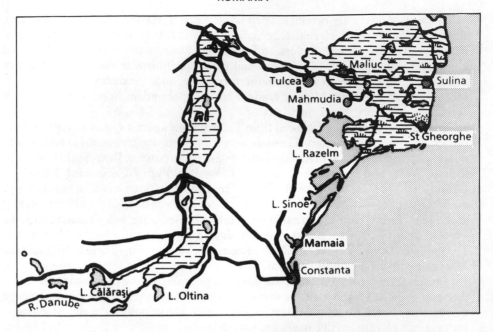

ROUTE: Constanţa has an international airport, and Mamaia offers package holidays. There is even a lagoon here with terns, gulls and waders from rear-facing hotel rooms.

Ditrău

This is a small village in the central Carpathians that makes a suitable base for those wishing to explore further than the delta and marshes of the Danube. Here the hills rise to nearly 2000 m (6560 feet), with deep valleys and extensive conifer forests creating an almost 'alpine' landscape. The birds are also typically alpine, with Nutcracker, Black Redstart, Sombre Tit and raptors that may include Golden Eagle. This area is not well explored, but it does have potential and full reports would be welcomed.

SUMMER: Golden Eagle, Honey Buzzard, Capercaillie, Black Grouse, Hoopoe, Nut-cracker, Grey Wagtail, Ring Ouzel, Sombre Tit, Crested Tit, Black Redstart, Firecrest, Crossbill, Raven.

ACCESS: The mountains and forests to the north of Ditrău, the Călimani and Rodna, are among the best for a variety of species. They are the only places for Black Grouse in Romania. Even Dotterel may breed in Rodna.

ROUTE: Via Bacău, then northwest on Route 15 to Bicaz, thence southwest to Gheor-gheni on Route 12C to join Route 12 north to Ditrău.

Satchinez

In the extreme west of Romania, the land drops from the heights of the Carpathians to the steppes of the Hungarian plain. Here the tributaries of the River Tisza meander over the level ground, slowly finding their way to the main river and ultimately to the Danube. Seasonal floods, oxbow lakes, pools and backwaters all created a marsh landscape that was systematically drained during the eighteenth century. Reedbeds which contained Glossy Ibis and Spoonbill until 1914 have given way to vast fields of cereals, and the sedge thickets and primeval oak forests have disappeared. Only in the area around Satchinez, 25 km (15½ miles) northwest of Timişoara, has any area of marsh remained. The pools and marshes here were declared a Monument of Nature in 1942, and 40 ha (100 acres) now form the Satchinez Bird Reserve. The area is noted mainly as a breeding haunt of herons — Purple Heron, Night Heron, Little Egret, Squacco Heron and Little Bittern — and these are found principally at Rîtul Dutin and Rîtul Mărăşeşti. The reserve also harbours a range of other species that are rare in this part of the country, including Greylag Goose, Ferruginous Duck, Marsh Harrier and White-winged Black Tern. The pond surrounds are the haunt of Penduline Tit, Bluethroat and an interesting collection of warblers, including Reed, Marsh and Savi's. The surrounding drained area is one of the best in Romania for Great Bustard.

SUMMER: Purple Heron, Little Egret, Squacco Heron, Night Heron, Little Bittern, White Stork, Greylag Goose, Ferruginous Duck, Marsh Harrier, White-winged Black Tern, Great Bustard, Penduline Tit, Bluethroat, Savi's Warbler, Reed Warbler, Marsh Warbler.

ACCESS: Leave Timişoara northwards on Route 69, and fork left to Sînandrei and Satchinez just outside the town. The main marsh and pools lie south of the village and are a reserve, though in fact the reserve covers a very small part of the area and most of the birds can also be seen outside it.

ROUTE: Timişoara is connected by air and train to other major Romanian cities.

SPAIN

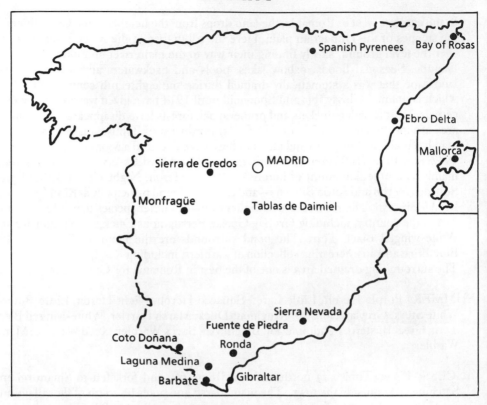

Spanish Pyrenees   Bay of Rosas

Ebro Delta

Mallorca

Sierra de Gredos   ○ MADRID

Monfragüe   Tablas de Daimiel

Sierra Nevada
Fuente de Piedra
Coto Doñana   Ronda
Laguna Medina
Barbate   Gibraltar

Barbate

Barbate is best known as the centre of the Spanish tuna-fish industry and is a busy, unpicturesque, easily forgotten little town. It is, however, an excellent base for exploring a variety of splendid birding areas along the Atlantic coast of southern Andalucía. To the west lies the famous Cape Trafalgar, with its old lighthouse, splendid beaches, spring lagoons and enough bushy cover to shelter migrants. Seabird passage may be exciting, with Gannet, shearwaters, skuas and terns all passing in numbers in suitable conditions. This is an excellent area for Audouin's Gull, often seen loafing on the beach, as well as Kentish Plover and Black-winged Stilt. Tawny Pipit is regular. Between Barbate and Trafalgar there is an excellent road through a fine forest of pines, with Woodlark, Dartford, Sardinian and Orphean Warblers, Hoopoe and migrants in season.

To the north is the beautiful hilltop town of Vejer de la Frontera, with Jackdaw and Lesser Kestrel, while to the south, through a military zone (do not stop and peer through binoculars or 'scopes), lies Zahara de los Atunes. Continue southwards along the coast beyond Zahara to a rocky peninsula, the Sierra de la Plata, which is the home of Europe's first colony of White-rumped Swifts. These birds breed in the disused nests of

182

Red-rumped Swallow in caves alongside the road that zigzags up the headland through a modern villa development. They arrive and breed late — June is probably the most reliable month.

Inland, the flat arable and grazing land east of the main N340 south of Tahivilla is the home of a few pairs of Great Bustard (very elusive: may take days to find them) and the more numerous Little Bustard. Further south still lies the Ojen valley, with lush groves, acres of scrub, high ridges and even a dam combining to produce one of those special places. Birds of a wide variety of species include Griffon and Egyptian Vultures, Short-toed and Booted Eagles and (with luck) Bonelli's Eagle, Montagu's Harrier, Buzzard, Red Kite and a wealth of small birds including Great Spotted Woodpecker.

Just south of Barbate, along the road to Zahara, is the tiny estuary of the Barbate River, with a modern bridge offering excellent vantage points over the mudbanks and the adjacent saltpans. Birds here often include Caspian Tern and Audouin's Gull, as well as several passage waders plus the occasional Spoonbill.

SUMMER: Cory's Shearwater, Manx Shearwater, Gannet, Cattle Egret, Little Egret, White Stork, Griffon Vulture, Egyptian Vulture, Booted Eagle, Bonelli's Eagle, Short-toed Eagle, Marsh Harrier, Montagu's Harrier, Sparrowhawk, Goshawk, Lesser Kestrel, Peregrine, Black-winged Stilt, Kentish Plover, Sandwich Tern, Caspian Tern, Audouin's Gull, Collared Pratincole, Bee-eater, Roller, Golden Oriole, Red-necked Nightjar, Calandra Lark, Short-toed Lark, Crested Lark, Woodlark, Thekla Lark,

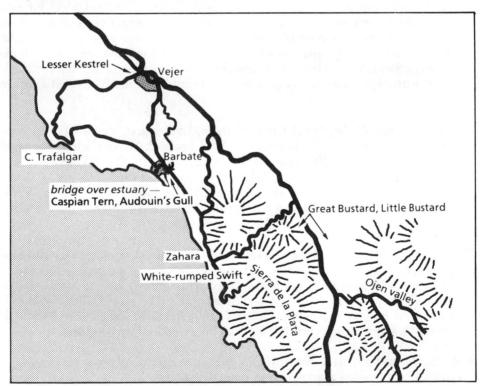

Tawny Pipit, Cetti's Warbler, Fan-tailed Warbler, Dartford Warbler, Sardinian Warbler, Orphean Warbler, Woodchat Shrike, Stonechat, Corn Bunting, Spotless Starling.

ACCESS: The whole area can be explored by road, with walking confined to the bushy area at Cape Trafalgar and the pine woods above Barbate. The Ojen valley can be motored to emerge above Los Barrios near Algeciras, though one of the best areas is by the dam near the western end of the valley.

ROUTE: Airports at Sevilla, Gibraltar and Málaga.

Las Tablas de Daimiel

In the Mancha region of Spain, the word *tablas* is used to indicate an area of flooding where rivers regularly overflow their banks to create uncontrolled marshland. As part of their conservation programme, the Spanish government have declared Las Tablas de Daimiel the smallest national park in the country. Here the waters of two rivers, the Ciguela and the Guadiana, overflow to create a huge network of waterways, lagoons and floating reedbeds. There is an excellent, modern park information centre, and it may be possible to arrange exploration by boat. In any case, the birds of the marshes and surrounding land are relatively easy to work via paths and roads.

Dominant are quite extraordinary numbers of Red-crested Pochard, which is far and away the most abundant duck species; others include Shoveler and Gadwall. Marsh and Montagu's Harriers are relatively common, and Hobby more or less regular. Other waterbirds include Little and Great Crested Grebes, Little Egret and Purple Heron, and White Storks are regular foragers here. Water Rail, Black-winged Stilt, Pratincole, plus a variety of passage waders can be seen, and Gull-billed and Whiskered Terns are regular.

SUMMER: Little Grebe, Great Crested Grebe, Little Egret, Purple Heron, White Stork, Gadwall, Shoveler, Red-crested Pochard, Pochard, Marsh Harrier, Montagu's Harrier, Hobby, Quail, Black-winged Stilt, Stone-curlew, Collared Pratincole, Little Ringed Plover, Gull-billed Tern, Whiskered Tern, Bee-eater, Hoopoe, Calandra Lark, Woodlark, Woodchat Shrike, Great Grey Shrike, Cetti's Warbler, Savi's Warbler, Moustached Warbler, Great Reed Warbler, Olivaceous Warbler, Bonelli's Warbler, Black-eared Wheatear, Bearded Tit, Reed Bunting.

ACCESS: Leave the main Madrid–Sevilla road westwards (signposted to Cuidad Real) at Manzanares or Puerto Lapice for Daimiel. From here the national park lies to the northwest over rough roads, but it is signposted. If in doubt ask for 'La Parque Nacional por favor', and be prepared for a volley of Manchegan directions and much pointing; the latter are the best clues to follow. The park centre has maps and guidebooks, and the staff will be able to help secure the best from this remarkably rich wetland.

ROUTE: Madrid airport is linked via the N1V, the main road southwards from the capital, which now has a fast motorway through its centre.

Coto Doñana

Named after Doña Ana, the wife of the Duke of Medina Sidonia who commanded the Spanish Armada, the Coto Doñana is one of Europe's top birding areas, visited by thousands of birders every year. Along this coast, the Atlantic has built up a huge dune beach that has diverted and restricted the outlet of the River Guadalquivir, creating behind it a huge area of seasonal floods known as the *marismas*. From late autumn, through the winter until the following summer, this area is covered by water which gradually dries out to leave islands (*vetas*) and later huge expanses of mud.

Taking a cross-section from west to east across the Coto, there is first the sea, which attracts a variety of seabirds including terns and marauding skuas, Gannet and large flocks of Scoter. The beach may be full of Sanderlings and Oystercatchers, with seasonal influxes of Whimbrel and other waders and a variable population of gulls that often includes Audouin's. Kentish Plovers breed. Then there are the dunes, varying in width from 100 m to 1 km or more (110–1000+ yards). They have a variable growth of stone pines and scrub, but are highly mobile. Defensive towers along the beach often hold Peregrine, and there are Short-toed Eagle, Stone-curlew, and Dartford and Sardinian Warblers. The next area, which lies between the dunes and the *marismas*, is wooded, with open glades often creating a parkland effect. Huge numbers of birds breed, including Europe's greatest concentration of raptors, and it is here that Imperial and Booted Eagles must be sought among the hordes of Black and Red Kites. Right alongside the wet *marismas* the largest colonies of herons and egrets can be found: species include Little and Cattle Egrets, Night and Purple Herons, Spoonbill and White Stork. The *marismas* are the great feeding ground on which all of these birds ultimately depend. In winter they are full of geese and duck, but as spring comes they are alive with migrant and breeding waders, Whiskered and Gull-billed Terns and the more recently established Flamingoes. Collared Pratincole is often numerous and Marsh Harrier abundant.

Across the *marismas* lie further areas of wood and grassland where raptors are again abundant and where visiting vultures are more often seen. Much of this land is being converted to agriculture, but some excellent areas of dwarf pines and scrub remain where Azure-winged Magpie and Great Spotted Cuckoo abound. There is even a recently (1986) established pair of Black-winged Kites, plus several Bee-eater colonies.

SUMMER: Purple Heron, Little Egret, Squacco Heron, Cattle Egret, Night Heron, Little Bittern, White Stork, Spoonbill, Flamingo, Marbled Teal, Red-crested Pochard, Egyptian Vulture, Griffon Vulture, Imperial Eagle, Booted Eagle, Red Kite, Black Kite, Short-toed Eagle, Peregrine, Black-winged Kite, Purple Gallinule, Avocet, Black-winged Stilt, Collared Pratincole, Slender-billed Gull, Audouin's Gull, Whiskered Tern, Gull-billed Tern, Great Spotted Cuckoo, Scops Owl, Red-necked Nightjar, Bee-eater, Roller, Hoopoe, Calandra Lark, Short-toed Lark, Crested Lark, Golden Oriole, Azure-winged Magpie, Green Woodpecker, Cetti's Warbler, Savi's Warbler, Great Reed Warbler, Melodious Warbler, Orphean Warbler, Sardinian Warbler, Subalpine Warbler, Spectacled Warbler, Dartford Warbler, Fan-tailed Warbler, Crested Tit, Tawny Pipit, Great Grey Shrike, Woodchat Shrike, Spotless Starling, Hawfinch, Serin.

SPRING: Black-tailed Godwit, Ruff, Greenshank, Spotted Redshank, Wood Sandpiper, Little Stint, Marsh Sandpiper, Black Tern.

WINTER: Geese, duck.

ACCESS: Large parts of the area are now contained within the Parc Nacional de Doñana, with its headquarters at the Acebuche Centre, while the main egret colonies and the heart of the Coto are a scientific reserve with restricted access. The Co-operativa of El Rocio runs half-day excursions by four-wheel-drive vehicles through the Parc Nacional, but these are often fully booked by tourists with no interest in wildlife and are expensive and pointless for birding. Fortunately much can be seen without leaving rights of way, and I suggest the following areas as offering the best birding opportunities.

El Rocio: The bridge at El Rocio is outstanding so long as there is water in the *marismas*. Excellent views of huge variety of birds from the roadside. Late evening produces flights of Night Heron.

La Rocina Centre: A sub-centre of the Parc, with an excellent hide overlooking the marsh west of El Rocio. Good for Little Bittern, Savi's and Great Reed Warblers. English-speaking receptionist will advise.

Acebuche Centre: The Parc HQ where the Co-operativa is based. Excellent shop, refreshment area, educational displays and free hides for watching for Purple Gallinule — almost the only 'good' spot for this species. Red-necked Nightjars sit out on the track after dark and there are many scrub birds here.

Palacio del Rey: In El Rocio (do not miss fabulous church except during last week of May, when 2 million 'pilgrims' hold a festival here), find the main 'square', and with your back to the bar-restaurant 'La Rocina' head eastwards along the left-hand side. After leaving the square, take the second left past the football 'stadium' to a modern concrete bridge. Continue out over a wooden bridge (excellent wader spot) to a rough track along the northern edge of the *marismas* towards Palacio del Rey. Explore woods, watch for raptors. Before the Palacio, fork right on to an ever-roughening track out into the *marismas*. With four-wheel-drive vehicles it is possible to reach a reservoir area, but this is a long, tough ride and not really necessary unless Crested Coot must be seen.

Beach: Drive as far south in Matalascanas as possible and park. Walk southwards along the beach for waders, gulls and terns. In a long day (and a very long walk), the mouth of the Guadalquivir may be reached opposite Sanlúcar de la Barrameda: watch for Slender-billed Gull.

Western Park: Take the Matalascanas — Huelva road, and after a few kilometres watch for a building on the right. Take the next right for typical scrub birds, plus Bee-eater (nesting under the track) and raptors. Also explore tracks on the left among the beach pines for Azure-winged Magpie etc.

ROUTE: Airports at Sevilla and Faro (Portugal). Leave the autoroute from Sevilla to Huelva signposted to Ballullos (not the Ballullos a few kilometres from Sevilla) and Almonte. Drive straight to El Rocio and on to Matalascanas.

186

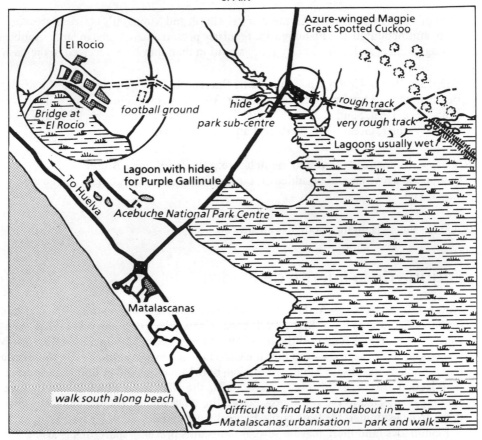

Ebro Delta

Despite its obvious attractions, the delta of the Ebro on Spain's Mediterranean coast remains sadly neglected by northern birders. Over 1200 ha (3000 acres) are now a game reserve protecting some of the country's most important seabird colonies, yet still visitors pass by on their way to what are seen as better birding areas. Perhaps this is because the Ebro delta lacks any 'special' birds, species that cannot be found elsewhere in Spain. Yet careful searching has produced breeding Lesser Crested Tern, some of the first in Europe, pre-dating the Farne Islands revelations of the BBC. Here then is a great wetland and the greatest unspoilt area on Spain's Mediterranean coast.

The delta consists of large lagoons, reedbeds, channels, ricefields and seasonally flooded areas of scrub. Though each should be thoroughly searched, it is the area nearest the sea that is of greatest attraction. Here, the lagoons shelter great breeding colonies of terns, including good numbers of Sandwich and Little, centred on Punta de Fangal. Gull-billed breed at Punta de la Baña, while Whiskered are widespread over the ricefields. Buda Island has Purple Herons in its vast reedbeds and, though numbers

187

vary, this is an important site for the species. Marsh and Montagu's Harriers are usually seen, and Spoonbill and Flamingo are regularly present, sometimes in large numbers. Passage waders and terns deserve more attention than they have received in the past.

SUMMER: Purple Heron, Spoonbill, Little Bittern, Red-crested Pochard, Marsh Harrier, Montagu's Harrier, Black-winged Stilt, Avocet, Kentish Plover, Gull-billed Tern, Whiskered Tern, Sandwich Tern, Little Tern, Lesser Crested Tern, Cetti's Warbler, Savi's Warbler, Great Reed Warbler, Fan-tailed Warbler.

ACCESS: Minor roads lead into the delta from the N340 near Amposta. To the areas mentioned above should be added an exploration of La Encanizada, La Tancada and Canal Vell.

ROUTE: Valencia, to the south, has an airport.

Laguna de la Fuente de Piedra

Now protected by ICONA, this unique saline lagoon can at last be treated fully, rather than hidden away as it was in the 1970 book of this title. For many years it has been a well-known secret that this was the second breeding place of Flamingoes in Europe (the Camargue being the first — and now the Coto Doñana makes a third). The trouble was that the colony was always liable to predation, both by natural and by human plunderers. The lagoon also dries up very quickly, and if the islands on which the birds breed become connected to the lakeshores before the chicks hatch the whole colony abandons. In late summer, the lagoon may be totally dry and devoid of birds.

Flamingoes (and there may be several thousands present) apart, this is also a good spot for Slender-billed Gull, Gull-billed Tern, Avocet, Black-winged Stilt and Red-crested Pochard. The surrounding fields and olive groves hold the species one would expect in this part of Spain.

A somewhat awkward drive to the north, near Aquilar, brings one to the Laguna de Zonar, which holds water throughout the summer when all around it is bone-dry. There are some areas of reed with the usual species, and Red-crested Pochard, grebes and other waterbirds can be found. Zonar is, however, one of the famous places for pure, wild White-headed Duck. Further north, the area west of the N331 around San Sebastian de los Ballesteros holds Little Bustard. These areas are not included in the checklist that follows.

SUMMER: Flamingo, Red-crested Pochard, Marsh Harrier, Avocet, Black-winged Stilt, Gull-billed Tern, Hoopoe, Woodchat Shrike.

ACCESS: From Antequera, take the N334 Sevilla road to Fuente de Piedra. Drive through this small town, cross the railway, and take a track on the left to the rubbish dump and to a small hill beyond which gives excellent views over the northern part of the lagoon. Early morning is best before heat haze makes viewing impossible. Return to the road and continue around the northern shore to other roadside viewpoints at the northwestern corner.

ROUTE: Málaga airport, then directly northward to Antequera. This is a must for anyone using Málaga as an entry port for a Doñana trip.

Gibraltar

Gibraltar is a tiny piece of Britain in Andalucía and has all the usual attractions associated with the British abroad: Watney's Red Barrel, fish and chips, discos, plus tall helmeted policemen! It has, however, the saving grace of experiencing one of the most dramatic migrations of birds of prey in Europe, with more birds passing overhead even than at the more famous Bosporus. Most numerous are Black Kite and Honey Buzzard, which often pass over in flocks several hundred strong on the short (25-km/15½-mile) crossing to and from North Africa. Short-toed and Booted Eagles, Goshawk and Sparrowhawk, harriers and, of course, White Stork are also numerous. No fewer than 17 species of raptor regularly pass over Gibraltar. Numbers are largest in autumn, but the birds tend to be higher than in the spring. White Stork is the earliest spring migrant, with Honey Buzzard the latest. Best seasons are late March and late September for the widest variety of species.

Warning: migration is always best with a westerly wind. If an easterly, the Levanter, is blowing, it is better to cross the border and travel westwards in Spain to the rubbish tip on the right-hand side of the N340 before Tarifa, or to the viewpoint on the left-hand side slightly earlier. In either case, Griffon Vulture will be an added bonus.

Best places to watch are Jew's Gate in spring (Peregrines on display almost continuously) and Princess Caroline's Battery and the Upper Galleries in autumn. Other good birds can also be seen, including an excellent passage of seabirds from Europa Point and Barbary Partridge at St Bernard's Chapel, especially in the evening. Grounded migrants may be sought anywhere on the Rock where there is cover.

PASSAGE: Cory's Shearwater, Manx Shearwater, Gannet, White Stork, Short-toed Eagle, Booted Eagle, Osprey, Goshawk, Sparrowhawk, Black Kite, Honey Buzzard, Montagu's Harrier, Barbary Partridge, Sardinian Warbler, Hoopoe.

ACCESS: Local maps of the Rock are available free at tourist information centres and at most hotels. Taxis are cheap and have a fixed-rate system. Most have radios, so even an occupied cab can be waved down and asked to request another to pick you up from any part of Gibraltar. Car hire is unnecessary, except for trips to Spain. Best excursions are towards Tarifa (see above) and to the lovely Castellar de la Frontera. Pass through the frontier to La Linea and take the Algeciras road. At the junction with the N340 turn left, and then after 3 km (nearly 2 miles) right towards Jimena. After 10 km (6 miles) fork left and climb to Castellar for Griffon, Lesser Kestrel and much more.

ROUTE: Gibraltar has an international airport with an exciting runway extending into the sea. (See map on page 190.)

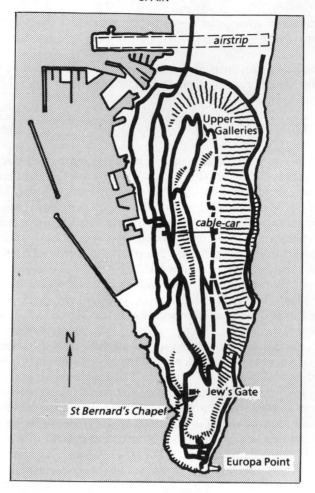

Sierra de Gredos

To the north and west of Madrid lies a long ridge of high mountains running more or less parallel with the road (the NV1) from the capital to Trujillo. In the west this is known as the Sierra de Gredos, in the east as the Sierra de Guadarrama. The whole is one of the best areas for raptors in Spain, and also has many of the other species that make this part of Europe so attractive to birders.

Guadarrama lies only 60 km (37 miles) north of Madrid, and rises to over 8000 feet (2440 m) at Peñalara. The high passes (even the main A6 passes over the hills here) provide excellent access through the pine forests, the green mountain meadows and to some first-rate raptor watchpoints. Griffon Vultures are easily seen and the variety of eagles includes Short-toed and Booted, as well as the more elusive Golden and Bonelli's. Even Black Vultures find a stronghold here and both kites, both buzzards and Goshawk are regularly seen. Much of Guadarrama is heavily forested, and the woods

190

should be explored along with the roadside scrub for smaller birds, including Golden Oriole, Firecrest, Bonelli's Warbler and Citril Finch, as well as Dartford Warbler, Rock Bunting and Great Grey Shrike.

The Sierra de Gredos is more remote and has the added advantage of a lowland area along the River Tietar at Candeleda. The area north of Arenas has much the same raptors as Guadarrama, but the hills are less wooded and open country and scrub birds predominate. Nevertheless, there are still Crested Tit and Crossbill, along with Black Vulture. Around Candeleda the river is lined with alders, poplars and oaks, and these are the haunt of Cetti's Warbler, Hoopoe and Golden Oriole as well as Bee-eater. There are Azure-winged Magpie, Red-rumped Swallow, Tawny Pipit, Woodchat and in some areas Rufous Bush Chat.

SUMMER: White Stork, Griffon Vulture, Black Vulture, Golden Eagle, Bonelli's Eagle, Booted Eagle, Short-toed Eagle, Buzzard, Honey Buzzard, Red Kite, Black Kite, Goshawk, Hobby, Peregrine, Common Sandpiper, Stone-curlew, Quail, Azure-winged Magpie, Golden Oriole, Hoopoe, Bee-eater, Roller, Woodchat Shrike, Green Woodpecker, Lesser Spotted Woodpecker, Red-necked Nightjar, Thekla Lark, Calandra Lark, Tawny Pipit, Crag Martin, Red-rumped Swallow, Short-toed Tree-creeper, Rock Thrush, Blue Rock Thrush, Firecrest, Melodious Warbler, Bonelli's Warbler, Dartford Warbler, Subalpine Warbler, Crested Tit, Citril Finch, Crossbill, Cirl Bunting, Rock Bunting, Rock Sparrow.

ACCESS: Sierra de Guadarrama can be explored from the main NV1, leaving the A6 at Guadarrama town. Further north, the old road looks over a huge basin of forest with soaring raptors passing from east to west. The minor roads to Navacerrada are excellent, and a turn left (north) to the Puerto de Navacerrada produces more raptors over more forested areas. The Lozoya valley is thoroughly recommended, especially for raptors. Though the reservoirs here and at Manzanares to the southeast are high-level waters, they do still produce a few duck and, in any case, their surrounds are full of Azure-winged Magpies. Ornitho-culture buffs should not miss Segovia and El Escorial.

Sierra de Gredos can be reached by a variety of roads heading westwards just south of Guadarrama via El Escorial. By taking the C600 to Avila, the possibility of two routes to Arenas is opened up. The C502 traverses the Puerto de Menga, whereas the C500 is less used. In either case, the area around Arenas is spectacular and should not be hurried. Candeleda is reached by the N501 some 20 km (12 miles) west of Arenas. The road from this town south to the River Tietar is excellent, and most birders then walk along the river-reservoir banks.

ROUTE: Madrid airport is within easy reach of both areas, and there are good hotels in all areas.

Mallorca

Mallorca is the largest of the Spanish Balearic Islands and one of the world's top tourist centres. From July to September it is crowded with mainly British and German visitors, though at other times it can be pleasantly empty. The island has also always been a popular birding site and worth a week or even a fortnight of exploration. Most birding visitors come in spring, from March to May, and stay in the north of Mallorca in the Puerto Pollensa area. This is undoubtedly the best bird area, as well as one of the most pleasant parts of the island, even if it is, at times, a bit like a warm 'Minsmere'. Do not despair if you are heading for another area; there are excellent bird spots scattered through the island.

Mallorca offers three major ornitho-attractions. Black Vulture finds one of its strongholds here, and is regularly seen in the mountains that occupy the northwestern part of the island. Eleonora's Falcon breeds at several places, and Marmora's Warbler can be found locally here and there. Additionally, there are several exciting migration spots that regularly produce superb birds, and the range of breeding species includes Osprey, Peregrine, Booted Eagle, Scops Owl and so on.

Based at Puerto Pollensa, the visitor is within easy reach of the Boquer valley for excellent migrants, as well as Blue Rock Thrush and Rock Sparrow. To the north lies Cape Formentor, with its Eleonora's Falcon, Marmora's Warbler and excellent seabird passage. To the east is the Albufereta and the Albufera Marsh, now an ICONA reserve and Mallorca's most famous bird spot. Here are Purple Heron, Little Egret, Osprey, Marsh Harrier plus many warblers. The Albufera is also a noted feeding ground of Eleonora's Falcon. Even the best spots for Black Vulture are only a short distance away. The lovely wooded Ternelles valley produces these birds, as does the road immediately west of Tomir, a substantial peak on the road between Pollensa and Soller. Vultures also appear at the two reservoirs beyond Tomir, where there are Rock Thrushes too. In the south of Mallorca there are several habitats, including the excellent Salinas de Levante. Here, Flamingo, Avocet and Kentish Plover can be found alongside many migrant waders. Porto Colom is another fine area, with Marmora's Warbler and Thekla Lark among others. This is also one of the better places for Audouin's Gull.

SUMMER: Manx Shearwater, Cory's Shearwater, Purple Heron, Little Egret, Little Bittern, Flamingo, Black Vulture, Marsh Harrier, Osprey, Eleonora's Falcon, Peregrine, Red Kite, Booted Eagle, Stone-curlew, Kentish Plover, Avocet, Black-winged Stilt, Audouin's Gull, Scops Owl, Hoopoe, Woodchat Shrike, Pallid Swift, Crag Martin, Short-toed Lark, Thekla Lark, Blue Rock Thrush, Rock Thrush, Tawny Pipit, Fan-tailed Warbler, Great Reed Warbler, Cetti's Warbler, Moustached Warbler, Marmora's Warbler, Sardinian Warbler, Serin, Cirl Bunting, Raven.

ACCESS: Cape Formentor is reached by road out of Puerto Pollensa. At the far end a path leads from the lighthouse to an excellent seawatching spot near the cliffs, but Eleonora's can be seen from the road just before the lighthouse. It is worth stopping at several points between Puerto Pollensa and Cape Formentor, especially where the road approaches the western cliffs, for Marmora's Warbler. Pleasure boats from Puerto Pollensa to Cala San Vicente pass around the cape and can give excellent views.

Boquer valley is a short walk from Puerto Pollensa along the road towards Formentor, turning left along a track between two rows of pines. Simply follow the track through the farm to the valley and eventually to the sea.

Sierras: the tactics in searching for Black Vulture are to drive along the road between Pollensa and Soller to Tomir peak and beyond. Alternatively, walk the Ternelles valley, which is signposted from the main road just north of Pollensa town. Permits must be obtained on Mondays from the Banca Marco in Pollensa; they are valid day of issue only. There is very limited car parking at a set of private gates.

For Albufera, drive eastwards from Puerto Pollensa to Alcudia and continue along the coast road towards Artá. The marsh will be found just past the Esperanza Hotel. Park and walk (drive) inland along the southern bank of a wide drainage channel to the farm; ask the staff for news. Continue back towards the sea along one of two tracks. Finish by walking back to the Esperanza along the main road.

For Salinas de Levante, find your way to Petra in the southeast of Mallorca and then check carefully that you take the road signposted to Vila Franca and Felanitx. In Campos, follow signs for Colonia San Jordi and continue to the salinas. The main entrance is on the right 1 km (just over ½ mile) after a sharp S-bend. Access is highly restricted and liable to change. Birdwatchers have recently been denied access.

Porto Colom lies in the southeast of Mallorca, and the main area of interest is easily found by turning left on reaching the harbour and proceeding along the peninsula to the lighthouse. The scrub is good for Marmora's as are the fields for Thekla Lark. The harbour produces Andouin's Gull.

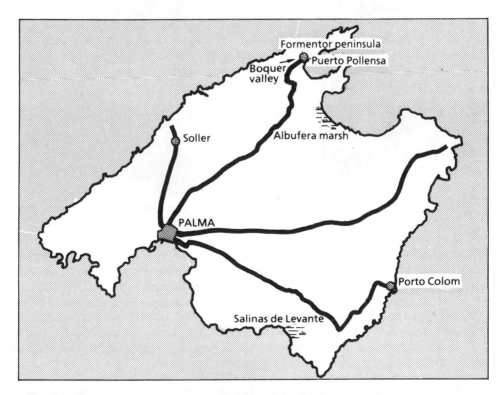

ROUTE: Abundant flights to Palma and easy car hire.

Laguna Medina

The Laguna Medina is one of those little places that looks as if it may be worth a stop, but which is actually a little gem deserving at least a full day. It is an ICONA reserve, well managed though with free public access, and lies to the southeast of Jerez just across the A4 autoroute. Medina is a natural, shallow lake, fringed with reeds and with broad shallow margins. Though principally a haunt of duck, it also attracts passage waders and terns, the occasional raptor and is a noted haunt of the rare White-headed Duck and Black-necked Grebe. Crested Coot is almost certainly a thing of the past.

Red-crested Pochard, Shoveler and Garganey are regular, and Black-winged Stilt, Ruff and Whiskered and Black Terns appear in season.

SUMMER: Black-necked Grebe, Little Grebe, Little Egret, Cattle Egret, Shoveler, Gadwall, Garganey, Teal, Pochard, Red-crested Pochard, White-headed Duck, Marsh Harrier, Montagu's Harrier, Short-toed Eagle, Red-legged Partridge, Black-winged Stilt, Hoopoe, Crested Lark, Short-toed Lark, Great Reed Warbler, Cetti's Warbler, Fan-tailed Warbler, Melodious Warbler, Sardinian Warbler.

PASSAGE: Ruff, Greenshank, Wood Sandpiper, Little Stint, Whiskered Tern, Gull-billed Tern, Black Tern, Mediterranean Gull.

ACCESS: The Laguna lies alongside the C440 eastwards of its junction with the A4 towards Medina Sidonia near Jerez. Access is free to the surrounding paths and picnic area — avoid summer weekends. Walk all the way along the western (right-hand) shore, as well as the northern shore with its more extensive reedbeds.

ROUTE: Airport at Sevilla, and easily combined with exploration of other areas of southern Andalucía.

Monfragüe

Monfragüe (the ü is pronounced as a w) is a natural park centred on a precipitous ridge running roughly west to east north of Trujillo alongside the now dammed River Tajo. However, we also include here the huge area of rolling plains around Trujillo itself and extending westwards to Cáceres. The two areas are quite distinct, and offer quite different types of birds. Monfragüe is one of Spain's outstanding raptor haunts; the plains to the south are for bustards and other open-country species.

Above all else, Monfragüe is known as one of the strongholds of the Black Vulture. These birds may be seen at almost any point in the park, but the best watchpoint is from the Embalse de Torrejon southwards along the ridge of the Sierra de las Corchuelas. This same spot is also good for Imperial, Golden and Short-toed Eagles, Black Kite and Griffon and Egyptian Vultures. The most spectacular birding, however, can be had at the rocky pinnacle of Peñafalcón. Here Griffon and Egyptian Vultures breed, and soar endlessly overhead viewed from the road on the eastern side of the Tajo. The pinnacle also holds Black Stork — look into low cracks on the right-hand side — and Eagle Owl, which is almost impossible to see. Here too there are Chough, Crag Martin, Red-rumped Swallow, Alpine Swift and Black-eared Wheatear. The road running east-wards along the southern side of the River Tietar descends into a wooded valley with cork oaks that has Cetti's Warbler, Hawfinch, Azure-winged Magpie, Woodchat Shrike, Booted Eagle and Black-winged Kite.

To the south, Trujillo is famed as the birthplace of Pizarro and for its beautiful town square — enjoy an evening drink, with White Stork, Pallid Swift and numerous Lesser Kestrels. To the south are rolling plains that hold Great and Little Bustard and both Pin-tailed and Black-bellied Sandgrouse. These plains extend to and beyond Cáceres, and areas recommended are those where others have been regularly successful — not the only places where the birds occur. There are also Calandra Lark, Montagu's Harrier, White Stork and Black Kite.

SUMMER: White Stork, Black Stork, Egyptian Vulture, Griffon Vulture, Black Vulture, Golden Eagle, Imperial Eagle, Booted Eagle, Red Kite, Black Kite, Short-toed Eagle, Black-winged Kite, Lesser Kestrel, Great Bustard, Little Bustard, Pin-tailed Sand-grouse, Black-bellied Sandgrouse, Pallid Swift, Alpine Swift, Hoopoe, Calandra Lark, Crag Martin, Red-rumped Swallow, Golden Oriole, Azure-winged Magpie, Great Spotted Cuckoo, Cetti's Warbler, Sardinian Warbler, Blackcap, Woodchat Shrike, Great Grey Shrike, Hawfinch, Chough.

ACCESS: Some areas of the park are closed to traffic, but all of the birds can be seen from a good network of public highways. To the south roads penetrate through the plains, though some walking to protect car springs from damage is advised.

Monfragüe has a tiny park HQ with a resident naturalist at Villareal de San Carlos; also a couple of cheap bar-restaurants. The park itself is reached along the Plasencia road from Trujillo where it crosses the River Tajo.

Peñafalcón is across the dammed river on a vicious hairpin bend in the main road. Park before or beyond and watch vultures and raptors; search the low caves on the right-hand side for Black Stork.

Saltos de Torrejon is the dam where a road crosses the empoundment. Continue on the north side, climbing steeply until a parking area is seen on the right. Look southward over the Sierra de las Corchuelas for Imperial and Golden Eagles and Black Vulture. Black Stork may overfly the reservoir to the north. Further viewpoints are northward along this road, which runs south and east of the River Tietar. Further north still, the road descends towards Bazagona through good forest for Black-winged Kite.

Castillo: this castle atop the Sierra de las Corchuelas is reached via a motorable track on the right-hand side about 1 km (just over ½ mile) before reaching Peñafalcón. It is excellent for vultures, including Black.

From Trujillo, for bustards, leave the town towards Madrid and turn right after 2 km (1¼ miles) in Belen. Continue to the village and follow to the hilltop beyond, where views of rolling plains can be had. Scan with telescope for Great and Little Bustards, Montagu's Harrier, and watch for Calandra Lark etc.

All the plains around the unattractive town of Cáceres hold bustards, as well as both sandgrouse. By taking the following route, all can be explored in a day. Leave the city eastwards toward Trujillo on the N521 and turn right after 8 km (5 miles) to Sierra de

Black-winged Kite

Fuentes (top Great Bustard spot). Continue to join C520 and turn right, back to Cáceres. Turn left in the town and take the N630 towards Mérida. At Valdesalor take a right at the end of a small housing development to 'Estacion de Valduelnas'. Peer over the railway to the plains beyond. For well-sprung vehicles, return to the main road and continue southwards to the Rio Salor. Just before the bridge, a track on the right leads over an old bridge and thence on past a farm into the plains. Return to Cáceres once more, but in the suburbs turn sharp left toward Badajoz. After a garage and café on the left (Rollers on the right), watch for the Rio Salor. Cross the bridge and in 100 m, among a line of eucalypts, turn right and park. Finally, return to Cáceres and take the new bypass north of the town east towards Trujillo. At a set of traffic lights turn left towards 'Talavan' on the CC912. After 10 km (6¼ miles) turn right towards Magasca. About 7 km (4½ miles) along, to the south, lies Las Encinillas, a farm where a track leads to bustard country.

ROUTE: Airports at Madrid and Lisbon (Portugal). Trujillo and Cáceres lie on the E4 (NV) joining the two.

Sierra Nevada

Reaching over 3350 m (11,000 feet), within 40 km (25 miles) of the Mediterranean, and now well developed as a ski resort, the Sierra Nevada is one of the easiest high-altitude regions of Spain to explore for birds. It is also well situated for those for whom a trip to Andalucía would not be complete without a visit to Granada to see the

196

Alhambra and the Generalife. WARNING: these sites are so overrun with tourists (would inundated be a better word?) that early-morning visits are essential for self-preservation. Nevertheless, they are fabulous.

Granada is the gateway to the Sierra Nevada, and a narrow mountain road twists and turns its way upward from the southeastern suburbs of the city. At first it passes through an agricultural valley, but later there are pine woods, grazing meadows and ultimately the bare mountain itself. Each habitat is worth exploring, with different species at different levels until at the top there is not much more than Alpine Accentor — though these are common birds outside the Parador Hotel.

SUMMER: Golden Eagle, Peregrine, Chough, Short-toed Lark, Alpine Swift, Crag Martin, Alpine Accentor, Black Wheatear, Woodchat Shrike, Hoopoe, Rock Thrush, Sardinian Warbler, Serin, Rock Bunting, Ortolan Bunting.

ACCESS: The Parador in the Sierra Nevada is well signposted from Granada. There are several large skiing hotels, but the Parador must be booked in advance.

ROUTE: From Málaga airport, drive eastward through the city and take the coastal road to Nerja and Motril. Turn left to Granada.

Spanish Pyrenees

The Pyrenees are considerably more than a handy boundary between France and Spain. These are real mountains, with high, snow-capped peaks, barren screes, dense pine forests and green mountain meadows; in fact, not what the average person thinks of as Spain at all. Here too is one of the best birding spots in Europe, with birds of prey in both number and variety together with a wealth of other mountain, as well as lowland, birds. Declining in other parts of Iberia, several species find their last stronghold among the mountain massifs.

Outstanding is the Lammergeier in one of its two last European strongholds. With one exception, these are the only Lammergeiers left in Iberia. There are other vultures, plus a variety of raptors which includes Golden, Bonelli's, Booted and Short-toed Eagles, Peregrine, Hobby, Red and Black Kites and Montagu's Harrier. Other species of particular interest include Black Woodpecker, Alpine Accentor, Citril Finch and the elusive Wallcreeper, but there are plenty of other, more widespread birds as well.

As with all mountain areas, the essential is to explore fully at various altitudes, from the lush meadows and streams via the forests to the high passes. By and large, there is no need to trek into remote areas or climb high peaks.

SUMMER: Lammergeier, Griffon Vulture, Egyptian Vulture, Golden Eagle, Short-toed Eagle, Bonelli's Eagle, Booted Eagle, Buzzard, Red Kite, Black Kite, Montagu's Harrier, Peregrine, Sparrowhawk, Black Woodpecker, White-backed Woodpecker, Alpine Swift, Crag Martin, Golden Oriole, Alpine Accentor, Dipper, Wallcreeper, Woodchat Shrike, Blue Rock Thrush, Rock Thrush, Black Wheatear, Bonelli's Warbler, Melodious Warbler, Crested Tit, Citril Finch, Rock Sparrow, Chough.

197

ACCESS: A good base is the town of Jaca, though the village of Torla is right in the mountains and perfect for the Ordesa National Park.

Ordesa has long been the most famous area in the Pyrenees and was, at one time, regarded as the most reliable Lammergeier site in Europe. It still produces this bird, as well as Griffon, Booted Eagle and, among the lower pine forests, Black Woodpecker and Crested Tit. From Torla, which lies east of Jaca, simply follow the road northwards then east to the head of the valley. There are plentiful walks and a good guidebook detailing tracks, paths and a variety of overnight accommodation for those who wish to walk through the park.

For San Juan and Riglos, head westward from Jaca on the C134 to the turning on the left (south) towards San Juan de la Peña. This magnificent road has breeding Griffon and Lammergeier before San Juan Monastery. At Bernues turn right to Santa Maria. Here turn left toward Ayerbe and watch for pinnacled red rocks on the left. Take the next turning to Riglos. Drive as far as possible and continue to the church. Watch the cliffs ahead. Here are Lammergeier, Griffon Vulture and one of the best spots for Wallcreeper; also Blue Rock Thrush, Black Wheatear, and Rock Sparrow in the church tower.

Fos de Biniés is a dramatic gorge with close-up views of Griffon, plus Chough, Alpine Swift and Dipper. Leave Jaca westward on the C134 to Berdun, turn right (north) to Biniés and continue to the gorge. Follow this road to just before Ansó and turn right to Hecho for possible Lammergeier and Golden Eagle, plus Griffon, Red Kite and Booted Eagle. At Hecho, turn right again for Melodious Warbler and Woodchat Shrike. Continue back to the N240.

For Fos de Arbayun, head west from Jaca, passing Berdun and the huge Yesa Reservoir, and watch for the turning to the right (north) to Lumbier. In this village fork right to the Fos de Arbayun, which holds vultures, both kites, Booted Eagle, Golden Oriole and both rock thrushes.

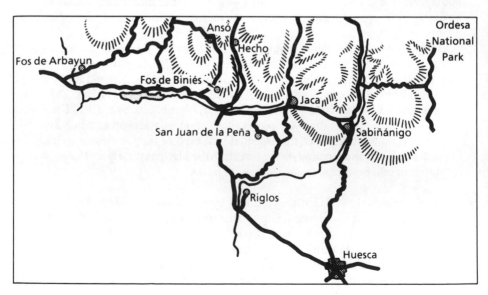

ROUTE: Nearest airports are Bilbao and San Sebastian, but do not ignore the possibilities of a French connection via Toulouse.

Ronda

For many years Ronda was regarded as the best area for mountain birds in Andalucía, and even today the town remains a splendid centre for the exploration of the sierras of this part of Spain. The town, divided in two by its deep gorge, is unique and has attracted tourists for generations. Today there are more hotels and hostels in the area, and the scope for exploration is considerably greater as a result. Many of the birds remain and, though the vultures of Ronda have disappeared, they can still be seen in many areas. The town still has Chough, Lesser Kestrel and Crag Martin, and the surrounding mountains hold Golden, Short-toed, Bonelli's and Booted Eagles, Peregrine, Goshawk, Egyptian Vulture, Black Wheatear, Blue Rock Thrush and Rock Bunting. Eagle Owls can also be found here, but as ever they are elusive.

SUMMER: Griffon Vulture, Egyptian Vulture, Golden Eagle, Short-toed Eagle, Booted Eagle, Bonelli's Eagle, Buzzard, Goshawk, Sparrowhawk, Peregrine, Lesser Kestrel, Little Owl, Eagle Owl, Alpine Swift, Woodlark, Blue Rock Thrush, Black Wheatear, Crag Martin, Red-rumped Swallow, Grey Wagtail, Chough, Raven, Rock Sparrow, Cirl Bunting, Rock Bunting.

ACCESS: Almost any one of the minor mountain roads radiating from Ronda will produce birds, and exploration of the high passes is strongly advised. A favoured area lies south of the C339 to the west of Ronda, in the area of the Sierra Margarita south to the Sierra Ubrique and bounded in the west by El Bosque. The Puerto del Boyor above Grazalema is excellent down to Benamahoma — the C344. The hills here have all the raptors, and the valleys produce the smaller birds. The tiny CA531 from Grazalema to Zahara is likewise first-class, with vultures, eagles, Choughs and many other typical birds. Further south the C341 leads southwest from Ronda, with minor turnings to the right such as the MA549 and MA548 and MA511 being particularly worthwhile.

Ronda offers a variety of accommodation, but do take a drink at the bar of the Reina Christina for magnificent views from the clifftop gardens. Ice-cold beer and Lesser Kestrel at a few yards — delicious!

ROUTE: Airports at Málaga and Gibraltar are roughly equidistant, and the route then follows the dreadful Costa del Sol to San Pedro. Although it then winds through the village, it is fast beyond there.

Rosas

The Costa Brava has become, along with Benidorm and the Costa del Sol, an international playground for the people of northern Europe. The development of high-rise hotels, along with all the other paraphernalia of modern tourism, has changed the Mediterranean coastline in a short 30 years. Estartit and La Escala, which once gave so many birders their first taste of Spanish birding, are now almost uninhabitable by birds. Fortunately, the marshes just along the coast, to the north of the Roman town of Ampurias, remained 'difficult' to develop and have now been accorded reserve status by the Catalan government. Since October 1983, the marshes around the mouths of the Rivers Fluvia and Muga have been known as the Aiguamolls de l'Emporda.

Inland lie areas of lagoons and floods, while there are extensive saltmarshes nearer the sea. Even the beach here is relatively unfrequented, though visiting birders should be careful not to direct binoculars too close to the intrepid nudists, who still make the long trek for a bit of peace and quiet. Almost 300 species have been recorded and, with greater management, there is hope that an increasing number will stay to breed. Penduline Tit, Purple Heron, Cetti's, Savi's and Fan-tailed Warblers, as well as many less specialised wetland birds such as Lesser Grey Shrike, already fall into this category. Waders are often plentiful on passage, and both Cattle and Little Egrets are often abundant. Flamingoes are regular visitors, and raptors include Marsh Harrier and Short-toed Eagle. The sea is a regular winter haunt of divers and sea-duck, so there is something for everyone throughout the year at this splendid reserve.

The surrounding countryside, though much despoiled, is still interesting enough a little way inland. In particular, the hills between La Escala and Estartit are still full of warblers in the scrub and backing pine forests. Here is a likely spot for Marmora's Warbler, Black Wheatear and occasional Eleonora's Falcon.

SUMMER: Little Egret, Cattle Egret, Purple Heron, Little Bittern, Flamingo, Marsh Harrier, Short-toed Eagle, Kentish Plover, Stone-curlew, Black-winged Stilt, Little Tern, Scops Owl, Bee-eater, Hoopoe, Short-toed Lark, Blue Rock Thrush, Alpine Swift, Pallid Swift, Red-rumped Swallow, Tawny Pipit, Lesser Grey Shrike, Woodchat Shrike, Penduline Tit, Black Wheatear, Black-eared Wheatear, Savi's Warbler, Cetti's Warbler, Fan-tailed Warbler, Great Reed Warbler, Moustached Warbler, Orphean Warbler, Spectacled Warbler, Sardinian Warbler, Subalpine Warbler, Dartford Warbler, Marmora's Warbler, Olivaceous Warbler, Serin.

ACCESS: From La Escala, drive northwards to Ampurias and continue on foot into the reserve. There are signs indicating routes, but access may change — so enquire locally. Alternatively, the reserve may be approached from the north through Rosas. For scrub and forest, leave La Escala southward along the shore road and continue towards Estartit. The best areas are near the coast and, in the southern part, inland of Estartit where roads lead into forest areas.

ROUTE: Gerona airport is only a short drive away, and there is plenty of accommodation.

SWEDEN

Abisko

Twenty years ago, Abisko was one of the most remote birding spots in Europe. It remains so today. There are plans for a road to pass through the area, but this seems to be a long time coming. Abisko lies 170 km (106 miles) north of the Arctic Circle near the Norwegian border and can be visited only by rail. The iron-ore deposits of Kiruna are carried westwards to the port of Narvik during the winter, when the Gulf of Bothnia is closed by ice. The trains run some five times a day and exploration is on foot.

The area is simply beautiful, with mountains rising steeply from the shores of Lake Torneträsk. In the distance is the 'Lap Gate', a prominently raised U-shaped valley. A full exploration of the area is essential. The high tops are basically tundra, with Shore Lark, Snow Bunting, Long-tailed Skua, Ptarmigan and Dotterel. Descending to the edge of the tree line, there are Lapland Bunting and Arctic Warbler, the latter a

201

speciality of the area. The woods are full of Willow Warblers and Arctic Redpolls, while the marshes hold Bluethroat, Whimbrel, Greenshank and Rough-legged Buzzard. Red-necked Phalarope breeds, but Broad-billed Sandpiper and Temminck's Stint are no more than spring migrants.

'As a visit to Abisko requires considerable planning and equipment, it would also be a good idea to check on the likelihood of the season turning out to be a 'lemming year'. Visitors during such seasons will enjoy far greater numbers of the major raptors and breeding skuas.

SUMMER: Black-throated Diver, Long-tailed Duck, Rough-legged Buzzard, Merlin, Ptarmigan, Willow Grouse, Golden Plover, Dotterel, Whimbrel, Greenshank, Temminck's Stint, Broad-billed Sandpiper, Red-necked Phalarope, Long-tailed Skua, Hawk Owl, Shore Lark, Redwing, Fieldfare, Ring Ouzel, Bluethroat, Wheatear, Arctic Warbler, Willow Warbler, Pied Flycatcher, Red-throated Pipit, Rock Pipit, Great Grey Shrike, Arctic Redpoll, Pine Grosbeak, Brambling, Lapland Bunting, Snow Bunting.

ACCESS: To get the best from Abisko, one must be fit, prepared to walk and carry a hefty rucksack all day. Hiking is the main summer sport of the Abisko National Park, and the Swedish Touring Club has established a network of huts at walkable distances to enable tourists to explore the area. These huts vary from the very simple to comfortable, wardened places, but they all require visitors to bring their own sleeping bags, food, cutlery and crockery (plastic?) and to look after themselves. Though they cannot be booked in advance, they have the reputation of never turning anyone away, a reassuring policy that can lead to overcrowding. Do not venture into this area without: walking boots, proper waterproofs, survival rations, compass, map (BD6), and mosquito repellent (best purchased in Sweden).

The Abisko Turiststation, 980 24 Abisko, is actually a hotel that can be booked via Svenska Turistförening, Stureplan 2, Fack, 108 80, Stockholm (tel: 08 22 72 00). It opens from mid-June until near the end of September and is decidedly expensive. Next door is a two-dormitory 'hut'. The best time to visit is June, preferably the second two weeks. There is a ski-lift that makes access to the high tops quite simple.

ROUTE: By rail from Sweden or Norway five times a day. The railway has many small stops and it is a good idea to get a return ticket to Narvik when purchasing it so that one can explore stations westwards on the same ticket as that used for access to Abisko. Note: Abisko Turiststation, not Abisko Östra, is the correct station at which to get off.

Ånnsjön

This is a large shallow lake in central Sweden lying near the Norwegian frontier west of Östersund. It has some surrounding hills and quite extensive forests, but the main ornitho-interest is centred on the surrounding peat marshes and deltas, where a quite excellent collection of breeding birds can be found. These include Whimbrel, Red-necked Phalarope, Ruff, Temminck's Stint and, sometimes, Broad-billed Sandpiper.

Cranes regularly breed here, as do both divers and both scoters. Most of these birds breed on the northern and eastern sides of the lake, but Red-necked Phalarope can be found along the shore south of Ånn and at the delta at Handöl. The woodland holds a good variety of species, including the elusive Hazelhen.

SUMMER: Black-throated Diver, Red-throated Diver, Scaup, Goldeneye, Velvet Scoter, Scoter, Long-tailed Duck, Osprey, Rough-legged Buzzard, Merlin, Willow Grouse, Black Grouse, Capercaillie, Hazelhen, Crane, Long-tailed Skua, Whimbrel, Wood Sandpiper, Temminck's Stint, Great Snipe, Broad-billed Sandpiper, Purple Sandpiper, Ruff, Red-necked Phalarope, Pygmy Owl, Tengmalm's Owl, Hawk Owl, Great Grey Shrike, Three-toed Woodpecker, Black Woodpecker, Grey-headed Woodpecker, White-backed Woodpecker, Siberian Jay, Bluethroat, Arctic Redpoll, Crossbill.

ACCESS: The area is best explored via the roads that meet at Ånn. Handöl, with its delta, is about 8 km (5 miles) away. There is simple accommodation available at the youth hostel in Ånn, and there are cabins at the camping site 1 km (just over ½ mile) west; there are also cabins at Handöl. The nearest town is Enafors, where there are two reasonable hotels.

A recent development is Klocka Gård, a wildlife centre that offers accommodation, food and birding excursions. Write to Arne Madsen, Klocka Gård, 1372-830 15 Duved, Sweden. This organisation offers all-in bird holidays with transport and guides, and seems to know what it is doing.

ROUTE: Ånn can be reached by road on the E75 from Östersund. There is, however, a railway station at Ånn and all trains stop there and at Enafors. Join the railway at Östersund. Both means of transport can also be started from Trondheim in Norway, but beware overloaded cars on the steep hills encountered from this direction.

Arjeplog and Ammarnäs

These two areas of southern Swedish Lapland lie just below the Arctic Circle and are treated together, though by road they are almost 200 km (125 miles) apart. Even as the Gyrfalcon flies they are separated by well over 100 km (62 miles). Nevertheless, they do offer similar birds in similar habitats. There are vast areas of woodland, birch-lined lakes, swamps and bogs and high, semi-tundra-topped hills and plateaux. But while Arjeplog is accessible and offers comparatively civilised birding, Ammarnäs is decidedly a backwater. Those intent on 'doing' Lapland will probably try the former; those who do not mind 100 km of unmade road and exploring on foot will choose the latter. Ammarnäs is much frequented by Swedish birders in early June, when many species wait in the valley for the snow to clear from the hills. Gyrfalcons, incidentally, do exist here, but are decidedly rare in their appearances.

Arjeplog has many lakes and several important quaking bogs where Whimbrel, Wood Sandpiper and Jack Snipe can be found. There are a few breeding Smew here, and the

203

woods hold Siberian Jay and Siberian Tit, as well as a few Waxwings in the damper places.

Ammarnäs offers a few Lesser White-fronted Geese, an occasional White-tailed Eagle, and Great Snipe, Spotted Redshank, Purple and Broad-billed Sandpipers, Hawk Owl, Shore Lark and Arctic Warbler. The main bird haunt is the delta in late May or early June, but a thorough exploration of the woods, mountains and lakes is needed to find all the specialities. A total of 216 species has been seen, including some 130 breeding birds.

SUMMER (Arjeplog): Black-throated Diver, Smew, Scaup, Goldeneye, Rough-legged Buzzard, Whimbrel, Jack Snipe, Spotted Redshank, Wood Sandpiper, Greenshank, Siberian Jay, Waxwing, Siberian Tit, Great Grey Shrike.

SUMMER (Ammarnäs): Lesser White-fronted Goose, Scaup, Long-tailed Duck, Scoter, Golden Eagle, Rough-legged Buzzard, White-tailed Eagle, Hen Harrier, Merlin, Ptarmigan, Hazelhen, Capercaillie, Dotterel, Great Snipe, Spotted Redshank, Greenshank, Purple Sandpiper, Temminck's Stint, Broad-billed Sandpiper, Red-necked Phalarope, Long-tailed Skua, Hawk Owl, Tengmalm's Owl, Three-toed Woodpecker, Shore Lark, Siberian Tit, Bluethroat, Arctic Warbler, Great Grey Shrike, Lapland Bunting, Pine Grosbeak, Parrot Crossbill.

ACCESS: Arjeplog is a particularly good centre, with roads leading in several directions to facilitate exploration. To the east, the woods and lakes at Stensund are good, and the village of Laisvall to the west is also recommended. There are several hotels, as well as a youth hostel.

Ammarnäs has two hotels, one of which also has cabins. Exploration is mainly on foot, with Marsivagge good for waders, Högbacken for high-altitude species and the slopes along the northern shore of Tjulträsk for Arctic Warbler. The village can be reached by mailbus from Sorsele (90 km/56 miles), which connects with the train: one of each per day. The hotel, however, can arrange to meet its guests at Sorsele, thus cutting down on a nasty three-hour drive: the address is Ammarnäsgården, Box 8, 920 75 Ammarnäs, Sweden (tel: 0952 600 03).

ROUTE: By rail or road from Norway or south Sweden.

Getterön

Getterön is a peninsula to the northwest of Varberg on the Swedish west coast. Formerly an island, it has been joined to the mainland by the dumping of dredged mud and this now forms an important marsh for both breeding and passage birds. About 50 pairs of Avocet plus Ruff and Black-tailed Godwit breed, while passage periods bring larger numbers of these and many other waders. Spotted Redshank, both stints, Broad-billed Sandpiper, Caspian Tern etc pass through, and there are regular Red-throated Pipits here. Smaller breeding birds include Thrush Nightingale, Black Red-start and Wryneck, all little more than a short walk from the town. A fair number of rarities have been noted, including Steller's and King Eiders and Gyrfalcon. Passage of seabirds following southwesterly winds is often quite impressive in autumn.

SUMMER: Garganey, Pintail, Eider, Marsh Harrier, Hobby, Spotted Crake, Black-tailed Godwit, Ruff, Avocet, Wryneck, Black Redstart, Thrush Nightingale, Blue-headed Wagtail, Red-backed Shrike.

PASSAGE: Red-throated Diver, Goldeneye, Bean Goose, Brent Goose, Whooper Swan, Sparrowhawk, Honey Buzzard, Hen Harrier, Osprey, Peregrine, Crane, Bar-tailed Godwit, Spotted Redshank, Little Stint, Temminck's Stint, Broad-billed Sand-piper, Red-necked Phalarope, Caspian Tern, Short-eared Owl, Bluethroat.

ACCESS: The road westwards from the E6 north of Varberg passes a rubbish tip then the southern side of the reserve. There is a bird tower at the southwestern corner of the reserve, which is the only access point during the breeding season. Continuing west-ward, there is a turning on the right past the airfield that leads to a bay for waders. Further west, the peninsula ends at a good seawatching spot. Usually regarded as somewhat better for seabird passage is the island of Hönö, some 25 km (15½ miles) west of Gothenburg. Here, following southwesterly winds in autumn, Manx and Sooty Shearwaters can be seen, along with Gannet, Storm Petrel, Little Auk and skuas.

ROUTE: Varberg is an ideal base. It lies 75 km (47 miles) south of Gothenburg on the E6.

Gotland

Gotland is the largest of the Baltic islands. It is 130 km (80 miles) long and 50 km (31 miles) wide and has the mildest climate in Scandinavia. The influence of the sea can also be seen in the ruggedness of the limestone cliffs, caves and stacks that are the dominating feature of the shoreline. Off the west coast are the two islands of Stora and Lilla Karlsö, where the limestone has been eroded into ledges favoured by breeding seabirds. To the north of Gotland, the adjacent island of Fårö is a military security zone and foreigners are not allowed access. This is unfortunate, as the island is the only Swedish breeding site of Roller. Nevertheless, there are many other attractions and several species are right on the northern fringe of their range. The Collared Flycatcher, for instance, is found nowhere further north in the world.

SUMMER: Greylag Goose, Crane, Osprey, Goshawk, Black-tailed Godwit, Ruff, Avocet, Green Sandpiper, Little Gull, Black Tern, Caspian Tern, Guillemot, Black Guillemot, Razorbill, Black Woodpecker, Thrush Nightingale, Redwing, Icterine Warbler, Marsh Warbler, Great Reed Warbler, Collared Flycatcher.

ACCESS: Allekvia äng is a small deciduous wood with large areas of open grassland. It is an interesting place because of the mixture of southern and northern species that meet here, including Collared Flycatcher (more than ten pairs) and Redwing. Take Route

Collared Flycatcher

147 from Visby and turn right (signposted Dalhem) afer 3 km (2 miles). In 6 km (3¾ miles) there is a small green sign on the right-hand side of the road that shows the way to Allekvia äng.

Lina myr is a marshland area with a growth of reeds surrounded by large wet meadows. It holds an excellent collection of regular breeding birds that includes Ruff and Black-tailed Godwit, but in some years River Warbler, Great Reed Warbler and Marsh Warbler occur. Take Route 147 eastwards from Visby and turn right after 35 km (22 miles) on to Route 146. After 10 km (6 miles) turn right for 1.5 km (1 mile) and fork right. Pass the bridge over the Gothemsån, and after 1.5 km turn left on to a road which goes straight down to the marsh.

Gothems storsund, an attractive lake set in a coniferous wood, has a bird tower on the southern shore giving views over the lake, which has emergent vegetation and attracts a wide variety of marsh birds. The most outstanding are Crane and Greylag Goose, but there are also Osprey, Caspian Tern and Little Gull. Casual non-breeding visitors include White-tailed Eagle and Great Reed Warbler. The surrounding woodland holds Black Woodpecker, Goshawk and Green Sandpiper, which can often be seen near the bird tower. Leave Visby eastwards on Route 147 and turn right after 35 km (22 miles) on to Route 146. After 12 km (7½ miles) pass Gothem church and in 1.5 km (1 mile) is the road to Botvaldevik. Soon after there is a small track going off to the left to a car park. The bird tower can be seen from there.

Stockviken, a shallow marshy lake with fringe vegetation and wet meadows, has a bird tower to the east of the lake which gives excellent views. Though the breeding marsh birds are the main attraction and include Greylag Goose and Avocet, the area is noted for the number and variety of rarities that turn up, probably a result of its strategic position in the south of the island. Vagrants have included Blue-cheeked Bee-eater, Little Bittern, Greater Flamingo and Black Stork. From Burgsvik in the south of Gotland, take the last road eastwards on the south side of the village and fork right after

2 km (1¼ miles). Continue 3 km (nearly 2 miles) southwards to the Stockville signpost, and in 2 km the bird tower can be seen to the right.

Stora Karlsö and Lilla Karlsö are Sweden's only seabird colonies. The latter is a nature reserve of the Svenska Naturskyddsföreningen covering 152 ha (375 acres) of sheep pasture. Both lie a few kilometres off the west coast south of Klintehamn, and hold breeding auks. A regular passage of passerines often includes Greenish Warbler and Scarlet Rosefinch, and Red-breasted Flycatcher is a summer visitor.

ROUTE: There are daily ferries (a four-to-five-hour crossing) from the mainland towns of Södertälje, Nynäshamn, Västervik and Oskarshamn to Visby and in some cases to Kappelshamn and Klintehamn. Gotland is only an hour by air from Stockholm. Because of the mild climate, interesting buildings and beautiful scenery, the island is a favourite holiday resort and there is plenty of accommodation.

Hammarsjön and Araslövssjön

These two shallow lakes lie south and north of Kristianstad respectively, in the east of Skåne in southern Sweden. They are easily reached from Malmö and by visitors to Falsterbo. Both lakes have extensive reedbeds and the surrounding meadows are excellent for breeding birds. The Håslövs Ängar to the east of Hammarsjön are carefully protected for breeding Black-tailed Godwit and Ruff, both numbering about 50 pairs. A smaller number of Black Terns also breed, along with Marsh Harrier, Spotted Crake and Bittern. Ospreys are regular summer visitors, and there are Bean Geese and Whooper Swan in autumn.

SUMMER: Bittern, Garganey, Pintail, Marsh Harrier, Hobby, Osprey, Spotted Crake, Corncrake, Black-tailed Godwit, Ruff, Black Tern.

AUTUMN: Goosander, Bean Goose, Whooper Swan.

ACCESS: Hammarsjön lies immediately south of Kristianstad, and the northern shore is the most accessible. There are bird-observation towers just south of the town and on the western shore near Norra Assum. There is a footpath around Håslövs Ängar. Araslövssjön is best watched from the observation tower on the southern shore near the car park. This is open at weekends, but not always on weekdays owing to military activities. No photography.

ROUTE: Kristianstad is easily reached by Route 15 from Malmö.

Hjälstaviken

This shallow lake was once part of the huge Ekolsund bay of Lake Mälaren, but is now a separate water. It lies just north of the E18 some 70 km (43 miles) west of Stockholm and is a noted haunt of breeding birds, with some excellent passage wildfowl and waders. Slavonian Grebe, Bittern, Marsh Harrier, Osprey, Spotted Crake and Ortolan Bunting all breed, and Jack Snipe regularly display in May. Passage waders include Temminck's Stint, and both Bluethroat and Red-throated Pipit are local migrant specialities.

SUMMER: Slavonian Grebe, Bittern, Garganey, Marsh Harrier, Osprey, Spotted Crake, Jack Snipe, Long-eared Owl, Ortolan Bunting.

PASSAGE: Bean Goose, Rough-legged Buzzard, Sparrowhawk, Hen Harrier, Hobby, Jack Snipe, Bluethroat, Red-throated Pipit, Lapland Bunting, Snow Bunting.

ACCESS: The extensive growth of reeds around the lake makes observation awkward, although there is a path right around the lake starting from a car park off the E18 in the southeastern corner. The adjacent hill of Kvarnberget gives excellent views from the southeast, and another hill in the north, Enbärsbacken, serves a similar purpose.

ROUTE: 70 km (43 miles) on the E18 from Stockholm. Watch for the lake on the right on emerging from an extensive pine forest.

Hornborgasjön

This famous lake lies south of route 49 between Skara and Skövde about 130 km (80 miles) from Gothenburg. Attempts to drain the lake over the last hundred years have resulted in total failure, and instead the creation of a reed and willow marsh of international importance. Restoration, involving management of the water level, has helped to restore some of its former glory. Although 100 species breed in the area, Hornborgasjön is famous for the migration of Cranes in spring. From 10 to 25 April, up to 2,500 of these splendid birds may be seen feeding (and displaying) on the potato fields southwest of the lake and flighting to roost between Bjurum church and Dagsnäs en route to the lake. At other seasons the eastern shoreline is best, and there is a bird tower at Fågeludden. This is an excellent spot for Slavonian Grebe, some 40 pairs of which breed here. There are also a few Black-necked Grebe, plus Marsh Harrier, Bittern, Osprey, Wood Sandpiper and Ruff.

SUMMER: Black-necked Grebe, Slavonian Grebe, Garganey, Pintail, Bittern, Marsh Harrier, Hobby, Osprey, Water Rail, Spotted Crake, Wood Sandpiper, Ruff, Long-eared Owl, Short-eared Owl, Blue-headed Wagtail.

SPRING: Crane.

AUTUMN: Hen Harrier, Spotted Redshank.

ACCESS: View the Cranes early in the morning or late in the evening as they flight across the road between Dagsnäs and Bjurum church. They can also be seen feeding, by taking the road from Bjurum church to the southwest. Fågeludden is reached by leaving the road along the eastern side of Hornborgasjön 1 km (just over ½ mile) north of Broddetorp church on a track leading westward. There are hotels in Skara and Falköping.

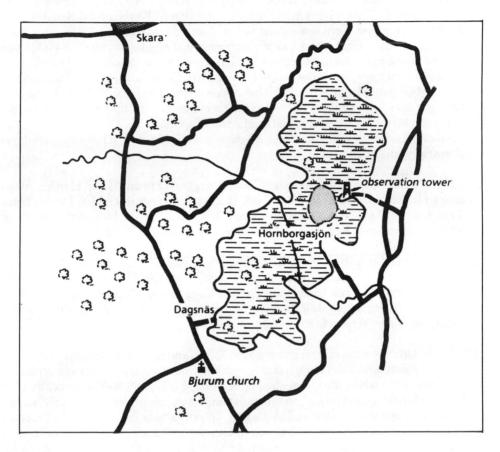

ROUTE: Take the E3 from either Gothenburg or Stockholm to Skara, then follow signs toward Falköping past the lake at the Crane corner. It is illegal to enter the Crane feeding fields.

Öland

Öland is an island in the Baltic just off the eastern coast of Sweden and joined to it by a road bridge and a ferry system. It is 137 km (85 miles) long, but only 16 km (10 miles) wide, and runs north to south parallel with the mainland. The west has a range of limestone cliffs and the land gradually falls away to the low-lying east coast. There are some huge areas of woodland, areas of grazing with dry-stone walls, and a characteristic limestone heathland called *alvar*.

Though perhaps best known for migrants — the bird observatory at Ottenby at the southern tip — Öland offers really splendid birding at all seasons. Among summer birds there are Slavonian Grebe, Marsh and Montagu's Harriers, Hobby, Corncrake, Ruff, Avocet, Black-tailed Godwit, Black Tern, Red-backed Shrike and exciting eastern species such as Thrush Nightingale, Icterine and Barred Warblers and Red-breasted Flycatcher. Caspian Tern is a regular visitor. During passage periods there are good numbers of geese, Crane, plus a variety of raptors that regularly includes both Golden and White-tailed Eagles in November. Waders are excellent, especially at Ottenby, and the number of migrating Eider is simply staggering. Daily spring totals of the latter of over 50,000 (late March–early April) have been counted, along with 30,000 returning birds per day (early October). Rarities usually occur in May and the first half of June, but migration here is both dramatic and productive of species.

Öland has many distinct sites, each of which is outlined below. It is worth a holiday at almost any time of the year.

SUMMER: Slavonian Grebe, Greylag Goose, Garganey, Pintail, Marsh Harrier, Montagu's Harrier, Corncrake, Avocet, Ruff, Black-tailed Godwit, Golden Plover, Black Tern, Caspian Tern, Wryneck, Red-backed Shrike, Icterine Warbler, Barred Warbler, Thrush Nightingale, Red-breasted Flycatcher, Bearded Tit, Penduline Tit.

PASSAGE: Black-throated Diver, Red-throated Diver, Long-tailed Duck, Velvet Scoter, Scoter, Eider, Bean Goose, Brent Goose, Barnacle Goose, Whooper Swan, Bewick's Swan, Golden Eagle, White-tailed Eagle, Rough-legged Buzzard, Crane, Whimbrel, Bar-tailed Godwit, Spotted Redshank, Greenshank, Knot, Ruff, Broadbilled Sandpiper, Wryneck, Ring Ouzel.

ACCESS: Ottenby is the southernmost area of Öland and the bird observatory is situated near the lighthouse. Visible migration is watched from the southern tip and grounded migrants in the whole area. Ottenby Fågelstation, Pl 37, 380 66 Ventlinge, Sweden (tel: 0485 610 93), has limited accommodation. There are passage geese on Västrevet to the west, and the meadowland to the east, known as Schäferiängarna, is a breeding ground of Avocet and Ruff. The woods of Ottenby Lund are a stronghold of Icterine Warbler and a few pairs of Red-breasted Flycatchers. To the west is an area called Tokmarken, where Barred Warblers breed. There are two observation towers: one at the southern end of Ottenby Lund near the car park, the other in the north at the end of the east–west Allevägen. Both are open to the public. The woods to the north of this road are also open via a gate near the youth hostel in the north and a tall stile further south. Bee-eater and Roller no longer breed, but do appear from time to time. Accommodation is limited, and there are few shops.

Beijershamn is an area around an old causeway on the western shore with interesting marshland and some splendid wildfowl and wader passage. This is one of the best spots for breeding Marsh Harrier, Ruff, Black Tern, and visiting Caspian. Passage of geese and duck, viewed from the end of the breakwater, can be dramatic, and passage waders may include Broad-billed Sandpiper. The adjacent woods and scrub are a stronghold of Thrush Nightingale and Icterine Warbler and, with care and patience, a Barred Warbler may be located.

Stora Rör is the ferry terminal opposite Revsudden north of Kalmar. Either spot makes an excellent base for watching the spectacular movements of wildfowl, divers, waders etc in spring and autumn.

Möckelmossen is a shallow lake 5 km (3 miles) east of Resmo church. It holds breeding Slavonian Grebe, Black Tern and Black-tailed Godwit, and is an autumn stop-over for Crane. Please view from the road along the southern shore to minimise disturbance.

Södviken is a shallow, sandy shore backed by meadows situated on the east coast in the north of Öland. Breeding birds include Avocet, and the area is excellent for migrant waders.

Mellby Ör is a small island connected to the east coast of southern Öland. It has breeding Black Tern, Avocet and Ruff and an excellent passage of waders, particularly at the southern tip. It is easily reached from the village of Mellby.

Betgärde Träsk is a reedy marsh some 15 km (9 miles) north of Borgholm. Breeding species include Little Gull, Black Tern, Godwit, Marsh and Montagu's Harriers, and Bearded and Penduline Tits. There is a bird tower on the right-hand side of the road north of Löt. The road to Stacktorp is a little further on. Paths are marked.

Kapelludden lies on the east coast opposite Borgholm, the only town on Öland. The meadows along the shore hold Avocet and are excellent for migratory waders. There is a lighthouse and easy access.

ROUTE: The bridge to Öland is at Kalmar, which also has a provincial airport. Accommodation is available at several places on Öland, including Borgholm, and there are summer cottages to rent. Contact Ölands Turistförening, Box 115, 380 70 Borgholm (tel: 0485 302 60).

Sappisaasi

This area lies 120 km (75 miles) north of the Arctic Circle and 45 km (28 miles) east of the industrial town of Kiruna. It is, however, much lower than Abisko and its consequent richer vegetation holds a significantly different avifauna. The three dominant Lapland habitats are found. The vast area of marshes to the east of the village holds breeding Crane and Whooper Swan, while Bean Geese breed in the damp forests. Waders, however, are dominant, with Spotted Redshank and Broad-billed Sandpiper the most interesting species. Alongside the road and separating it from the marshes is a narrow belt of woodland, while the lower slopes of the hill to the north are covered with conifers. Pine Grosbeak and Siberian Tit are the most interesting species. Climbing the hill of Ounistunturi (not to be confused with the Ounastunturi National Park 100 km/62 miles east across the Finnish border) gives excellent views over the surrounding woods and marshes.

Caution should be exercised when walking over the quaking bogs that are a feature of the marshes. In particular the areas around the occasional small lakes are to be avoided, but with waterproof footwear and a little care there is no danger.

SUMMER: Crane, Whooper Swan, Bean Goose, Osprey, Spotted Redshank, Wood

Sandpiper, Broad-billed Sandpiper, Hazelhen, Siberian Tit, Pine Grosbeak, Ortolan Bunting.

ACCESS: The area lies on Route 396 — the Vittangi–Karesuando road — 20 km (12½ miles) north of Vittangi. There is a ferry immediately north of Vittangi which is a good place for Ospreys and Ortolans. Vittangi is the best place for accommodation, though it is not a large town and hotels are few and small. Sappisaasi itself is only a derelict cottage.

ROUTE: By road or train to Kiruna from southern Sweden.

Skåne

Skåne is the southernmost province of Sweden and is one of the country's best areas for birds. Though best known for its migrants, especially waders and birds of prey at Falsterbo, there are several lakeland areas that attract breeding birds which are otherwise decidedly scarce as far north as this. Best of these are Red Kite and Golden Oriole.

Falsterbo lies at the end of a peninsula south of Malmö and faces westward towards Denmark. Here the two coastlines of Scandinavia come together, and migrating birds of prey have no choice but to set out over the sea. In autumn these birds gain height by circling over the heath of Ljungen, and numbers are often very impressive indeed. Though lacking the variety of Gibraltar or the Bosporus, numbers are certainly greater, with over 14,000 birds counted on an exceptional day and over 1,000 a day occurring several times a season. Early September is best for Honey Buzzard and October for Buzzard and Rough-legged Buzzard. Other species include Sparrowhawk, Osprey, Marsh Harrier, Red Kite plus the odd Spotted or White-tailed Eagle. Best weather is clear and sunny with light westerly winds. When winds are from the south or southeast, birds cross the straits on a broad front.

Falsterbo Bird Observatory is situated just south of the village and has an active ringing programme. To the south lies the small hill of Kolabacken, a good raptor-watching spot, while just to the west is the lighthouse with its garden, good for small passerines. Visible migration of small birds in October can be very dramatic, with 100,000 passing through on a good day. Waders are concentrated mainly at the northern end of the peninsula at Slusan, Bakdjupet and Revlarna. The latter is particularly good, but easily disturbed. Birds include Temminck's and Little Stints, Spotted Redshank and even Broad-billed Sandpiper. The inlet of Foteviken in the north at the base of the peninsula is also good for these species, and both Avocet and Kentish Plover breed.

Inland are the lakes of Börringesjön, Hackebergar, Krankesjön and Vombsjön. Though mostly worked over by summer visitors, these waters should not be ignored during migration. The woods at Börringesjön have Red Kite, Golden Oriole and Thrush Nightingale, while the marsh at the northern end has breeding Black Tern. Bean Geese and sometimes Crane appear on passage, as do many birds of prey. Krankesjön has extensive reedbeds, with breeding Bittern, Marsh Harrier, Black Tern and occasionally Great Reed Warbler. Vombsjön has breeding Black-tailed Godwit, plus passage Bean and White-fronted Geese. Eagles regularly winter, and Cranes use the area as a September stop-over. Clearly there is much to be enjoyed in southernmost Sweden throughout the year.

SUMMER: Black-necked Grebe, Red Kite, Marsh Harrier, Osprey, Sparrowhawk, Bittern, Kentish Plover, Avocet, Ruff, Black-tailed Godwit, Black Tern, Golden Oriole, Thrush Nightingale, Great Reed Warbler, Marsh Warbler, Bearded Tit, Penduline Tit.

AUTUMN: Honey Buzzard, Osprey, Buzzard, Rough-legged Buzzard, Hen Harrier, Marsh Harrier, Sparrowhawk, Peregrine, Hobby, Crane, Spotted Redshank, Temminck's Stint, Little Stint, Broad-billed Sandpiper, Red-throated Pipit, Two-barred Crossbill.

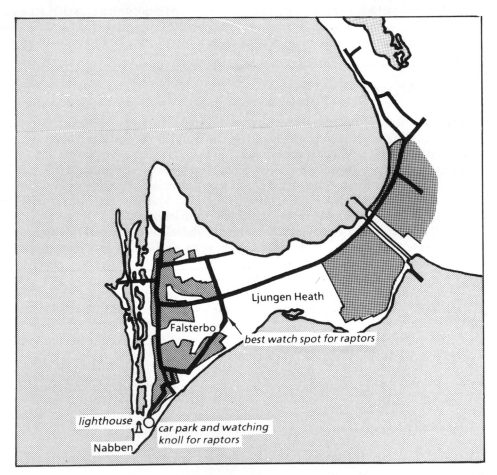

WINTER: Bean Goose, White-fronted Goose, Golden Eagle, White-tailed Eagle, Rough-legged Buzzard.

ACCESS: The Falsterbo area is well built-up and of open access. There are two hotels, and the bird observatory that caters for the serious birder: Gunnar Roos, Falkvägen 21, 230 10 Skanör, Sweden. All tend to be fully booked during September. There are also camping sites, but they close in mid-September. The best place for raptor-watching is along the north-to-south road that extends along the western side of Ljungen. Waders are concentrated in the northern part of the peninsula, north and west of Skanör. The southern point Nabben is always popular. Foteviken, the wader bay, is easily reached between Höllviksnäs and Vellinge.

For the lakes, follow country roads with the aid of a map. Börringesjön is near Börringekloster. From there, turn north to Hackebergar at Dalby. From here, take minor roads to Silvåkra for Krankesjön, while Vombsjön lies 4 km (2½ miles) east of Krankesjön.

ROUTE: Falsterbo and the lakes are easily found from Malmö, which is itself reached by ferry from Copenhagen, or by road from Gothenburg. Ferries across the North Sea will determine which is the best route. Malmö does, however, have an airport for those in a hurry.

Store Mosse

This huge peat bog lies in southern Sweden, yet is more typical of the landscape of the far north. Huge marshy areas with poor vegetation and ill-defined lakes, often well out of sight, make this a difficult place to watch, but as the landscape is typically northern so are the birds. Store Mosse is thus a very convenient place to see breeding birds such as Crane, Whooper Swan, Long-tailed Duck, Jack Snipe, Wood Sandpiper and Ruff. It also has Tengmalm's Owl, Hazelhen and Three-toed Woodpecker in the surrounding woodland. But note! These are very difficult birds to locate.

In the middle of the Mosse lies Kävsjön, a splendid lake with a remarkably useful bird tower — take a telescope. Some other areas of open water can be seen from roads.

SUMMER: Red-throated Diver, Goldeneye, Long-tailed Duck, Whooper Swan, Goshawk, Marsh Harrier, Osprey, Hobby, Merlin, Hazelhen, Crane, Golden Plover, Jack Snipe, Wood Sandpiper, Ruff, Tengmalm's Owl, Three-toed Woodpecker.

ACCESS: The road between Hillerstorp and Värnamo passes the centre of the area near Kävsjön, where the bird tower lies east of the road.

ROUTE: The E4 between Hälsingborg and Jönköping passes through Värnamo.

Tåkern

This shallow lake is one of the best-known bird resorts in central Sweden and lies

214

immediately east of the huge Lake Vättern. It is the combination of emergent vegetation and surrounding marshes that has produced such an enviable list of both breeding birds and migrant species. Among the former are Red-necked, Black-necked and Slavonian Grebes, Bittern, Osprey, Black Tern, Great Reed Warbler and Parrot Crossbill. Bearded Tits previously bred in their thousands here, but recent hard winters have seriously reduced their numbers. Even Penduline Tit may breed. Migrants include thousands of Bean Geese, Whooper Swan and Caspian Tern. The numbers of breeding birds have been increasing in recent years, and the numbers of duck in spring and autumn are quite outstanding — perhaps hundreds of thousands. The Bean Geese are often accompanied by a few Whitefronts, and there is invariably a good selection of raptors present. Reedbeds restrict visibility in many areas and comparatively little can be seen from the surrounding roads. Fortunately there are bird towers, in the north and the south. Waders are generally rather few.

SUMMER: Red-necked Grebe, Black-necked Grebe, Slavonian Grebe, Bittern, Garganey, Marsh Harrier, Osprey, Water Rail, Spotted Crake, Black Tern, Icterine Warbler, Great Reed Warbler, Bearded Tit, Penduline Tit, Parrot Crossbill.

PASSAGE: Bean Goose, White-fronted Goose, Whooper Swan, Hen Harrier, Caspian Tern, Short-eared Owl.

ACCESS: From the south, take the E4 and then fork left on to Route 50 at Ödeshög. Minor roads to the right lead right around the lake, with other minor roads leading to the lake and to the two bird towers.

ROUTE: Gothenburg is 250 km (155 miles) and Stockholm 350 km (217 miles). Jönköping has a provincial airport.

SWITZERLAND

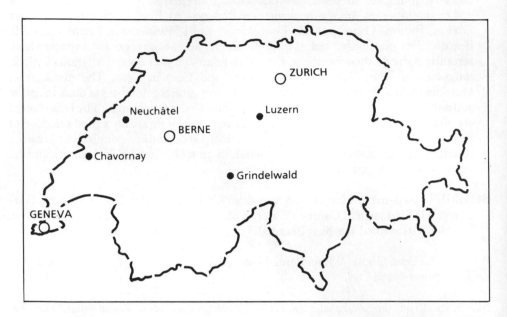

Chavornay

For the lower part of its course, before joining Lac de Neuchâtel, the River Orbe runs over a flat plain that is particularly liable to flooding in spring. Here too are the old clay pits around Chavornay with their reedbeds, willow thickets and permanent open water. During the early part of spring the area is a favourite haunt of duck, but as the water level drops it offers fine opportunities for migrating waders. Birds such as Temminck's Stint and Marsh Sandpiper are regular and in most years there is a scattering of herons, including Little Egret and Night Heron. In fact, species as varied as Hobby, Baillon's Crake and Red-necked Phalarope use this lowland 'channel' to pass between the Jura and the Alps on their way northward.

Of course, most visitors will bird this area during the summer on their way to the mountains, and at this time there are plentiful Black Kite, Hobby and Great Reed Warbler to be seen.

PASSAGE: Little Egret, Night Heron, Honey Buzzard, Marsh Harrier, Wood Sandpiper, Marsh Sandpiper, Temminck's Stint, Red-necked Phalarope, Bluethroat.

SUMMER: Black Kite, Hobby, Little Bittern, Great Reed Warbler.

ACCESS: Leave the Chavornay–Orbe road northwards 2 km (1¼ miles) west of Chavornay on a narrow road to the pits. The whole of the area along the Orbe between Bavois and Yverdon is worth exploring at any season.

ROUTE: Northwards from Lausanne.

Grindelwald

This ski resort in the Bernese Oberland is the place where summer tourists touting binoculars should not be confused with fellow birders. They gather here to watch the intrepid perform on the North Face of the Eiger. Though decidedly touristy, Grindelwald makes an ideal base for alpine birding, with ski-lifts for easy access to the high slopes and a railway that actually runs inside the Eiger itself to Jungfraujoch at high altitude. Most of the facilities do not operate between the end of the ski season in mid-April and the start of the summer season in June.

The town itself has Alpine Chough and Black Redstart, while the odd Golden Eagle occasionally glides overhead. The first chair-lift to the north of the town has Peregrine, Nutcracker, Crested Tit, Firecrest, Crossbill and Citril Finch. Higher up there are Alpine Accentor and Snow Finch, while in the woods around the town there are Grey-headed Woodpecker and Fieldfare.

Down the valley near Interlaken, the rack-and-pinion railway at Wilderswil rises to Schnige Platte, with Honey Buzzard, Alpine Chough and Citril Finch. The Brienzer See, east of Interlaken, has Goosander as well as the ubiquitous Red and Black Kites. Further east, beyond Brienz, is Meiringen and the nearby Reichenbach Falls. The woods here have both kites and Honey Buzzard, with Wallcreeper on the waterfall itself.

SUMMER: Goosander, Buzzard, Honey Buzzard, Black Kite, Red Kite, Grey-headed Woodpecker, Alpine Swift, Alpine Accentor, Ring Ouzel, Fieldfare, Water Pipit, Red-backed Shrike, Wallcreeper, Crested Tit, Redstart, Black Redstart, Firecrest, Citril Finch, Snow Finch, Nutcracker, Alpine Chough.

ACCESS: As detailed above, with plentiful and easy access to the tops.

ROUTE: Southeast on Route 6 from Berne.

Luzern

Luzern is a good centre from which to explore in every direction . . . including upwards. It also connects easily with the Grindelwald area, offering further opportunities of finding alpine birds. In that direction, southwest, is the Sarner See, where woodlands hold both buzzards and both kites. In Luzern itself the tower of the old bridge has Alpine Swift, while the parks and woodland along the northern shore of the lake have Black and Green Woodpeckers, together with Golden Oriole and Wood Warbler.

To the south, beyond Stans, is the ski resort of Engelberg, with Alpine Chough, Water Pipit and Rock Bunting together with a selection of raptors that includes Golden Eagle and Goshawk. To the east the lake turns sharply southwards through a wooded gorge, with Peregrine, both 'green' woodpeckers and breeding Red Kite. The best spot in this area is Seelisberg on the southern (western!) shore. Further south Goldeneye summer around Flüelen, while at nearby Altdorf a road leads eastward to the Klausen Pass, with Nutcracker, Rock Thrush, Snow Finch and Alpine Chough.

SUMMER: Goldeneye, Golden Eagle, Black Kite, Red Kite, Buzzard, Honey Buzzard, Goshawk, Peregrine, Black Woodpecker, Green Woodpecker, Grey-headed Wood-pecker, Alpine Swift, Water Pipit, Tree Pipit, Golden Oriole, Wood Warbler, Black Redstart, Rock Thrush, Nutcracker, Alpine Chough, Snow Finch, Rock Bunting.

ACCESS: Sites detailed above.

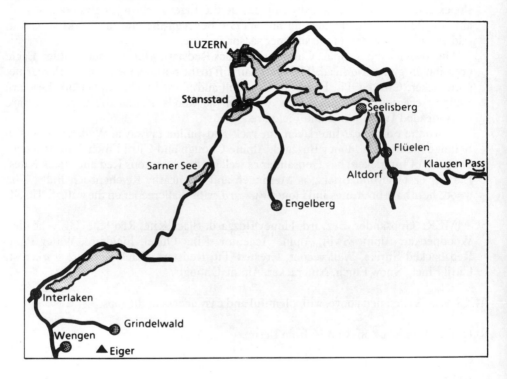

ROUTE: Luzern lies a short drive south of Zurich with its international communications.

Neuchâtel

The northern end of Lac de Neuchâtel has extensive marshy margins extending for many kilometres along the shore between Neuchâtel town and Portalban. These are arguably the most important wetlands in Switzerland, both for breeding and for migrant birds. Waders flock the shoreline, and the damp marshes and the larger reedbeds hold Swiss rarities such as Little Bittern and Purple Heron. There are always Black Kites here and Marsh Harrier is a regular passage visitor.

The nearby hills are not high by local standards, but their woods hold many species

218

including Bonelli's Warbler, Crested Tit and Pied Flycatcher. At Le Fanel, a reserve covers both marsh and woodland and is as good a place as any to start working the area.

SUMMER: Black-necked Grebe, Purple Heron, Little Bittern, Shoveler, Pochard, Black Kite, Bonelli's Warbler, Pied Flycatcher, Crested Tit.

PASSAGE: Marsh Harrier, Little Stint, Temminck's Stint.

ACCESS: Start by walking the embankments along the canalised Broye River. These turn westwards off the road between Campelin and Cudrefin 16.5 km (10¼ miles) southeast of Neuchâtel. Le Fanel is administered by the Société Romande pour l'Etude et la Protection des Oiseaux, Case Postale 548, 1401 Yverdon, CCP 20-117 Neuchâtel, which issues permits.

ROUTE: South and west from Neuchâtel.

TUNISIA

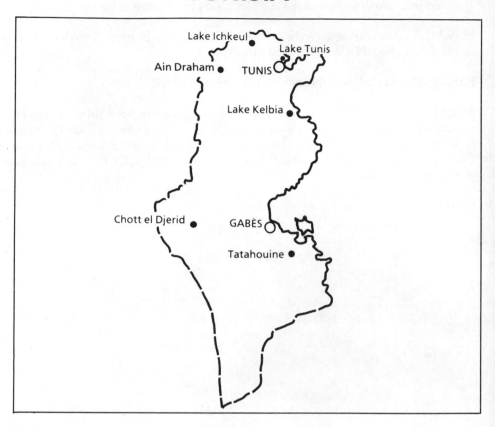

Lake Ichkeul
Lake Tunis
Ain Draham
TUNIS
Lake Kelbia
Chott el Djerid
GABÈS
Tatahouine

Ain Draham

The road GP17 between Tabarka on the north coast and Jendouba to the south passes through an excellent area of rugged hills reaching the highest point at the Col des Ruines, near Ain Draham. The forests here are extensive and well worth exploring for what may be common species in northern Europe but highly localised birds in Tunisia. Both the Col and the village have produced good things such as three species of woodpecker, including Levaillant's, Bulbul, Blue Rock Thrush, Crossbill and Hawfinch. Doubtless there are more birds to be found by anyone prepared to give the area more than a couple of hours.

SUMMER: Woodpigeon, Tawny Owl, Levaillant's Woodpecker, Great Spotted Woodpecker, Lesser Spotted Woodpecker, Jay, Bulbul, Blackcap, Sardinian Warbler, Blue Rock Thrush, Blackbird, Song Thrush, Short-toed Treecreeper, Chaffinch, Crossbill, Hawfinch, Cirl Bunting.

ACCESS: Drive to Ain Draham and continue northwards towards Col des Ruines. After

1.5 km (1 mile) stop and explore the woods. The woods south of Ain Draham are also worth exploring wherever there are large oaks.

ROUTE: Jendouba is reached from Tunis on the GP6. Some groups link this area with Lake Ichkeul via Beja.

Chott el Djerid

Djerid lies in central western Tunisia near the Algerian border, and is a vast salt lake that is variably flooded in winter. On occasion Flamingo and Ruddy Shelduck breed and there may be an interesting passage of waders, but mostly this shallow lake remains dry and is virtually devoid of birds. Its inclusion in this guide depends more on its surroundings than on the lake itself, for the Sahara is nearby and the whole area is one of the best in North Africa for desert and semi-desert species. The two main areas of interest lie to the northwest, around Tozeur, and to the southeast around Douz. Both should be included in any Tunisian itinerary.

The oasis at Tozeur supports Palm Dove and Olivaceous Warbler, with House Bunting in the town itself. An exploration of the surrounding area should produce Red-rumped Wheatear (common), with Desert, Mourning and White-crowned Black Wheatears. Desert and Bar-tailed Desert Larks along with Bifasciated, and sand-grouse, Courser and Trumpeter Finch complete the normal desert species. Peregrine, Lanner and Long-legged Buzzard are all possible, and the edge of Djerid beyond Kriz has produced Houbara Bustard.

During most seasons it is possible to drive the GP16 road across the northern edge of Djerid to Kebili, with more larks, wheatears, falcons and some Little Swifts. South of Kebili, the road to Douz passes through oases with Fulvous Babbler, while at Douz itself there are Brown-necked Ravens on the rubbish tip. From Douz, a road leads to Hessai Oasis and then out into the desert. This route will almost certainly be blocked by sand, but it is worth exploring on foot for Tristram's, Desert and Scrub Warblers and Desert Sparrow. The latter breeds at the end of the road at Ksar Rhilane, but this spot requires an expedition or a specially chartered vehicle, driver and guide.

All in all, this area offers a splendid alternative to sub-Saharan Morocco for desert species. It deserves more attention than it has so far received.

SUMMER: Flamingo, Ruddy Shelduck, Long-legged Buzzard, Lanner, Peregrine, Barbary Falcon, Houbara Bustard, Stone-curlew, Spotted Sandgrouse, Palm Dove, Little Swift, Desert Lark, Bar-tailed Desert Lark, Bifasciated Lark, Crested Lark, Thekla Lark, Spotless Starling, Raven, Brown-necked Raven, Bulbul, Sardinian Warbler, Spectacled Warbler, Tristram's Warbler, Desert Warbler, Scrub Warbler, Marmora's Warbler, Fan-tailed Warbler, Mourning Wheatear, Desert Wheatear, Red-rumped Wheatear, Black Wheatear, White-crowned Black Wheatear, Blue Rock Thrush, Moussier's Redstart, Fulvous Babbler, Rock Sparrow, Desert Sparrow, Trumpeter Finch, House Bunting.

ACCESS: From Tozeur, the desert can be explored along the various roads by seeking out different types of terrain. It is certainly worth driving to within a short distance of the

Algerian border, as well as out towards Kriz. To the north, the Gorges de Seldja is reached from the road towards Gafsa; watch for a sign saying Thildja. This gorge has Marmora's Warbler, Little Swift and Rock Sparrow. The Tozeur area is certainly worth a couple of days.

The road across Djerid produces many wheatears and larks, as well as Little Swift and Trumpeter Finch. At Kebili turn south toward Douz, inspecting oases for Fulvous Babbler, and on arrival drive through the town watching for a National Guard camp on the right. Turn left and continue to Hessai Oasis. Carry on out into the desert for a few kilometres, then turn left (south) at the National Guard camp to the rubbish tip. Continue on the road toward Zafrane and turn right towards Naxil. The Chott of the same name is on the left after 5 km (3 miles) — for duck, herons etc.

ROUTE: Gabès is the nearest substantial town and the GP16 road is the main approach.

Ichkeul Lake

This large lake near the north coast lies a few kilometres inland from Bizerte and is connected to the sea via the lake of that name. Five separate rivers run into Ichkeul, flushing through the lake each autumn and considerably increasing its size. Thereafter the water level drops until the following autumn, though some sea water flows into the lake when it is at its lowest. For years, Ichkeul has been acknowledged as a major wetland and a primary staging post for migrants crossing the Mediterranean and Sahara. In spring there is an enormous passage of waders, especially Ruff, while in winter huge numbers of geese make this their traditional home.

In fact there are birds at all seasons at Ichkeul, with breeders including Marbled Teal and White-headed Duck, egrets and herons, Marsh Harrier and many warblers.

White-headed Duck

During spring and autumn the wader flocks regularly include large numbers of Little Stint and Curlew Sandpiper and a few Marsh Sandpipers. There are Avocets and quite substantial flocks of Flamingo and, in late summer, Eleonora's Falcon regularly appears here.

The local countryside provides a good introduction to Tunisian birds. The Jebel Ichkeul to the south rises to over 450 m (1500 feet) and holds a few species, such as Crag Martin, that help build up a substantial list. Long-legged Buzzards use the mountain as a winter roost.

PASSAGE: Flamingo, Osprey, Avocet, Kentish Plover, Little Stint, Temminck's Stint, Curlew Sandpiper, Ruff, Spotted Redshank, Marsh Sandpiper, Greenshank, Sandwich Tern, Yellow Wagtail.

SUMMER: Cattle Egret, Little Egret, Marbled Teal, White-headed Duck, Marsh Harrier, Lanner, Eleonora's Falcon, Water Rail, Purple Gallinule, Kentish Plover, Little Owl, Kingfisher, Crag Martin, Lesser Short-toed Lark, Thekla Lark, Bulbul, Cetti's Warbler, Fan-tailed Warbler, Moussier's Redstart, Spanish Sparrow.

WINTER: Little Egret, Flamingo, Wigeon, Teal, Pintail, Shoveler, Pochard, Marsh Harrier, Long-legged Buzzard, Barbary Falcon, Peregrine, Avocet, Golden Plover, Red-throated Pipit.

ACCESS: The village of Tindja lies on the eastern shore and is an ideal starting point. To the north, the MC57 road offers many viewpoints and it is easy to stop and explore. In particular, the various river mouths are often productive. In the south, the Jebel Ichkeul involves leaving the Tindja–Mateur road and exploring westward along the southern shore. This is an easily worked area that is as good as most other wetlands in the Mediterranean.

ROUTE: Though Bizerte makes the ideal base, most visitors arrive from Tunis on the GP7. Turn right on the MC54 12 km (7½ miles) before Mateur to Tindja.

Kelbia Lake

Ranked within the top category of wetlands of international importance, Kelbia is a substantial lake that has the advantage of being close to the main tourist areas of the Tunisian coast. Sousse is about 35 km (22 miles) distant and the airport at Monastir about 20 km (12½ miles) further. It is thus frequently visited by birders with families and, as a first stop, by those using a package holiday as the base for a birding trip. Its size varies according to season and rainfall and it does, sometimes, dry up completely. In normal circumstances, its emergent vegetation holds a good collection of breeding birds, including Squacco Heron, White-headed Duck, Purple Gallinule and Black-winged Stilt. It can, depending on water levels, also be a major wintering ground for a wide variety of species, often including Flamingo and Crane, and on passage wader numbers are often very impressive. The usual species include both stints, Ruff,

223

Greenshank and Spotted Redshank, but there is often a concentration of Kentish Plovers and outstandingly a regular flock of Dotterel. Birds of prey are often noted, and there are frequently interesting terns to be seen. Collared Pratincole may be present in large flocks and there are resident Crested and Thekla Larks. The arid hills to the west are worthy of more than a cursory look. Black-bellied Sandgrouse and Coursers have been noted here.

SUMMER: Squacco Heron, Little Egret, Shelduck, White-headed Duck, Purple Galli-nule, Black-winged Stilt, Crested Lark, Thekla Lark, Fan-tailed Warbler.

PASSAGE AND WINTER: Flamingo, Little Egret, Squacco Heron, Glossy Ibis, White-headed Duck, Osprey, Bonelli's Eagle, Hen Harrier, Lanner, Peregrine, Crane, Purple Gallinule, Kentish Plover, Dotterel, Little Stint, Temminck's Stint, Ruff, Greenshank, Caspian Tern, Gull-billed Tern, Collared Pratincole, Black-bellied Sandgrouse, Cream-coloured Courser, Calandra Lark, Short-toed Lark, Crested Lark, Thekla Lark, Marmora's Warbler, Spectacled Warbler, Fan-tailed Warbler.

ACCESS: The best access point is at the northwestern corner on the GP2 near the junction with the MC48. From here, a walk southwards along the shore will produce most of the birds of the area. Because of the variable water level, there are no particular 'hot spots' and a general exploration is required.

ROUTE: Leave Sousse northwards and turn left beyond Hamman-Sousse towards Kebira on the MC48. Monastir is the nearest airport.

Tatahouine

This is an alternative site to Chott el Djerid for sub-desert species and is particularly convenient to anyone staying on the Isle of Djerba, or working the shorebirds, terns and gulls of Bahiret El Biban. Oases and semi-desert areas can be found north and south of the town, as well as along the minor roads and tracks that extend in all directions. Tatahouine is thus more a base for exploration than a bird spot itself. To the north of the town is an area of dry fields with Trumpeter Finch, Desert Lark and Temminck's Horned Lark. To the south is a dry river valley with Tristram's, Desert and Scrub Warblers and more besides.

SUMMER: Lanner, Long-legged Buzzard, Stone-curlew, Desert Lark, Bifasciated Lark, Temminck's Horned Lark, Brown-necked Raven, Tristram's Warbler, Desert Warbler, Scrub Warbler, Trumpeter Finch.

ACCESS: There is no reason to suppose that the areas mentioned are outstanding or even particularly worth visiting. They are simply spots where others have seen birds that are almost certainly more widespread. A full report on an exploration of this area would be most welcome. North of Tatahouine, watch the kilometre stones and stop halfway between km 23 and km 24. A sandy track leads eastward. Park and walk north for 200 m

(220 yards) to an area of fields for Temminck's Horned and Desert Larks. The Oued Dekouk crosses the GP19 road 25 km (15½ miles) south of Tatahouine. This is excellent for all the warblers.

Bifasciated Lark

ROUTE: Medenine is the nearest large town some 49 km (30½ miles) due north on the GP19. Ben Guerdane lies near the coast to the east — access via the MC111 — and could prove interesting.

Tunis Lake

The visitor to Tunis with only a little time available has one of the best wetlands in the country just beyond the hotel doorstep. A quick taxi ride to the esplanade, north of the port area, and there is the lake and the birds. Two roads lead out towards the coast, and both provide excellent birding.

Lake Tunis is a saltwater lagoon connected to the Mediterranean and, therefore, a home to many seabirds. It often has several thousand wintering Flamingoes, is Tunisia's major haunt of Cormorant (about 5,000), has several hundred Black-necked Grebes and a good population of wintering duck. Egrets and waders are present during passage periods, and gulls regularly include Slender-billed. At the end of the road lie the ruins of Carthage — so birding and culture combine.

PASSAGE AND WINTER: Black-necked Grebe, Cormorant, Little Egret, Flamingo, Teal, Avocet, Kentish Plover, Little Stint, Slender-billed Gull, Sandwich Tern.

225

ACCESS: Take either the road along the northern shore or the road through the lagoon towards Carthage and La Marsa, both eastward out of the city.

ROUTE: Tunis environment.

TURKEY

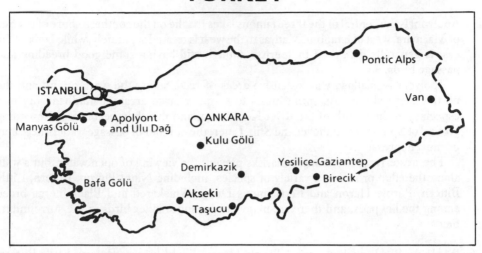

Akseki

Akseki is noted for its unfriendly hotel, its prison and its graveyard. The first is unfortunate, the second is a good landmark, and the third is full of interesting birds and especially Olive-tree Warbler. This is one of the three specialities of this otherwise not too spectacular area, the others being White-backed Woodpecker and Krüper's Nuthatch. There are other birds here too, including Rüppell's Warbler, Masked Shrike, Great Spotted Cuckoo and Cretzschmar's Bunting.

SUMMER: Long-legged Buzzard, Booted Eagle, Short-toed Eagle, Syrian Woodpecker, White-backed Woodpecker, Krüper's Nuthatch, Great Spotted Cuckoo, Masked Shrike, Roller, Blue Rock Thrush, Orphean Warbler, Rüppell's Warbler, Subalpine Warbler, Olive-tree Warbler, Cretzschmar's Bunting.

ACCESS: The graveyard is opposite the prison in the southeast corner of the town: Olive-tree Warbler and Masked Shrike here. Take the Konya road for 7.9 km (4.9 miles) to a lay-by on the right. There is a clearing among the woods across the road with White-backed Woodpecker. About 50 m further along the road a path leads left towards a radar station. After 600 m (650 yards) there is another clearing for the 'pecker. Krüper's Nuthatch is numerous hereabouts.

South of Akseki there are Rüppell's, and after 8 km (5 miles) there is a small conifer wood on the left followed by a turning on the right. Olive-tree Warbler can be seen among the scattered trees behind the plantation, as can Masked Shrike and Great Spotted Cuckoo. A track heading eastward from the southern side of the conifer plantation leads to a rocky area beyond a small village for raptors.

ROUTE: Konya has an airport.

Apolyont, Ulu Dağ and the Kocabas Delta

Apolyont is the central of the three famous lakes that lie on the southern shore of the Sea of Marmara, west of Istanbul. Manyas to the west is treated separately, while Iznik to the east is generally disturbed by tourists, though still having some good breeding and passage birds.

Apolyont is shallow, with extensive areas of reeds along the western end and the northwestern shores. As spring turns to summer large areas of mudbank dry out, especially at the mouth of the River Kemalpaşa, and this then becomes the breeding ground of Spur-winged Plover and Stilt. Later, the number of passage waders here may be most impressive.

The western reedbeds and tamarisks prevent the viewing of open water, but a walk along the edge produces a variety of species, including Night Heron, Bittern, Little Bittern, Purple Heron and Ferruginous Duck. Whiskered and Black Terns breed among the lily pads, and there are many interesting smaller birds in the surrounding fields.

SUMMER: Black-necked Grebe, Purple Heron, Night Heron, Bittern, Little Bittern, Little Egret, Ferruginous Duck, Lesser Kestrel, Whiskered Tern, Black Tern, Black-winged Stilt, Kentish Plover, Spur-winged Plover, Common Tern, Rüppell's Warbler, Olivaceous Warbler.

ACCESS: Leave Route 2 at Ulubat, which is the birthplace of Hassam, the first to scale the walls of Istanbul in 1453. A statue in his memory marks the track that leads to the lakeshore.

Ulu Dağ is a significant mountain rising to almost 700 feet (213 m) above Bursa. It is a

Krüper's Nuthatch

228

national park and has good road access and even a cable-car. Its fame rests on its convenient situation adjacent to the well-known lakes and within easy distance of Istanbul. Here is one of the best areas to see Krüper's Nuthatch, Red-fronted Serin and Lammergeier.

SUMMER: Golden Eagle, Lammergeier, Alpine Accentor, Rock Thrush, Shore Lark, Krüper's Nuthatch, Red-fronted Serin.

ACCESS: Leave Bursa westwards and turn left past the airport to Huseymalani. Turn left to Ulu Dağ.

The Kocabas delta lies at the mouth of the Koca River that drains Apolyont Gölü. Two large lakes, Arapciftligi and Dalyan Gölü, lie adjacent to the river and shoreline and the whole area offers some of the best birding to be found in the western part of the country. As with so many other good bird areas, it is the variety of habitat that accounts for its richness. Shoreline, lakes, reeds, mud, flooded woodland and fields and scrub-covered hillsides are all found within a small area. The result is a remarkable variety of species for such a generally underworked area. Stilt, Ruddy Shelduck, Stone-curlew and Kentish Plover breed, as does a decent-sized colony of Pratincole along with a few Tawny Pipits and Short-toed Larks.

To the west of Dalyan Gölü is a superb area of flooded forest over which Lesser Spotted Eagle and Honey Buzzard display, and where a thorough investigation may produce Olive-tree Warbler, White-backed Woodpecker, Masked Shrike and River Warbler. There are really outstanding numbers of birds here, with Nightingale and Red-backed Shrike dominating.

SUMMER: Ruddy Shelduck, Lesser Spotted Eagle, Honey Buzzard, Kentish Plover, Stone-curlew, Pratincole, Short-toed Lark, Tawny Pipit, Golden Oriole, Roller, Red-backed Shrike, Masked Shrike, White-backed Woodpecker, Nightingale, Olivaceous Warbler, Olive-tree Warbler, River Warbler.

ACCESS: The road from Karacabey to the coast more or less follows the river to its delta. It would be good to have a full list of birds and a sketch map of this area from anyone inspired to explore it thoroughly.

ROUTE: Bursa is the best centre for all sites and is easily reached from Istanbul. There is a hotel at Ulu Dağ that saves the tedious trek up and back each day.

Bafa Gölü

This splendid area lies on the coast of southwestern Turkey, and consists of the large Bafa Gölü, plus the nearby coastal Karine Gölü and the mouth of the River Büyük Menderes. The whole was formerly the delta-estuary of the Menderes, but has been extensively reclaimed for cotton-growing. It is particularly attractive to those taking a package holiday along this coast (many mass-holiday companies feature Izmir and its surroundings).

The bird list is extensive, with Bafa Gölü regularly producing Pygmy Cormorant, Dalmatian Pelican, a variety of herons and egrets, Ruddy Shelduck, Spur-winged Plover, Penduline Tit, and both the sought-after kingfishers. Migrants include Hobby, White-winged Black Tern and waders, and the only drawback to the area is the apparently ferocious dog near the main access point.

Between Bafa Gölü and Karine Gölü lies an area of fields, bounded in the north by interesting but relatively unexplored mountains (Peregrine and eagles) and in the south by scrub-covered hills with Cretzschmar's Bunting. This area regularly produces Fan-tailed Warbler, Bee-eater and Eleonora's Falcon. The latter is also found at Karine Gölü, along with Flamingo and more pelicans, and this is probably the roost for the herons that fly westwards from Bafa at dusk. Clearly the collection of breeding and passage birds makes this an excellent and accessible area, but in winter the numbers of duck rise to a staggering 300,000, with additional numbers of geese. Outstanding are over 100,000 Wigeon, 60,000 Pintail, 3,000 Red-crested Pochard, plus 3,500 Great Crested Grebe. The whole area is quite beautiful.

SUMMER: Pygmy Cormorant, Dalmatian Pelican, Little Egret, Squacco Heron, Night Heron, Purple Heron, Little Bittern, Flamingo, Ruddy Shelduck, Peregrine, Hobby, Eleonora's Falcon, Mediterranean Gull, Kentish Plover, Spur-winged Plover, Black-winged Stilt, Alpine Swift, Great Spotted Cuckoo, Bee-eater, Rufous Bush Chat, Cetti's Warbler, Fan-tailed Warbler, Icterine Warbler, Penduline Tit, Lesser Pied Kingfisher, Smyrna Kingfisher, Cretzschmar's Bunting.

WINTER: Great Crested Grebe, Cormorant, Pygmy Cormorant, Dalmatian Pelican, Great White Egret, Teal, Mallard, Wigeon, Pintail, Shoveler, Red-crested Pochard, Pochard, Ruddy Shelduck, White-fronted Goose, Curlew.

ACCESS: Take the road southwards from Söke to the bridge over the Menderes River. Stop at the next turning on the right (leading to Akköy) and turn left, past the tea house, on a track for 2 km (1¼ miles) to a dilapidated farmhouse (ferocious dog). Walk to the shores of Bafa Gölü with reedbeds for Penduline Tit etc. A scrubby hill south of the track leads to Cretzschmar's Bunting etc. North of the Menderes bridge a motorable embankment can be taken eastwards to the lakeshores. Only this southwestern corner of Bafa Gölü has reeds and cover.

Return to the bridge and tea house and take the turning to Akköy. Turn right in the village and cross the Menderes again. Walking the river may produce the kingfishers. The track continues along the landward side of Karine Gölü and at the end joins an east–west track between Doganbey on the beach and the main Söke road.

ROUTE: There is an airport north of Izmir.

Birecik

Birecik is a small village in eastern Turkey just a few kilometres north of the Syrian border. It has achieved ornitho-eminence by virtue of the colony of Bald Ibis that breed on the crags above the village, but repeated visits by Ibis-twitchers have produced a good range of Anatolian species in the immediate area. The Ibis (often called Waldrapp) are now the subject of a breeding project by the WWF and free-flying birds, as well as captives, can be seen throughout the area, as well as on the cliffs 2 km (1¼ miles) to the north. With the recent population crash in Morocco, this species is becoming ever more difficult to see.

Bald Ibis

Other local specialities include Bruce's Scops Owl in the tiny park in the south of the town, and two species of sandgrouse that regularly fly in from the east at dawn to drink from the River Euphrates on islands north of the town. Lesser Pied and Smyrna Kingfishers haunt the river, and Ménétries' and Graceful Warblers are common along the adjacent scrub. An extensive wadi just north of the captive Bald Ibis spot is worth exploring for both species of rock sparrow, and there is often an Eagle Owl present. Blue-cheeked Bee-eater can be found on the west bank north of an enclosed wood, as well as in sand pits some 5 km (3 miles) to the south on the eastern bank. The latter also hold Dead Sea Sparrow, which is, however, common among the orchards and scrub to the north of the wadi. Other species of note include Desert Finch, Chukar and See-see Partridges, Desert and Bimaculated Larks and even regular Long-eared Owl.

SUMMER: Bald Ibis, Short-toed Eagle, Chukar, See-see Partridge, Little Ringed Plover, Ringed Plover, Black-bellied Sandgrouse, Pin-tailed Sandgrouse, Palm Dove, Nightjar, Bruce's Scops Owl, Long-eared Owl, Little Swift, Lesser Pied Kingfisher, Smyrna Kingfisher, Blue-cheeked Bee-eater, Syrian Woodpecker, Desert Lark, Short-toed Lark, Lesser Short-toed Lark, Bimaculated Lark, Rufous Bush Chat, Black-eared Wheatear, Graceful Warbler, Great Reed Warbler, Olivaceous Warbler,

Upcher's Warbler, Ménétries' Warbler, Spanish Sparrow, Dead Sea Sparrow, Pale Rock Sparrow, Yellow-throated Sparrow, Rock Sparrow, Black-headed Bunting.

ACCESS: There is a hotel in Birecik, as well as a bank and an 'excellent' restaurant. The main areas are the small park in the southern part of the town and the sand pits some 5 km (3 miles) south on the east bank. To the north, there is a track leading northwards just beyond a café on the west bank. The east bank, north of the town, is the best, with the main wadi about 3 km (nearly 2 miles) away with Ibis etc. Continuing north, a small stream joins the Euphrates and beyond here is an area of scrub and orchards. Allow two or three days here.

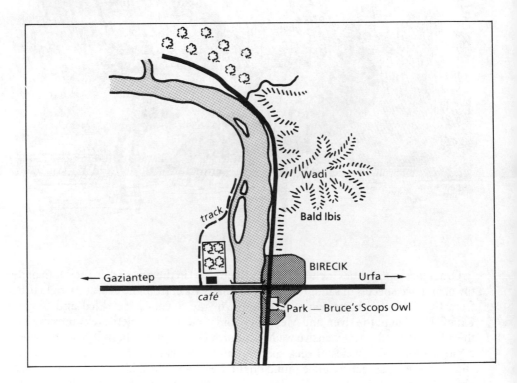

ROUTE: Gaziantep, some 60 km (37 miles) to the west, is the nearest town. As everywhere in Turkey, there is a bus service.

Demirkazik

This high mountain area is noted as the best place in Turkey for Caspian Snowcock, but it also offers a good range of high-altitude species to those intrepid enough to face the efforts of searching for them. The Snowcock are far from obliging. Firstly, one must leave for a 1½–2½-hour hike in darkness to arrive at the high snowfields before dawn.

Then, as the light emerges, listen for the 'Curlew-like' call and locate the birds before they climb up among the screes and crags. Once they have done that, there is little chance of finding them again. Calling stops by about 8 a.m. in mid-May, while by mid-June the snow is disappearing and with it any reasonable chance of this bird. There is, however, much more to Demirkazik than this species. Radde's Accentor is regularly seen, along with Finsch's Wheatear, Shore Lark, Rock Bunting and Red-fronted Serin. The gorges are one of the most reliable places for Wallcreeper, and there are usually a few Lammergeier and Griffons to be seen. Other good birds include Crimson-winged Finch and Snow Finch, with Bimaculated Lark and Isabelline Wheatear lower down.

SUMMER: White Stork, Griffon Vulture, Lammergeier, Golden Eagle, Caspian Snow-cock, Chukar, Scops Owl, Alpine Swift, Bimaculated Lark, Short-toed Lark, Shore Lark, Crag Martin, Water Pipit, Grey Wagtail, Alpine Accentor, Radde's Accentor, Black Redstart, Isabelline Wheatear, Wheatear, Finsch's Wheatear, Rock Thrush, Cetti's Warbler, Rock Nuthatch, Wallcreeper, Alpine Chough, Chough, Snow Finch, Red-fronted Serin, Serin, Crimson-winged Finch, Rock Bunting.

ACCESS: The route in is off the E98 between Niğde and Kayseri. North of Niğde turn right just beyond Ovacik to Baldaras. Continue towards Camardi and watch for the hill village of Demirkazik to the left. Continue and turn left across the river (some 8 km/5 miles before Camardi), then proceed over a motorable track to the village. Beyond Demirkazik is a path to a mountain lodge which offers accommodation, but no food. Two gorges open out above the lodge. Take the right-hand one up to the snow line, allowing 1½–2½ hours prior to dawn for Snowcock. Cross to the left and descend down the second gorge back to the lodge. A cup-shaped hollow at the top of the second gorge holds Radde's Accentor, Finsch's Wheatear etc.

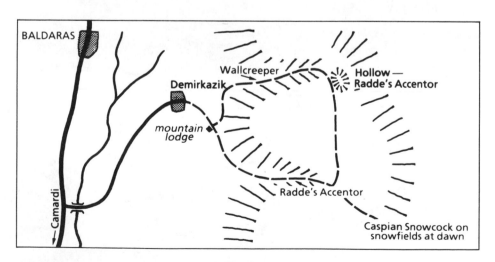

ROUTE: Kayseri has an airport with flights from Ankara.

233

Istanbul and the Bosporus

The spectacular migration of storks and birds of prey continues to attract hordes of birders every autumn. The main period is from late August, when Honey Buzzards reach peak numbers, until early October. Birds vary according to the period of watching, but generally mid-September is the best time for the largest variety, with up to 18 different species of raptor seen in a single day. At this time, Spotted and Lesser Spotted Eagles, Buzzard, Short-toed Eagle, Booted Eagle, Levant Sparrowhawk and Black Kite are regularly seen. White Storks pass over in their thousands, but much earlier in the season. Return passage is lighter, but still produces the species variety from mid-March to early April.

Though these birds are the main attraction, there are many other migrants in the area. These include *yelkouan* Shearwater, while among small birds in the bushes are Red-breasted Flycatcher and the occasional Green Warbler. Istanbul itself is noted for Palm Dove and Alpine Swift.

AUTUMN: Manx Shearwater, White Stork, Black Stork, Lesser Spotted Eagle, Spotted Eagle, Short-toed Eagle, Booted Eagle, Buzzard, Honey Buzzard, Griffon Vulture, Egyptian Vulture, Levant Sparrowhawk, Black Kite, Red Kite, Hobby, Lesser Kestrel, Red-footed Falcon, Wryneck, Alpine Swift, Palm Dove, Redstart, Red-breasted Flycatcher.

ACCESS: Istanbul has many hotels and restaurants, and is connected to the Asian shore by a modern bridge and by frequent ferry services. The main watchpoint is a café on Buçuk Çamlıca, the larger of the Çamlıca Hills. This can be reached by following signs to Kisikli on the Asian side of the bridge, or by bus from Üsküdar reached by ferry across the Bosporus. In peak season all the café tables will be occupied by birders: arrival at 10 a.m. is fine.

White Storks

ROUTE: Istanbul has international flights.

Kulu Gölü

This small (by Turkish standards) lake lies south of Ankara and is generally regarded as an essential ingredient in any tour of Turkey. It is easily found, relatively easy to work, and regularly produces a variety of breeding and passage birds. The shallow margins hold passage waders and the reedbeds produce the odd heron and occasional Thick-billed Reed Bunting. The flock of White-headed Duck is significant and may on occasion exceed 100 birds in summer. Flamingo is also regular and other interesting species include Gull-billed and White-winged Black Terns, Slender-billed Gull, Ruddy Shelduck, Glossy Ibis, plus a variety of waders that includes Marsh Sandpiper, Red-necked Phalarope and, outstandingly, Greater Sand Plover. The most abundant pipit is usually Red-throated, and Citrine Wagtail is sometimes seen.

SUMMER: Black-necked Grebe, Purple Heron, Squacco Heron, Glossy Ibis, Flamingo, Ruddy Shelduck, Gadwall, Garganey, Pintail, Red-crested Pochard, White-headed Duck, Red-footed Falcon, Hobby, Great Bustard, Avocet, Black-winged Stilt, Kentish Plover, Greater Sand Plover, Temminck's Stint, Little Stint, Red-necked Phalarope, Ruff, Marsh Sandpiper, Collared Pratincole, Little Gull, Slender-billed Gull, Gull-billed Tern, White-winged Black Tern, Black-bellied Sandgrouse, Roller, Short-toed Lark, Lesser Short-toed Lark, Calandra Lark, Bimaculated Lark, Red-throated Pipit, Tawny Pipit, Citrine Wagtail, Great Reed Warbler, Isabelline Wheatear.

ACCESS: Leave the E5 south of Ankara on Route 35 towards Konya. Stop in Kulu and turn left past the Turkish I.S. Bank. Continue over a stream on a gravel track to the southwest corner of the lake. Walk from here along the western shore, the Sand Plovers often being found along the northern shore, and explore the reedbeds and fields. Return and explore the southern shore; a sandy spit often holds waders. There is a hotel in the town (poor reports).

ROUTE: Easily reached on the E5 from Ankara with its international airport.

Manyas Gölü

Lake Manyas has long been famous for both its breeding and its passage birds and is the site of Turkey's first bird reserve, Kuş Çenneti on the northeastern shore. This is mainly a reserve for breeding herons and egrets, with up to 2,500 pairs among the lakeside willows. These include Grey, Night and Purple together with Little Egret, Little Bittern and Spoonbill. Dalmatian Pelican also breeds and large numbers of White Pelican regularly pass through. The reedy woodland holds Pygmy Cormorant, Scops Owl, Penduline Tit and, in the more open areas, Great Reed and Savi's Warblers. There are Spur-winged Plover, Marsh Harrier, Roller, Bee-eater, Great Spotted Cuckoo and Rufous Bush Chat among the grand total of over 90 breeding species. All told, some 200 species have been noted at Manyas.

Passage often brings huge numbers of White Storks, and Red-footed Falcons may be present in significant flocks.

SUMMER: White Stork, Pygmy Cormorant, Dalmatian Pelican, Night Heron, Purple Heron, Little Egret, Little Bittern, Spoonbill, Lesser Kestrel, Spur-winged Plover, Kentish Plover, Scops Owl, Long-eared Owl, Roller, Bee-eater, Great Spotted Cuckoo, Penduline Tit, Great Reed Warbler, Savi's Warbler, Olivaceous Warbler, Rufous Bush Chat, Black-headed Bunting.

PASSAGE: White Stork, White Pelican, Glossy Ibis, Ferruginous Duck, Red-footed Falcon, Caspian Tern, White-winged Black Tern.

ACCESS: Kuş Çenneti is well signposted at the northeastern corner of the lake near Sigirciatik. It is well fenced and it may be necessary to raise the warden by making local enquiries. Most of the species can, however, be seen without entering the protected area at all.

ROUTE: Leave Route 2 south of Bandirma, which is on the Sea of Marmara.

Pontic Alps

The mountains that border the Black Sea coast of eastern Anatolia have through history generated a considerable range of names. The area referred to here lies north of the road from Gümüşhane to Erzurum and is still one of the least explored areas in the whole of Turkey. Though some parts are well known and attract birders every year, there is much more to explore and undoubtedly many more places that would produce the region's special birds.

As long ago as 1972, the author took a horse trip from near Gümüşhane up into the hills to a summer village, where Scarlet Rosefinch was the common bird and where Water Pipit, Shore Lark, Sombre Tit and a variety of eagles were easily seen. No doubt there are other, more accessible villages, where these and other species can be seen.

Sivri Kaya lies between Ispir and Ikizdere, high on the shoulder of Kirkla Dağ, and has become a prime spot for the highly elusive Caucasian Blackcock and the almost equally so Caspian Snowcock. Both can be found among the crags and rhododendron scrub high above the road to the north of the village. Access is decidedly difficult to find, and the approach must be made in darkness to ensure arrival in the correct area before dawn. Mountain Chiffchaff is another attraction here.

Ikizdere has a good woodland area where Green Warbler is a speciality, but this species is just as easily located at the famous Sumela Monastery near Macka inland from Trabzon, where there is also Red-breasted Flycatcher. In the other direction, Ispir is noted for its Semi-collared Flycatchers among the valley orchards to the north and south of the town. From here, a track leads through woodland for Syrian Woodpecker, Golden Oriole and Hobby.

SUMMER: Egyptian Vulture, Black Kite, Goshawk, Golden Eagle, Booted Eagle,

Hobby, Caucasian Blackcock, Caspian Snowcock, Hoopoe, Green Woodpecker, Great Spotted Woodpecker, Syrian Woodpecker, Shore Lark, Water Pipit, Grey Wagtail, Dipper, Alpine Accentor, Dunnock, Black-eared Wheatear, Black Redstart, Rock Thrush, Marsh Warbler, Green Warbler, Mountain Chiffchaff, Semi-collared Flycatcher, Chough, Scarlet Rosefinch, Crimson-winged Finch, Rock Bunting.

ACCESS: Sumela Monastery is easily reached from Trabzon via Macka. There is a zigzag path through lovely woodland, with Green Warbler and Rosefinch, to the monastery, which is set into a sheer rock face. Continue upwards, join a track to the left and descend back to the river (Dipper and Red-breasted Flycatcher) via another track.

Sivri Kaya lies on the Rize–Erzurum road between Ispir and Ikizdere. About 800 m (½ mile) on the Ispir side, an inconspicuous path leads up the hill, passes a few houses and continues into an area where small rhododendrons can be seen above and below. This spot, where the path disappears, is best for Snowcock and Blackcock; but you must be here before dawn. Mustapha Sari lives opposite the tea room in the village; arrange for him to act as guide — pay him! There is a hotel. Across the river, opposite the village, the conifer woods hold Mountain Chiffchaff.

About 1.5 km (1 mile) south of the village of Ikizdere, a bridge crosses the river. Take this, and turn back for 400 m (¼ mile) alongside the stream where a steep path zigzags through the woods for Green Warbler.

Ispir village lies just off the Erzurum–Rize main road. Take the village road and immediately search the orchards on the right near the river for Semi-collared Flycatchers. They may be elusive. They may also be sought in an orchard near the bus station north of the village. Continue along a track up the river valley for other species. Hotel here.

ROUTE: Airports at Trabzon and Erzurum with car-hire possibilities at the former.

Taşucu

Taşucu nestles in a small bay on the Turkish south coast and is one of the ferry ports for Turkish Cyprus. It is a handy place for exploring the largely reclaimed, but still significant, Göksu delta. All who have worked this area have found it a bit of a slog, and these include determined walkers as well as motorists prepared to drive along the beaches. The collection of species is what one could reasonably expect in this part of the Mediterranean, with Spur-winged Plover, Ruddy Shelduck, White Pelican and Marbled Teal heading the bill. There are, however, Purple Gallinule, White-tailed Plover and Graceful Warbler, and a good passage of waders that may include Greater Sand Plover. Crakes can be regularly seen crossing gaps in the reeds while one watches for Purple Gallinule. Audouin's Gull breeds along the coast and is regularly seen from Taşucu pier in the evening, while the hillsides above the village have Yellow-vented Bulbul.

Inland, the Göksu River has good, if undramatic, cliffs where vultures, eagles, and Bulbul and other rocky-based birds can be found. All in all, it is a good area for a few days' exploration.

SUMMER: Great Crested Grebe, Shag, Pygmy Cormorant, White Pelican, Squacco Heron, Little Bittern, Little Egret, Great White Egret, Purple Heron, White Stork, Glossy Ibis, Ruddy Shelduck, Marbled Teal, Egyptian Vulture, Griffon Vulture, Lesser Spotted Eagle, Short-toed Eagle, Hobby, Eleonora's Falcon, Chukar, Water Rail, Purple Gallinule, Little Crake, Baillon's Crake, Spotted Crake, Black-winged Stilt, Greater Sand Plover, Spur-winged Plover, White-tailed Plover, Little Stint, Curlew Sandpiper, Audouin's Gull, Syrian Woodpecker, Rock Nuthatch, Red-rumped Swallow, Crag Martin, Blue Rock Thrush, Yellow-vented Bulbul, Black-eared Wheatear, Graceful Warbler, Spanish Sparrow, Cretzschmar's Bunting.

ACCESS: The pier at Taşucu and the road northwards from Silifke towards Mut are easily found. The Göksu delta is more awkward. Leave Taşucu on the Silifke road, and after an extensive fenced-off factory area of about 2 km (1¼ miles) a track on the right leads to the beach. Motor or walk left, hopping over the dunes from time to time in the search for an extensive reed-fringed lagoon. A hired motorbike might prove the perfect way of exploring the whole of the estuary.

ROUTE: The E24 runs westwards from Adana, which has an airport.

Lake Van

Van is a huge inland sea in the far east of Turkey near the Russian border. It is a magnificent blue in colour and virtually devoid of birds. It does, however, have a number of small rivers running into it, plus a number of adjacent marshes that together hold a good variety of interesting birds. There are several islands, such as Aknamara, that hold breeding Herring Gull, Night Heron, Ruddy Shelduck plus Lesser Kestrel and Olivaceous Warbler.

Van town is a bustling place with several hotels that no-one could recommend. It is about 5 km (3 miles) from Van Citadel, which is a good spot for exploring the marshes to the south of the railway line. Crane, Marsh Harrier, Caspian Tern, Little Bittern, Roller, Moustached Warbler and White Stork can all be seen. The marshes to the north across the railway have waders and duck, including White-headed Duck.

To the east of Van, the railway runs through a gorge where Eagle Owl may be seen and where Grey-necked Bunting and Finsch's Wheatear are relatively common. Alternatively the road to Erçek has these species, as well as Lanner, Long-legged Buzzard, Crimson-winged Finch and Bimaculated Lark, with Red-necked and Black-necked Grebes, White-winged Black Tern, Ruddy Shelduck, Crane and Stilt on the various waters seen from the road.

In the northeastern corner of Van, just beyond where the road to Muradiye turns off, is the Bendi-Maki marsh. Here, there are often good concentrations of White Pelican, Gull-billed and Caspian Terns, White-headed Duck, Crane and Ruddy Shelduck, while Citrine Wagtail may be found among the areas of short grass. Rock Thrush may be quite common along the road to Ercis.

Several of the roads leaving Van lead through high-level passes and, while some are known to hold Radde's Accentor and Red-fronted Serin among others, there is no reason to suppose that others do not. There are several other excursions from Van that may be rewarding. To the north, Doğubayazit and adjacent Ishakpasa have Rock Nuthatch, Snow Finch, Rock Sparrow and Finsch's Wheatear, while further north still the marshes alongside Mount Ararat (Noah and the flood fame) have Marsh and Montagu's Harriers, Crane and Ruddy Shelduck.

One of the most outstanding birds of the Van area is generally regarded as worth the considerable effort involved in seeing it: the Demoiselle Crane. These birds may be found along the River Murat north of Bulanik, but it is a 6-km (3¾-mile) walk plus a possible 4-km (2½-mile) exploration to find them — even if they are there. Other birds include Crane, Pygmy Cormorant and Quail, plus possible Great Bustard. Bulanik marsh lies some 10 km (6 miles) to the west and is good for Glossy Ibis and Pygmy Cormorant.

There is still much to explore in the Van area.

SUMMER: Red-necked Grebe, Black-necked Grebe, Pygmy Cormorant, White Pelican, Little Bittern, Night Heron, Squacco Heron, Little Egret, Purple Heron, White Stork, Glossy Ibis, Flamingo, Ruddy Shelduck, Ferruginous Duck, White-headed Duck, Egyptian Vulture, Griffon Vulture, Marsh Harrier, Montagu's Harrier, Goshawk, Golden Eagle, Lesser Kestrel, Hobby, Quail, Crane, Demoiselle Crane, Black-winged Stilt, Avocet, Greater Sand Plover, Gull-billed Tern, Caspian Tern, Whiskered Tern, White-winged Black Tern, Black-bellied Sandgrouse, Calandra Lark, Bimaculated Lark, Citrine Wagtail, Isabelline Wheatear, Finsch's Wheatear, Bluethroat, Rock Thrush, Savi's Warbler, Marsh Warbler, Moustached Warbler, Great Reed Warbler, Olivaceous Warbler, Rock Nuthatch, Penduline Tit, Rock Sparrow, Red-fronted Serin, Crimson-winged Finch, Ortolan Bunting, Grey-necked Bunting.

ACCESS: The area of eastern Van is easily worked at the Citadel (see above), at Erçek Gölü and the other waters along the Van–Erçek road, and at Bendi-Maki marsh (see above). Baskale is a plateau above the army camp just north of the town, beyond which a track leads up to a hillside village with a narrow valley beyond for Radde's Accentor and Bluethroat. The hillside below the village has Grey-necked Bunting, while lower still are Crimson-winged Finch and Red-fronted Serin.

There are Cranes in many areas but Demoiselles are found at Bulanik. There is a dilapidated bridge across a river immediately north of the town, which is on Route 60 northwest of Lake Van. Watch for an 'orange'-coloured building. A track leads to the River Murat. At the river explore westwards. For Bulanik marsh, head westwards to the fork for Muş and Varto. At this point a path leads south to the marsh, which cannot be seen from the road.

ROUTE: There is an airport at Van and a train service from Ankara, and a train service also from Istanbul (on the Asian shore) to Tatvan. Regular ferries connect Tatvan and Van. There are hotels in most towns, but the standard of accommodation varies from unsatisfactory to downright disgusting. Take a padlock and key and/or large wooden wedges to ensure privacy.

239

Yesilice

Yesilice (or Büyük Arapter as it is sometimes called) lies 23 km (14¼ miles) northwest of Gaziantep and is, therefore, often worked by visitors to Birecik. It is an area of rocky outcrops and hillsides with fields and orchards, and is a strangely fruitful place for several otherwise decidedly elusive species. It may, however, be a little awkward to find, as some observers are unsure as to whether they visited the correct place or not! The interesting birds include Red-tailed Wheatear and Eastern Rock Nuthatch, as well as the more regular Upcher's Warbler (fairly common), Cinereous Bunting, Desert Finch and Pale Rock Sparrow.

SUMMER: Chukar, Bimaculated Lark, Rock Nuthatch, Eastern Rock Nuthatch, White-throated Robin, Red-tailed Wheatear, Black-eared Wheatear, Upcher's Warbler, Cinereous Bunting, Cretzschmar's Bunting, Desert Finch, Pale Rock Sparrow.

ACCESS: From the Gaziantep direction, continue through Yesilice and watch for a lime kiln on the right after 1.5 km (1 mile). A track on the left opposite this leads past a village and on up a valley with rocky outcrops and sides. Continue to the far end for Red-tailed Wheatear, with Eastern Rock Nuthatch on outcrops and Upcher's in orchards to the north. Pale Rock Sparrows are on the right-hand slopes of the valley.

If this fails, return towards Yesilice and take a track right 200 m (220 yards) before the town. Continue for 4 km (2½ miles) to a village and then, on foot, up a valley for Wheatear and Eastern Rock Nuthatch on crags.

If this also fails, head towards Gaziantep to about 1.5 km (1 mile) before the Maras fork, where a restaurant on the right is followed by a stream leading from a gorge. Here at least you should get Upcher's, Cinereous and Pale Rock Sparrow. There are no hotels in Yesilice, but several in Gaziantep.

ROUTE: Gaziantep is on the E24. The nearest airport is Malatya to the northeast.

YUGOSLAVIA

Babuna Gorge

The Babuna Gorge has been formed by the river of the same name as it flows eastwards over the edge of the Babuna Plateau. The town of Titov Veles lies only 4 km (2½ miles) to the north and the motorway E5 crosses the Babuna before that river joins the Vardar. The gorge has sheer cliffs 100 m (330 feet) or more high and is lined with nooks and crannies beloved of breeding birds. The surrounding hills are dry, with scanty vegetation, while the Vardar is lined by trees and bushes that add to the attraction. Birds here include Bee-eater, Hoopoe, Roller, Golden Oriole, Syrian and White-backed Woodpeckers and Penduline Tit.

The gorge itself has proved easy to find; or almost impossible, since first detailed in the earlier editions of *WWBBE*. Part of the problem stems from the construction of a Titov Veles bypass on the main road. New directions follow the seasonal bird lists.

The gorge is known mainly for its raptors, breeding and on passage, including two vultures, Golden, Booted and Short-toed Eagles, Long-legged Buzzard, Lanner, Lesser Kestrel, Red-footed Falcon, Goshawk and Levant Sparrowhawk. There are also regular Alpine Swift, Red-rumped Swallow and Crag Martin. Hillsides here hold Rock Partridge, Rock Nuthatch, Rock Thrush, Blue Rock Thrush, Black-eared

241

Wheatear and Olive-tree Warbler among others. In fact, the more this apparently undistinguished area is explored, the more it seems to produce. Certainly it is an excellent stop-over for anyone motoring through Yugoslavia and, in any case, Titov Veles is a good place to leave the main road for a detour to Lake Préspa (now treated under Greece).

Black-headed Bunting (male)

SUMMER: Griffon Vulture, Egyptian Vulture, Golden Eagle, Long-legged Buzzard, Peregrine, Lesser Kestrel, Alpine Swift, Red-rumped Swallow, Crag Martin, Rock Partridge, Rock Nuthatch, Hoopoe, Golden Oriole, Roller, White-backed Woodpecker, Syrian Woodpecker, Dipper, Penduline Tit, Sombre Tit, Rock Thrush, Blue Rock Thrush, Short-toed Lark, Black-eared Wheatear, Black Redstart, Tawny Pipit, Orphean Warbler, Subalpine Warbler, Olive-tree Warbler, Olivaceous Warbler, Icterine Warbler, Black-headed Bunting, Ortolan Bunting.

SPRING AND AUTUMN: Black Stork, Booted Eagle, Short-toed Eagle, Lanner, Red-footed Falcon, Goshawk, Levant Sparrowhawk, Marsh Harrier, Montagu's Harrier.

ACCESS: Travelling southwards on the E5, leave the road following signs to Titov Veles. Proceed through the town, cross the bridge over the River Vardar and follow signs towards Ohrid and Gevgelija. This is the 'old E5'. Continue on this road for some 4 km (2½ miles) south of town until the road crosses a bridge over the River Babuna (name plate!). There is a small factory and considerable rubbish here, and a track that leads off westward along the northern bank of the river. Walk the track, forking right to the gorge. Sit at the entrance or climb up into the hills. Do not forget the trees alongside the River

242

Vardar. Groups continue to camp 'wild' here, but Titov Veles has the Hotel International and other varied accommodation.

ROUTE: Off the E5 in the south of the country.

Carska Bara

This is an important marsh area near Zrenjanin north of Belgrade. It lies at the centre of an extensive wetland area, with the nearby marshes of Perleska Bara and Tiganjica nearby. Visitors should not miss the fishponds at Ečka. The outstanding feature of this shallow, reed-fringed lake is the heron colonies, which contain really good numbers of several species. Night Heron is particularly numerous, but there are also decent numbers of Purple Heron, both bitterns and even perhaps a few pairs of Spoonbill. Great White Egret now breeds and both storks are regular in their appearances.

SUMMER: Garganey, White Stork, Black Stork, Purple Heron, Squacco Heron, Night Heron, Great White Egret, Bittern, Little Bittern, Glossy Ibis, Marsh Harrier, Whiskered Tern, Lesser Grey Shrike, Red-backed Shrike, Syrian Woodpecker, Great Reed Warbler, Savi's Warbler, Golden Oriole.

ACCESS: A minor road westward leaves the Belgrade–Zrenjanin road at Ečka. Check the river from the bridge and continue to the west side of Carska Bara near Belo Blato.

ROUTE: Belgrade airport and easy car hire.

Kopački Rit

This is the marshland reserve at the confluence of the Rivers Danube and Drava, referred to as Baranja in earlier books of this title. The whole complex of channels and marshes here is as rich as any other area of northern Yugoslavia, but since it is so vast it is best to concentrate on one or two sites for all but the most extended of visits.

The area is seasonally flooded and, over the years, a vast network of channels, backwaters, oxbows, islands, bogs, reedbeds, marshy meadows, peat bogs and flooded woods has been created. Here there are colonies of grebes, Cormorant, Purple Heron, Little Bittern and Great White Egret. There are raptors, including White-tailed Eagle, and a huge array of smaller birds, including Penduline Tit and Savi's Warbler.

Though birds can be seen almost anywhere in the area, the reserve at Kopački Rit is undoubtedly best of all. A series of dykes allow exploration on foot over huge areas of the region, including vast tracts of flooded grassland. Across the river lies Veliki Rit, while to the north is Crna Bara near Bački Monoštor, both similar marshland reserves.

Flooded woodland, here as elsewhere, is very rich in breeding birds and should be thoroughly explored. Agricultural and village areas too have their special birds, including Lesser Grey Shrike, Hoopoe and White Stork. Finally, to the northeast near the Hungarian border, is Lake Ludas, a shallow reed-fringed water with good colonies of herons, duck and grebes.

243

SUMMER: Great Crested Grebe, Pygmy Cormorant, Black Stork, White Stork, Little Egret, Purple Heron, Great White Egret, Little Bittern, Glossy Ibis, Greylag Goose, Ferruginous Duck, White-tailed Eagle, Marsh Harrier, Spotted Crake, Penduline Tit, Hoopoe, Lesser Grey Shrike, Savi's Warbler, Great Reed Warbler.

ACCESS: Kopački Rit is reached from Osijek, which forms an ideal base, by leaving the town northwards to Bilje, then following signs to the right to Kapacevo. Thereafter watch for the restaurant 'Cormoran', from where access can be gained to the network of dykes overlooking all the good areas. The 'Zoo Park' is the centre of a Zoological Park (not a zoo as we know it) and offers regular boat trips for tourists — worth a go.

ROUTE: Osijek is just over 100 km (62 miles) from Belgrade, using the E94 and then turning right to Dakovo.

Metković

Metković is situated in the lower Neretva River 95 km (59 miles) northwest of Dubrovnik and 15 km (9 miles) from the sea. Below Gabela, the river flows across a marshy valley floor, though it has been extensively canalised near its mouth. The area of marsh is constantly being reduced by drainage, but the dykes among the water meadows are lined with reeds and the two large lakes of Deransko Jezero and Hutovo Blato are not threatened. The latter was declared a reserve in 1954. The surrounding hills rise to 530 m (1750 feet) and add a large number of birds to the area's list, which at present numbers about 300 species.

The most important marshes are the reserves at Hutovo Blato and Deransko Jezero and the nearby odd lakes and ponds. Then there are water meadows intersected by drainage ditches with a fringe of reeds, and agricultural cultivated areas mainly devoted to maize, vines and figs. The riverine scrub along the banks of the Neretva consists mainly of *Salix* and poplars. There are also woods and finally the estuary itself to explore.

The first and most dramatic area visited by birdwatchers is the Deransko Jezero, which holds a wealth of herons of which Squacco is the commonest, but Purple and Night Herons, Little Egret and both bitterns also breed. Other birds of this area include Pygmy Cormorant, Cetti's and Great Reed Warblers, as well as excellent numbers of waders and Black Terns on passage. The hills, of which Rujnica is the best explored, hold Rock Partridge on the lower slopes and Blue Rock Thrush, Rock Nuthatch and Alpine Chough higher up. Species such as the two vultures, White-tailed Eagle (said to breed), Short-toed Eagle (the commonest raptor) and Lanner Falcon can be seen almost anywhere. The area also holds several other interesting birds, among them Eagle Owl, Olivaceous and Olive-tree Warblers and Bee-eater.

Northwards, beyond Mostar, the Neretva flows through a splendid gorge with good raptors.

SUMMER: Pygmy Cormorant, Purple Heron, Little Egret, Squacco Heron, Night Heron, Little Bittern, Bittern, Ferruginous Duck, Egyptian Vulture, Griffon Vulture,

White-tailed Eagle, Marsh Harrier, Short-toed Eagle, Lanner Falcon, Rock Partridge, Quail, Scops Owl, Eagle Owl, Alpine Swift, Bee-eater, Hoopoe, Crested Lark, Tawny Pipit, Lesser Grey Shrike, Blue Rock Thrush, Black-eared Wheatear, Cetti's Warbler, Great Reed Warbler, Olivaceous Warbler, Olive-tree Warbler, Orphean Warbler, Sardinian Warbler, Subalpine Warbler, Sombre Tit, Rock Nuthatch, Black-headed Bunting, Ortolan Bunting, Golden Oriole, Alpine Chough.

WINTER: White-headed Duck.

ACCESS: This area is excellent for a single-centre holiday of exploration based on Metković. Access to most of the countryside is unrestricted. One can drive to Karaotok at the centre of the reserve, where there is a shelter and an ornithological museum.

ROUTE: Easy drive from Dubrovnik with its international airport.

Obedska Bara

Despite being thoroughly written up in the earlier editions of this guide, the reserve of Obedska Bara remains little visited by non-Yugoslavian birders. This is a pity, for the encouragement of local birders depends to a large extent on contact with enthusiastic visitors. Obedska Bara is a reserve on the northern banks of the River Sava, part of a larger area that is regularly inundated by the flooding of that river. The splashy marshes and woods gradually dry out during the summer months, but are always wet underfoot. The reserve is a horseshoe-shaped marsh some 12 km (7½ miles) long and 0.5 km (550 yards) wide lying between Obrež and Kupinova. The woods, flooded marshes, pools and meadows offer a variety of different habitats, which accounts for the richness of the fauna. To the east the woodlands of Kupinski (near Kupinova) are flooded, while on higher ground, as at Matijevica, they are dry and mostly well drained.

Over the years the number of raptors has sadly declined, and the visitor can no longer rely on either Imperial or White-tailed Eagle here. However, there are eagles still to be seen, including the occasional Golden and Lesser Spotted. Marsh Harrier, Black Kite and Hobby are all regular. Otherwise the selection of birds remains much as before, with storks, grebes, duck and a variety of good marshland birds, including Glossy Ibis, Purple and Squacco Herons, Penduline Tit, Great Reed and Icterine Warblers and large numbers of Golden Oriole.

SUMMER: Great Crested Grebe, Purple Heron, Little Egret, Night Heron, Spoonbill, Glossy Ibis, White Stork, Black Stork, Black Kite, Golden Eagle, Lesser Spotted Eagle, Marsh Harrier, Montagu's Harrier, Hobby, Spotted Crake, Black-tailed Godwit, Ruff, Long-eared Owl, Hoopoe, Syrian Woodpecker, Middle Spotted Woodpecker, Wryneck, Lesser Grey Shrike, Red-backed Shrike, Woodchat Shrike, Penduline Tit, Great Reed Warbler, Savi's Warbler, Olivaceous Warbler, Icterine Warbler, Bonelli's Warbler, Pied Flycatcher, Hawfinch, Golden Oriole.

ACCESS: On the eastern outskirts of Kupinova a track leads southward to the River

Sava, with flooded woods on the right, bushy areas to the left and flooded fields near the river. Turn left along the river for more woods. East of Obrež is a boardwalk into the area of reeds and pools with an adjacent elevated hide. There are two more of these at intervals eastward on the road towards Kupinova. To the north of the road are dry woods with a variety of species. The distance between the two towns is only 6 km (3¾ miles), making for easy exploration.

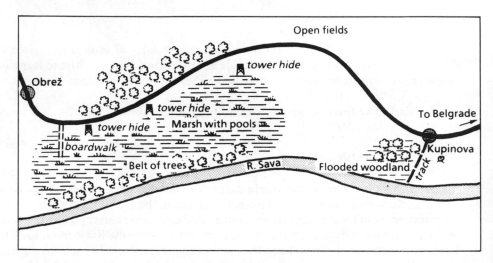

Fruška Gora, a range of wooded hills to the north between Obedska Bara and the Danube, has declined in importance with the disappearance of most of its raptors. There are still some birds hereabouts, including relatively common Collared Flycatcher, plus Middle Spotted Woodpecker and the occasional eagle. It is easy enough to visit for a day using one of the many roads that cross the hills from north to south.

ROUTE: Belgrade has an international airport with car hire. Drive westward on the E94 and turn left to Obrež.

Lake Préspa

Lake Préspa lies on the borders with Greece and Albania and offers first-class birding throughout the year. The Yugoslavian side is certainly as good as the Greek portion, but the birds are virtually the same and most visitors tend to work the Greek side. Thus Préspa has been detailed under Greece, and visitors to the more northern part of the lake should refer to that account for likely species.

Scutari Lake

Lake Scutari lies in the southwestern corner of Yugoslavia and is crossed by the boundary with Albania. It is a huge water covering 40,000 ha (99,000 acres), the majority of which is in Yugoslavia. Several of its feeder rivers, notably the Morača, have formed deltas on the northern shore, and a chain of marshes extends from the border to beyond the bridge at Virpazar. This area is a maze of lagoons, reedbeds and woodland that is regularly flooded. Inland is an agricultural plain extending as far as Titograd. Willows break up the plain, and there are extensive stands of hornbeams that attract woodpeckers and oaks that harbour warblers.

To the west, Scutari is separated from the sea by a range of mountains which fortunately is crossed by the road between Virpazar and Petrovac. Here there are several dry-scrub birds typical of the Mediterranean, as well as a quite impressive passage of raptors. Petrovac itself is still relatively unspoilt and makes the perfect base for exploration. It offers scrub and tree cover for migrants and has a good range of breeding birds. To the south, the marsh at Buljarica often holds good waterbirds.

A good excursion from Scutari is via the fine Morača Gorge to Lake Biograd. Here are good mountain birds, such as Wallcreeper, plus raptors and several woodpeckers, including Black, among the lakeside woods.

Of all the birds of the area, the colony of Dalmatian Pelicans is probably the most significant in international terms. The birds can be seen at several places around Scutari, though the mouth of the Morača is a favourite. Other important species include White-tailed and Golden Eagles, Lanner, Syrian Woodpecker, Olive-tree Warbler and Collared Flycatcher. All in all, this is an easily worked area with an excellent range of breeding and migrant species. Lake Scutari is an important wetland and a major attraction, but there is much more besides. In fact, it is by far the easiest area of Yugoslavia to work.

SUMMER: Black-necked Grebe, Dalmatian Pelican, Pygmy Cormorant, Purple Heron, Little Egret, Squacco Heron, Night Heron, Little Bittern, Bittern, White Stork, Ferruginous Duck, White-tailed Eagle, Red Kite, Black Kite, Short-toed Eagle, Levant Sparrowhawk, Goshawk, Honey Buzzard, Booted Eagle, Golden Eagle, Lesser Spotted Eagle, Egyptian Vulture, Griffon Vulture, Lanner, Hazelhen, Black-winged Stilt, Collared Pratincole, Black Tern, Eagle Owl, Scops Owl, Tengmalm's Owl, Ural Owl, Bee-eater, Roller, Black Woodpecker, Syrian Woodpecker, Middle Spotted Woodpecker, Three-toed Woodpecker, Alpine Accentor, Olivaceous Warbler, Olive-tree Warbler, Collared Flycatcher, Rock Thrush, Rufous Bush Chat, Sombre Tit, Wallcreeper, Black-headed Bunting, Golden Oriole, Nutcracker, Alpine Chough.

PASSAGE: Spoonbill, Osprey, Saker, Crane, Little Crake, Baillon's Crake, Marsh Sandpiper, Slender-billed Curlew, Great Snipe, Gull-billed Tern, White-winged Black Tern, Whiskered Tern, River Warbler, Aquatic Warbler, Red-breasted Flycatcher.

ACCESS: The road between Titograd and Virpazar is excellent for viewing the plains and marshes of Lake Scutari and for access to bushy thickets and woodland. There is a fine causeway 400 m (¼ mile) south of the level crossing that cuts across east of Virpazar. The village of Bijelo Polje has access eastwards toward the River Plavnica through huge reedbeds, while further north the Zeta railway station has Spanish Sparrow. Further north still, at Golubovci, is a right turn marked by a large monument. Follow signs to Motel Plavnica for excellent views over the lake.

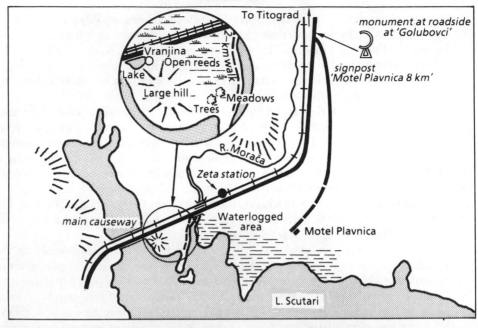

The mountains to the west can be explored on minor roads extending north and south from Virpazar. The one leading southwards to Zabes, Seoca and Godinje is probably best. Keeping left at various forks brings one to a large headland on either side of which are regular White-tailed Eagle feeding zones.

Petrovac is easily found, and the marsh at Buljarica lies immediately to the south. The main road continues southwards and eventually leads to some saltpans at Ulcinj. Unfortunately these require a permit, but the route continues southward through some excellent countryside well worth exploring. In particular, the Brsatski Gorge lies some 20 km (12½ miles) south of Petrovac where the railway runs close to the main coast road on a viaduct 1 km (just over ½ mile) from Sutomore. A walk along the path (leads under the viaduct and across the stream) through the gorge may produce Levant Sparrow-hawk, Golden Eagle, Eagle Owl and Olive-tree Warbler.

Continuing past Ulcinj to the mouth of the Bojave River near Ada Island can be rewarding: Pelican, Pygmy Cormorant, Great White Egret, Red-footed Falcon etc. Bear in mind that this is the Albanian border and that Ada Island is a naturist resort!

Morača Gorge lies along the road north of Titograd toward Kolašin. The area between tunnels 9 and 10 is good for Wallcreeper. Park on the right just after leaving tunnel 9. Continue northward to a sign for 'Biogradska Gora 4 km' and take a minor turning on the right for Lake Biograd. The Lovćen National Park area is north of Petrovac and is reached by taking the minor mountain road west of Cetinje. Not far away on the coast are the saltpans close to Tivat airport. Even when dry, the area is rich in species. It is reached by taking the track to the cement factory at the eastern end of the runway until the disused saltpans appear on the right, about 50 m beyond a café. From here, a causeway leads northwards. It is recommended that visitors carry their passports and bird books: the local police often check because of the adjacent airport.

248

ROUTE: The area is reached via Cilipi airport, which is a short distance south of Dubrovnik.

INDEX

Major localities mentioned within the texts are indexed. Figures in bold type refer to main site entries.